OTHER BOOKS BY GEORGE F. WILL

THE WOVEN FIGURE:
Conservatism and America's Fabric, 1994–1997

THE LEVELING WIND:
Politics, Culture and Other News, 1990–1994

RESTORATION:
Congress, Term Limits and the Recovery of Deliberative Democracy

SUDDENLY:
The American Idea Abroad and at Home, 1986–1990

MEN AT WORK:
The Craft of Baseball

THE NEW SEASON:
A Spectator's Guide to the 1988 Election

THE MORNING AFTER:
American Successes and Excesses, 1981–1986

STATECRAFT AS SOULCRAFT:
What Government Does

THE PURSUIT OF VIRTUE
AND OTHER TORY NOTIONS

THE PURSUIT OF HAPPINESS,
AND OTHER SOBERING THOUGHTS

GEORGE F. WILL

BUNTS

Curt Flood, Camden Yards, Pete Rose
and Other Reflections on Baseball

SCRIBNER

SCRIBNER
1230 Avenue of the Americas
New York, NY 10020

Copyright © 1998 by George F. Will

All rights reserved, including the right of reproduction in whole
or in part in any form.

SCRIBNER and design are trademarks of Simon & Schuster Inc.

DESIGNED BY ERICH HOBBING

Set in Adobe Garamond

Manufactured in the United States of America

1   3   5   7   9   10   8   6   4   2

Library of Congress Cataloging-in-Publication Data is available.

Due to space constrictions, art credits and text permissions can be found on page 351,
and should be considered an extension of this copyright page.

ISBN 0-684-83820-6

This book is dedicated to
DAVID MASENG WILL,
at age five, with the hope that baseball,
and the rest of life, will give him as much joy
as he gives to the author, his father.

CONTENTS

Contents

Contents

BUNTS

INTRODUCTION

It was October baseball at its best, played in the lengthening shadows of late afternoon and in the shadow cast by the long season that had led to this dramatic moment. An autumnal sense of winding down pervaded Baltimore's Camden Yards, with the light and warmth of summer seeping away amid hints of winter. The lights were on and so were sweaters and game six of the American League Championship Series was scoreless in the bottom of the seventh inning.

During the 1997 regular season the Orioles had become only the third "wire to wire" team in American League history—in first place from game 1 through game 162. But the Indians were leading the Series three games to two when shortstop Mike Bordick led off the seventh for the Orioles with a single. The next batter was Brady Anderson, who, on the first pitch, squared as though to bunt, but took a breaking ball for ball one. He did not want to bunt, but he wanted the Indians' pitcher, Charles Nagy, and catcher, Sandy Alomar, to think he might be bunting and to pitch to him with that in mind. Perhaps they did. The next pitch was a high fastball, a pitch easier to hit than to bunt. Anderson slapped it into right for a single. Bordick stopped at second.

If the Orioles could score Bordick, they would be six outs from forcing a seventh game. It would be a home game, so if they could advance Bordick 180 feet they would be favored to advance to the World Series. However, the Orioles were 0 for 8 with runners in scoring position in this game. The next batter, Orioles second baseman Roberto Alomar, Sandy's brother and one of baseball's better bunters, would try to move Bordick the 90 feet to third base, from which he could score on a sacrifice fly.

The inning, and perhaps the game, and even the season were coming down to one taut moment, a test of anticipation and execution by Roberto Alomar, and by brother Sandy and the rest of the Indians. Would Roberto Alomar drop down a bunt? And if so, where? That would depend on which bunt defense the Indians chose, and that choice would depend on what the Indians thought Roberto Alomar and the Orioles were thinking. So the first task for both teams was to get some information.

To that end, after Alomar got set in the batters box, Nagy, a righthander, stepped off the mound and looked to second. He was signaled to do so from the Indians' bench. Nowadays, managers call for "step-offs"—for the pitcher to step off the rubber—and throw-overs to first base, and pickoff plays. (Until relatively recently, managers did not involve themselves in such micromanagement of games. In 1948, the Indians won the American League pennant and the World Series under a player-manager, shortstop Lou Boudreau, who had a spectacular season, batting .355 with 18 home runs and 106 RBI. It is inconceivable that he could have called step-offs and throw-overs while playing shortstop.) Usually a step-off is called to see if some motion by the batter or by a base runner betrays the intentions of the team at bat.

Reflecting about that play, Davey Johnson, the Orioles' manager, recalls thinking that the Indians might be looking for evidence that the Orioles were going to try a hit-and-run. Such evidence, betrayed just before Nagy stepped off or in response to his doing so, might be some slight lean or start by Bordick or Anderson, or some adjustment by Alomar of his stance, or some slight movement of his bat.

The bat control that makes Alomar a deft bunter also makes him adept at the hit-and-run. Besides, Johnson does not often call for a bunt. On the other hand, in situations like this Alomar sometimes bunts on his own. He has been in baseball since he was in diapers (his father had a fifteen-year major league career) and he has abundant confidence in his situational judgments. Furthermore, he spent his first three seasons in the National League (with the Padres). In that league, for a number of reasons (principally, tradition, and bigger parks, and the absence of the designated hitter) there is somewhat less of an emphasis on "big bang," long-ball baseball, somewhat more willingness to give up an out to advance a runner 90 feet.

In any case, when Nagy stepped off, neither Bordick nor Anderson nor Alomar did anything that looked like evidence of a hit-and-run, or a bunt. But Mike Hargrove, the Indians' manager, was not suspecting a hit-and-run and did not doubt what Johnson had in mind and what Alomar was going to do. "The situation," Hargrove says, "was screaming bunt." If ever there was a time to play for one run, this was it.

Thinking back on this minidrama, Hargrove says the rush of decisions concerning Alomar's at bat is "a little bit of a blur," but he says the Nagy step-off might have been part of a pickoff play at second: The shortstop breaks for third, and perhaps the runner on second thinks he can and should lengthen his lead. The second baseman darts in behind the runner to take the throw from the pitcher. However, the pitcher does not have to throw to second when that play is put on, and Nagy did not throw.

Now it was time for the first pitch to Alomar, and it was Alomar's and the Orioles' turn to try to learn something. Alomar shortened up and partially squared to bunt, but he took the first pitch, a buntable breaking ball. His eyes were less on the pitch than on the left side of the Indians' infield, third baseman Matt Williams and shortstop Omar Vizquel. Both are among the best defensive players at their positions; both have won Gold Gloves. Together, they give a manager confidence to put on the "wheel" or "rotation" play in a situation like this.

But Mike Hargrove had not done so. Yet.

On the "wheel" or "rotation" play the third baseman charges the bunt, as does the first baseman, as the pitcher covers the middle of the infield. The second baseman sprints to cover second. And the shortstop breaks toward third, racing the runner on second and arriving at third—if all goes well—in time to force the lead runner. However, on the first pitch to Alomar, Williams had, in Johnson's words, "played it regular." Playing it "regular" means, Johnson says, that "the third baseman doesn't come until he sees [the ball] coming toward him." Williams had not charged. He had been edging in toward Alomar as Nagy prepared to deliver the first pitch, but then had held back.

So what information had the Orioles acquired? Precious little. They had learned that the wheel play was not on. Not on the first pitch, at least. Which did not surprise Johnson: "Our reports were that they did not run the wheel." When told that Johnson had assumed the Indians did not use that play, Hargrove said, laughing, "That's what you get for assuming."

The trouble is, in baseball, as in the rest of life, we live by assuming. We act all the time on assumptions about how children, the weather, stocks and other things are apt to behave. And in fact the Orioles' reports had been basically right. Hargrove says the Indians only use the wheel play "two or three times a year." But, he says, "we work at it all the time." They were about to work it for what Hargrove thinks was only the second time in 1997.

After Alomar took that first pitch, Williams looked in to the Indians' dugout on the third-base side of Camden Yards, then turned toward his teammates and went through a series of signs. Next, he went to the mound and, with his glove over his mouth to frustrate any lip-readers in the Orioles' dugout, spoke to Nagy. As Johnson said later, "Williams is a National League guy." He had spent the ten seasons prior to 1997 with the Giants, and the wheel play was a routine part of his defensive craftsmanship. So Alomar and the Orioles had to wonder whether Williams had signaled a new play—the wheel—or whether all this was just a charade to get the Orioles thinking that the Indians would not play the second pitch the way they had played the first. If the Indians were not going to use the wheel, Alomar's job would be to bunt the ball toward third hard enough that Williams, not Nagy, would have to field it, drawing him away from third, leaving the Indians with only the option of getting Alomar at first as Bordick and Anderson advanced.

Alomar bunted the second pitch toward third, and he and the Orioles instantly, and to their sorrow, had the answer to their question. This time Williams was charging and Vizquel was on the run to his right, toward third. Williams fielded the ball about 25 feet in front of the plate, whirled and threw to Vizquel, who beat Bordick to third by at least 15 feet for the force-out.

The time that had elapsed between Anderson's single touching the right-field grass and Williams' throw touching Vizquel's glove: one minute and fifty-nine seconds.

The Orioles still had a threat going, with Anderson—who is a lot faster than Bordick is going from second to home—on second and Alomar on first. But the Indians, having been challenged to anticipate correctly and execute flawlessly, had done so. The next batter, Geronimo Berroa, grounded the first pitch into a double play with Roberto Alomar out at second. The game remained scoreless until the eleventh inning, when the Indians' second baseman, Tony Fernandez, lofted a home run over the right-field scoreboard.

That, and one more inning of good relief pitching, sent the Indians to the World Series. However, the hinge of the game was the play four innings earlier.

It was not a baseball fan who said that God gave us memory so that we could have roses in winter. Roses are all very well, but real fans are warmed between the postseason and the preseason by the afterglow of episodes like Alomar's bunt and the Indians' businesslike but beautiful 5–6 putout in the seventh.

Bunts are modest and often useful things, although they are not always well understood, even by those who are supposed to know when and how to lay them down. In a baseball story in *McClure's* magazine in 1917, back when the ball was dead and bunting was an essential and admired skill, a manager marveled at a player's misconceptions:

"So I asks him, 'Young man, can you bunt?' 'Mr. Ryan,' says he, 'I don't

Tony Fernandez forces Roberto Alomar at second, and throws out Geronimo Berroa
at first, completing the inning-and-rally-ending double play in the seventh inning
of game 6 of the 1997 ALCS.

like to brag about myself, but I can bunt farther than any other man on the
team.' Them's his very words. Can you beat it?"

The origin of the word "bunt" is lost in the mists of history, which of
course does not inhibit either speculation or certitude. In the Church of Baseball, the mere absence of conclusive evidence is no impediment to belief.
Baseball fans are forever in the grip of originitis, a mild mental illness that
manifests itself in a powerful craving for usually unattainable knowledge of
when this or that practice originated. Baseball's most venerable "knowledge"
is the most preposterous: It is the Abner Doubleday myth, the story that in
the summer of 1839 young Abner sashayed into Farmer Phinney's pasture at
Cooperstown and said, "Let there be baseball," or words to that effect. There
is even a theory about the origin of the use of batting gloves. It is that in 1968
Ken Harrelson, then with the Bostons (concerning that way of speaking, see
the essay about Bill Rigney in this volume), assumed he was not expected to
play in a particular night game. So he played 36 holes of golf before going to
the ballpark, where he arrived with blistered hands and found his name on

the lineup card. (That is what you get for assuming.) So he wore his golf gloves to bat.

One theory about the origin of the word "bunt" is that it evolved from the word "butting," which is what Tim Murnane of the Boston Red Stockings called it when he used his flat-sided bat—such bats were legal back then—to put a ball into play without swinging. Another theory is that "bunt" derived from "buntling" to designate a baby hit. That is a particularly charming theory, so let's accept it until some spoilsport refutes it.

I have titled this collection of baseball writings *Bunts* because they are mostly small, most of them having been written for newspapers, magazines and book review publications. Baseball, unlike basketball or hockey or soccer, is a game of episodes, not of flow, and so lends itself to snapshots. These essays are verbal snapshots taken of baseball during a quarter of a century of usually exhilarating, sometimes exasperating but always affectionate observation of the game. The subjects of these essays range from the nobility of Curt Flood, to the torments of Billy Martin, to the self-destruction of Pete Rose. They range from what baseball has done exquisitely right—Camden Yards, for example—to what it has done ruinously wrong—labor relations. Two of the longer essays, the one on broadcaster Jon Miller and the concluding survey of the game at the end of the century, were written for this volume.

Connie Mack, who spent sixty-four years in Major League Baseball—fifty-three of them in dugouts, and fifty of those wearing a business suit and necktie and stiff collar and managing the Philadelphia Athletics—said near the end of his life, "I have never known a day when I didn't learn something new about this game." There is indeed a lot to learn. The writings in this volume contain much of what one fan has learned from a lifetime constantly refreshed by sips from the meandering stream of baseball's life.

I am sometimes asked when it was that I first came upon that stream which irrigates my life. I answer that I do not know, because I have no memory of life before baseball. My mother recalled that at age six, after listening to a broadcast of a 1947 World Series game that the Yankees lost, I asked her if the Yankees' mothers would be sad. (She said, "No." She should have said, "Not for long.") My interest in baseball was fed by radio. I grew up in Champaign-Urbana, Illinois, a university community, and radio was my connection with metropolitan America. As we lived more or less midway between Chicago and St. Louis, the family Philco crackled with the broadcasts of the Cubs (Burt Wilson), White Sox (Bob Elson), Cardinals (Harry Caray) and Browns (Buddy Blattner). Baseball was in the air.

For half a century, and especially in the almost quarter of a century covered by the columns and other essays in this volume, the national pastime has been a full participant in the three great dramas of the nation in that period. These dramas have concerned relations between the races, the temptations and stresses of prosperity and the aggressive assertion of new rights. In this period I have come of middle age, and baseball has grown up.

These rites of passage are supposed to be tinged with melancholy—farewell to innocence and all that—and baseball has in fact paid a price for its growth into an institution more complex and less intimate than it was. In a sense, baseball has become both more and less close to those of us who care about it. It is closer to us in the sense that we know more about its internal workings as a business, and we know more about (and there is more to know about) what the players and managers are doing during games. On the other hand, a certain social distance has opened up between the people on the field and the people in the stands. Players and managers are highly paid celebrities, with all the attendant demands on them, and often a certain wariness from them. The stakes of success and failure are much higher than they were.

So much has changed, but the most remarkable thing is that the essential feature—the enjoyment fans derive from a close connection with the game—has not. The following writings wend their way through the delights and, yes, exasperations of one fan's experiences with this American delight. The volume ends with a summing-up, an examination of baseball's evolution through the century. It is nice to know that my last words in this volume will not be the last word on anything, because baseball is a work in progress. If you don't believe me, just remember—and heed—the fan's familiar cry: "Wait 'til next year!"

THE CUBS
AND CONSERVATISM

March 21, 1974

A READER DEMANDS to know how I contracted the infectious conservatism for which he plans to horsewhip me. So if you have tears, prepare to shed them now as I reveal how my gloomy temperament received its conservative warp from early and prolonged exposure to the Chicago Cubs.

The differences between conservatives and liberals are as much a matter of temperament as ideas. Liberals are temperamentally inclined to see the world as a harmonious carnival of sweetness and light, where goodwill prevails, good intentions are rewarded, the race is to the swift and a benevolent Nature arranges a favorable balance of pleasure over pain. Conservatives (and Cub fans) know better.

Conservatives know the world is a dark and forbidding place where most new knowledge is false, most improvements are for the worse, the battle is not to the strong, nor riches to men of understanding and an unscrupulous Providence consigns innocents to suffering. I learned this early.

Out in central Illinois, where men are men and I am native, in 1948, at age seven, I made a mad, fateful blunder. I fell ankle over elbows in love with the Cubs. Barely advanced beyond the bib-and-cradle stage, I plighted my troth to a baseball team destined to dash the cup of life's joy from my lips.

Spring, Earth's renewal, a season of hope for the rest of mankind, became for me an experience comparable to being slapped around the mouth with a damp carp. Summer was like being bashed across the bridge of the nose with a crowbar—ninety times. My youth was like one long rainy Monday in Bayonne, New Jersey.

Each year the Cubs charged onto the field to challenge the theory that there are limits to the changes one can ring on pure incompetence. By mid-April, when other kids' teams were girding for Homeric battles at the top of the league, my heroes had wilted like salted slugs and begun their gadarene descent to the bottom. By September they had set a mark for ineptness at which others—but not next year's Cubs—would shoot in vain.

Every litter must have its runt, but my Cubs were almost all runts. Topps baseball gum cards always struggled to say something nice about each player. All they could say about the Cubs' infielder Eddie Miksis is that in 1951 he was tenth in the league in stolen bases, with eleven.

Like the boy who stood on the burning deck whence all but he had fled, I was loyal. And the downward trajectory of my life was set.

In 1949 I reported for Little League, the teams sponsored by local merchants. My friends played for teams like Rasmussen Masonry Braves and Kuhn's Department Store Cubs. Their team colors were bright red and vivid blue. I was a very late draft choice of the Mittendorf Funeral Home Panthers. Our color was black. An eight-year-old could not face these fires without being singed, unless he had the crust of an armadillo, and how many eight-year-olds do?

Of the sixteen teams that existed in 1949, all have since won league championships—all but the Cubs. And which of the old National League teams

EDDIE MIKSIS

Number 10 in the NL in stolen bases.
He had eleven.

was first to finish in tenth place behind even the expansion teams? Don't ask. Since 1949 the Cubs have lost more than 2,200 games. That's more than 6,000 hours of losing baseball. They never made me like losing, but they gave me superb training for 1964 when I cast my first vote for president, for Barry Goldwater.

My cruel addiction continued. In 1964 I chose to do three years of graduate study at Princeton because Princeton is midway between Philadelphia and New York—two National League cities. All I remember about my wedding day in 1967 is that the Cubs dropped a double-header.

But the gentleman with the horsewhip should stay his hand. I share his fervent desire that I should quit writing about politics. I still hope to reverse the career pattern of James Reston, who began working in baseball but has sunk to writing a political column (for *The New York Times*). I hope to rise as far as he has fallen. I want to be a baseball writer when I grow up.

As the 1998 season began, the Cubs had lost 4,120 games since opening day 1949, more than any other major league team. The second-losingest team in that space is the Athletics, who have lost 4,064.

THE FAN'S FUNNY SORT OF SERIOUSNESS

May 11, 1974

THE FEDERAL GOVERNMENT in all its majesty is worried that sports broadcasters do sinister things, like rooting for the home team.

Last year the Federal Communications Commission authorized an inquiry into sports broadcasting. The inquiry is a monument to the government's excessive energy and inadequate ability to make commonsense distinctions.

Most broadcasters are employed with the approval of, and sometimes by, the teams or leagues they cover. Critics suggest this involves two closely related problems.

The FCC's licensees—the stations—are supposed to maintain control over their programming. Broadcasters employed by or with the approval of professional sports organizations are supposed to compromise the licensees' control of programming. Critics say that this, in turn, produces inaccurate "news reporting" from the stadiums.

These two complaints fail for the same reason: Sports events are not "news" so sports broadcasts are not newscasts. There is "sports news," lots of it, but live broadcasts of sporting events are something else.

News events are automatically in the public domain. Obviously there can be no property right in news. The government could not auction off broadcasting rights for (say) a Senate hearing to the highest network bid.

But sports events are private property, and so are the rights to broadcast them. A radio station that carries (say) the Pittsburgh Pirates broadcasts is controlling its own programming. It is buying an entertainment package. No one is forced to listen to it, and the only people apt to listen are Pirate fans.

They hear—and adore—broadcaster Bob Prince, "The Voice of the Pirates." Like any fan worth the mustard on his hot dog, Prince suffers the torments of the damned when the Pirates lose and he enjoys transports of bliss when they win.

Prince encourages people to support the club by coming to the ballpark. And he does his best to help listeners *enjoy* the listening. Walter Cronkite doesn't try to make the news enjoyable. Prince's job is different.

The pertinent point was made well in a letter to the FCC from a Kansas City lady in whose presence I would *never* disparage the K.C. Royals baseball team:

"If there is dissension in the clubhouse or mismanagement in the front office, let the sports *reporter* dig it out and report it on the *news* programs and in the *news*papers. But for crying out loud, let the fans enjoy the games without some 'objective' announcer leading the booing when our favorite pitcher walks four in a row or our outfield comes unglued."

Of course there are instances of calculated, greedy broadcaster deceptiveness. But they do not much matter, for a reason that the government is prone to forget: The American people are not ninnies.

Some teams have forced broad-

Bob Prince, Pirates announcer
for twenty-eight years.

casters to lie about the weather, crowd size, or caliber of play, in attempts to lure customers to the ballpark. But the weather is common knowledge, attendance figures appear in the box scores and people who care enough to tune in broadcasts usually care enough to be exceptionally knowledgeable about the way the team is playing.

By worrying about sports broadcasting the government is taking sports too seriously, or at least seriously in the wrong way. Americans, myself emphatically included, are prone to forget that sports are only serious in a funny way. Part of the fun of having flaming passions about our favorite teams—the fun of being a "fan," short for *fanatic*—is the comic lack of proportion in it.

You hear the voice of the true sports fan in this letter to the FCC from Kalamazoo, Michigan:

"Most of the people who listen to Detroit Tiger broadcasts are Tiger fans. . . . I would think something was not quite right if the broadcaster on the radio for Tiger baseball couldn't show a little bias in favor of the Tigers. If I were a Boston Red Sox fan, I would not love it, but I'd be in enemy territory and would have to accept it."

"Enemy territory." I like that.

THE MOST CONSOLING WORD: "OVERDUE"

March 20, 1975

MY TRAINED SENSES tell me: Spring is near. For most of the world hope, given up for dead, stirs in its winding linen. But I, like Figaro, laugh that I may not weep.

Baseball season approaches. The weeds are about to reclaim the trellis of my life. For most fans, the saddest words of tongue or pen are: "Wait 'til next year." For us Cub fans, the saddest words are: "This is next year."

The Cubs haven't won a pennant since 1945, a year when the race was not to the swift because most of the swift athletes were dashing up Iwo Jima's beaches or across Remagen bridge. Then the war ended, and peace has been hell.

Korea and Vietnam taught a stern lesson: Limited wars are too limited to draft away enough athletes to restore the Cubs' vanished supremacy. When the Thousand Year Reich collapsed, the Cubs' one-year dynasty did, too.

Recently Roger Kahn wrote a fine book, *The Boys of Summer,* about the great Brooklyn Dodger stars of the late 1940s and early 1950s, their playing years, and what has happened to them since. It is a poignant story of middle-aged men who have passed through their glory years.

But where is the poet who can tell the even more poignant story of the Cubs I grew up with, who now are middle-aged men who never had glory years? Who will sing the song of Eddie Miksis? The ballad of Wayne Terwilliger? Who will be Boswell for Dee Fondy, Turk Lown, Harry Chiti?

A few years ago Simon and Garfunkel, in "Mrs. Robinson," sang this question: "Where have you gone, Joe DiMaggio? A nation turns its lonely eyes to you." No ballad will ever ask, "Where have you gone, Frankie Baumholtz?"

But avert your lonely eyes, America. Joltin' Joe DiMaggio, the Yankee Clipper, is on television flogging coffeemakers. Frankie Baumholtz hasn't sunk to that. Having been a Cub has its consolations: There are some depths to which you can plunge only from an Olympian height.

The other Cub consolation is Leo Durocher's celebrated aphorism: "Nice guys finish last." It is a limited consolation because Durocher missed the point, which is: People are quick to say that someone is a nice guy when they are sure he is a loser.

Loser or not, there is one Cub I cannot recall without a twinge of pain. Roy Smalley taught me, at age nine, why this is called a vale of tears.

Only a team named after baby bears would have a shortstop named Smalley—a right-handed hitter, if that is the word for a man who in his best year (1953) hit .249. From Smalley I learned the truth about the word "overdue."

A portrait of this columnist as a tad would show him with an ear pressed against a radio, listening to an announcer say: "The Cubs have the bases loaded. If Smalley gets on, the tying run will be on deck. And Smalley is overdue for a hit."

It was the most consoling word in the language, "overdue." It meant: In

Roy Smalley: Overdue.

the long run, everything is going to be all right. No one is really a .222 hitter. We are all good hitters, all winners. It is just that some of us are, well, "overdue" for a hit, or whatever.

Unfortunately, my father is a right-handed logician at the University of Illinois, and he knows more than it is nice to know about the theory of probability. With a lot of help from Smalley he convinced me that Smalley was not "overdue." Stan Musial batting .249 was overdue for a hot streak. Smalley batting .249 was doing his best.

Smalley retired after eleven seasons with a lifetime average of .227. He was still overdue.

I am sadder but wiser now, thanks to the Cubs. Still, the heart has its reasons that the mind cannot refute, so I say:

Do not go gently into this season, Cub fans; rage, rage against the blasting of our hopes. Had I but world enough, and time, this slowness, Cubs, would be no crime. But I am almost halfway through my allotted three score and ten and you, sirs, are overdue.

PLAYERS ARE BOUGHT AND SOLD? SAY IT AIN'T SO.

June 24, 1976

THE DUGOUT INTELLECTUAL who theorized that "good pitching will stop good hitting, and vice versa" may have thought he had plumbed baseball's depths. But he did not anticipate baseball's current complexity.

The business of America is business, and so, of course, is the national pastime. But more than half a century ago the Supreme Court succumbed to sentimentality and declared that baseball is not commerce. This made baseball exempt from antitrust prosecution. Hence owners enjoyed a form of control over their laborers comparable to the control briefly confirmed for some earlier masters by the Dred Scott decision.

Players were owned by a team until the team traded, sold or retired them. This prevented a free market in talent: No player could sell his services to the highest bidder. But now our heroes in spikes have broken the rod of the oppressor, with the help of one of the oppressors.

Charlie Finley, June 1976, outside Bowie Kuhn's office,
pleading for his right to devastate "baseball's reputation for integrity
and to public confidence in the game."

Charles Finley, owner of the Oakland A's, is the cause of baseball's Sturm und Drang. In 1974 he got into a contract dispute with an employee named Catfish Hunter. Baseball's arbitrator declared Hunter a free agent, and Hunter signed with the New York Yankees for $3 million.

Next, a Los Angeles Dodger, Andy Messersmith, played a season without a contract. Baseball's arbitrator said to him: "You are a free agent." Baseball's owners said to the arbitrator: "You are fired." Two federal courts said to the owners: "The arbitrator is right."

So Messersmith became an Atlanta Brave, and a millionaire. And this year perhaps fifty players—about two per team—will play the full season without contracts in order to become free agents and try their luck in the new free market.

Finley is neither the nicest nor the dumbest owner. He realized that at the end of this season he would lose his unsigned players to the free market, without getting a nickel for them. So a few days ago he sold three of them for cash, one to the Yankees for $1.5 million, two to the Red Sox for $2 million.

At this point, Bowie Kuhn entered. Kuhn is commissioner of baseball. He resembles the unimpressive catcher who moved Casey Stengel to remark, "He's twenty. In ten years he has a chance to be thirty."

Kuhn banned Finley's sales on the hilarious ground that they are "devastating to baseball's reputation for integrity and to public confidence in the game." Evidently fans are supposed to believe that Kuhn believes that fans would be devastated if they learned that players are bought and sold.

Kuhn is an employee of the owners, so the fact that he is opposed to Finley's sale probably means that most of the owners are too. It is no mystery why. Most of the owners are appalled because Finley and his New York and Boston trading partners have demonstrated, in public, to the public, and to other players, what the free market value of a star is.

Some fans grumble that "no player is worth a million dollars." But baseball owners are not running charitable organizations. If no players were worth that, no owners would pay it.

In their forlorn attempt to roll back players' rights, some owners will argue, as the football owners argued, that a free market in player talent will mean a rush of superstars to rich teams. But that is another self-serving theory killed by facts. This year only twenty-four football players became free agents on May 1. The three richest owners—those of the Dallas, Houston and Kansas City teams—signed none of the top stars.

Football owners fought tooth and nail, and unsuccessfully, against the players' union to prevent the emergence of something like a free market in talent. Every step of the way they argued that a free market would destroy "competitive balance," and that their only concern was "the good of the game."

But sports businessmen are businessmen, which means they are neither irrational nor altruistic. None of them will spend themselves into penury by irrationally stockpiling expensive talent. And they are nimble at rising above principles: Their passion for free enterprise stops just a bunt short of the point where a free market might cost them money.

WARREN BUFFETT MISSES
A GRAVY TRAIN

March 13, 1977

THE LETTER WAS SUITABLY TERSE: "We regret to inform you that you have been nominated for membership in the Emil Verban Memorial Society."

Verban was the Chicago Cubs' second baseman, 1948–50. Then he was sent to the Boston Braves and retired after four games to rest on his laurels. His most notable achievement was a remarkable ratio of home runs (1) to times at bat (2,911). Today he is a patron saint of Cub fans because he symbolizes mediocrity under pressure.

The sight of the first crocus, the song of spring's first robin are, for most people, harbingers of the lighter and brighter side of life. But for Cub fans, they are omens of hideous clarity—signs that the happy stagnation of winter is over and the season of suffering is beginning.

Spring is the winter of the Cub fan's soul. By June his lifeless eyes will resemble oysters on half shells; his complexion will be the color of Cream of Wheat. He must have Spartan stoicism and the skin of a rhino: The Cubs have lost 2,654 games since they last won a pennant, in 1945.

Undaunted, I recently resolved to buy one share of Cubs stock so that on my income tax form I could list my occupation as "baseball owner." While visiting Omaha, I confided this desire to Warren Buffett, who is a St. Louis Cardinal fan but not otherwise sinister. In a blaze of bonhomie uncharacteristic of Cardinal fans, he wrote to a friend in Des Moines, the estimable Joseph Rosenfield:

"Dear Joe: George Will, an otherwise quite competent young man, shares your irrationality regarding the Cubs. I mentioned to George that in this case it is possible to put your money where your aberrations are, and that it would be possible for him to buy stock in the club. Considering the fact that you and Phil Wrigley are the two largest shareholders, I don't see how he can help

Emil Verban:
Mediocrity under pressure.

but upgrade the present membership. Why don't you write George directly and explain to him precisely how to get aboard this gravy train."

Cardinal fans are by nature sarcastic. Cub fans are of sweet disposition. Rosenfield wrote to me offering help and counsel:

"If I were you, I would not consult Warren about the stock as he will give you a long, learned treatise on price-earnings ratios, return on capital, and a bunch of other hogwash which has no place in a transaction between two true sportsmen."

Well put, don't you think? And the benevolent Rosenfield continued:

"Before buying the stock, I would like to give you a word of caution based on personal experience. Some twenty-five years ago I was in a broker's office in Chicago and the trader, who knew of my interest in the Cubs, told me ten shares were available, which I bought as a kind of lark. However, I soon discovered that this was like taking your first shot of heroin, and I could not wait to increase my holdings. Every time stock appeared . . . I bought it and I kept pounding the brokers to find more.

"At the end of two years I had accumulated 274 shares and was otherwise bankrupt. After two unsuccessful holdup attempts in order to get additional buying power, I managed to kick the habit through sheer iron will and the help of three nationally known psychiatrists.

"However, the Cubs have given me something to live for. Some time ago Harry Reasoner was telling on the news about an old friend of his who had set as his goal to live until the Washington subway was completed. Being of a somewhat advanced age myself, I have determined to live until the Cubs win the National League pennant."

In the deepest sediment of my soul, I know that the Cubs have been good for me, too. They have taught me the first rule of reasonable living: Discern the unalterable and submit to it without tears.

The Cubs, although deeply painful to contemplate, symbolize Man's Fate. All of us are, like the Cubs, feathers on the breeze of Life, lonely sliders down the splintery banister of Eternity.

THE CHICAGO WATER BEETLES

June 27, 1977

A⊤ 7:17 A.M. (the moment is forever fixed in my memory) the drowsy stillness of the Will house was broken only by the voice of Ray Gandolf, the reporter of sports for the CBS morning news, giving baseball scores: ". . . the mighty Cubs beat . . ."

Mighty Chicago Cubs? I have waited decades to hear a sportscaster say something like that.

Unpleasant people say that this year's Cubs are like Hilaire Belloc's water beetle:

> *He flabbergasts the Human Race*
> *By gliding on the water's face*
> *With ease, celerity and grace;*
> *But if he ever stopped to think*
> *Of how he did it, he would sink.*

Stuff and nonsense. The Cubs' sudden ascent to greatness is the work of Providence. In the fullness of time it has come to pass, as the prophets prophesied: The meek, who have eaten the bread of affliction, are inheriting the earth.

The romantic saga of today's rampant Cubs is a nice counterpoint to unromantic baseball news, such as the trade of Tom Seaver from the New York Mets to the Cincinnati Reds. The Seaver trade, and the restless mobility of "free agent" superstars, strains fan loyalty. Baseball is a business but such unsentimental capitalism is bad business. Baseball capitalism that respects only market forces is profoundly destructive because it dissolves the glue of sentiment that binds fans to teams. Besides, as Jacques Barzun says, baseball is Greek because it is based on "rivalries of city-states." Athens would not have traded Pericles for Sparta's whole infield.

Scholars concede but cannot explain the amazing chemistry of Cub fans' loyalty. But their unique steadfastness through thin and thin has something to do with the team's Franciscan simplicity. The Cubs play on real grass, under real sunlight. Their scoreboard does not explode and they do not wear gaudy uniforms like those that have the Pittsburgh Pirates looking like the softball team from Ralph's Bar and Grill.

Iron has entered into the soul of this generation of Cub fans. World War II made the National League safe for the Cubs (they won in 1945, conscription having taken the able-bodied opposition), but since then rooting for the Cubs has been the moral equivalent of war: hell. I became a Cub fan in Champaign, Illinois, in my seventh year, 1948, the year the Cubs' management ran newspaper ads apologizing for the team. Thereafter, my youth was spent devising theories to take the sting out of summer, such as the theory that each team would score only a certain number of runs each season, so when the Cubs lost 22–0 the winner squandered twenty-one of its allotted runs.

Baseball always was a sobering experience for me. Many children who had been trusted playmates revealed shocking flimsiness of character: They sank to rooting for the St. Louis Cardinals. I regarded these opportunists with lofty disdain, as de Gaulle regarded Vichyites. But now I know they were more to be pitied than censured, because rooting for a successful team is ruinous.

Have you ever known a Yankee fan with real character? Twenty years ago rooting for the Yankees was like rooting for IBM. It was for cloying children who liked violin lessons and dreamed of being Secretary of the Treasury. What do Yankee fans know of the short and simple annals of the poor? Of lives of quiet desperation?

The most that can be said for most team loyalties is that they are poor

The 1948 Chicago Cubs: A train wreck about to leave the yard.

preparation for here or the Hereafter. But rooting for the old, unregenerate Cubs was a complete moral education. From 1946 through 1966 they finished seventh seven times and eighth six times. In 1962, the first year it was possible to finish ninth, the Cubs did, and the Mets had to extend themselves to a record 120 losses to wrest tenth from the Cubs. In 1966 the Cubs became the first nonexpansion National League team to finish tenth.

In those days, Cardinal fans reading *Who's Who in Baseball* found glowing descriptions of Stan Musial and Marty Marion. Cub fans read about their Lenny Merullo: "He is always on the verge of being ousted from his job because of his frequent erraticness—but he probably will be around this season." Bill Nicholson: "He has been in the clutches of a prolonged batting slump for three seasons." Paul Minner: "His wins were meager, but his stamina tremendous." Dutch McCall: He suffered from "disheartening support—and lack of endurance." Roy Smalley: "His errors at short are many, but he keeps trying." And Ralph Hamner: "The tall stringy hurler abounds in tough luck."

The Cubs' teams of this era taught their fans an invaluable lesson about the inevitable triumph of ineptitude over sincerity. From these Cubs we learned life's bitterest truth: Verily, man is born unto trouble, as the sparks fly upward. That is not news to Cub fans, who have seen a relief pitcher stride to the mound, promptly injure himself by falling off the mound and leave without having thrown a pitch. Today, a quarter of a century later, I am an embattled parent, convinced that babies are born plump as peaches because they are packed full of dubious ideas. It is never too soon for them to learn that the world is not their oyster, and *nothing* teaches that lesson quicker than loyalty to a train wreck like the 1948 Cubs.

Still, one summer of happiness can't do irreparable harm to me or the two rising Cub fans at the Will house. Yes, the paths of glory lead but to the grave, but so do all other paths. Yes, we bring nothing into the world and can take nothing out, but Ray Gandolf's sweet reference to "the mighty Cubs" is one thing no one can take away from us.

Water seeks its own level, and so did the 1977 Cubs, who, mighty in June, reverted to form by September and finished fourth, twenty games out of first.

ALEXANDER CARTWRIGHT AND THE JOY OF BASEBALL

April 2, 1978

WHEN LAST I ADDRESSED the subject of baseball, the lark was on the wing, the snail was on the thorn and my Chicago Cubs were in first place. That was last June. The lark and snail had good seasons, but the Cubs foundered. Now several sadists have called my attention to the fact that another season is at hand, and they have dared me to say anything cheerful.

That is a daunting challenge, but if the challengers had done their homework in the Will family archives, they would have known that we are a family rarely daunted. So here goes a cheerful thought: Not even practitioners as inartistic as the Cubs can spoil something as sublime as baseball.

To understand why this is so, you should begin at the beginning of baseball, and that does *not* mean Abner Doubleday. Doubleday, who was a captain of artillery in the Union army at Fort Sumter, was present at the creation of the Civil War, but not of baseball. His *New York Times* obituary did not even mention baseball. Such is the power of myth, however, that baseball's Hall of Fame is at Cooperstown, New York, because Doubleday was a schoolboy there.

Nevertheless, the Hall does contain a plaque honoring the one American whose achievements of mind rank with those of Aristotle, Newton, Hegel and Einstein. I refer, of course, to Alexander Cartwright, whose middle name was, appropriately, Joy. On the plaque, the list of his accomplishments begins: "Set the bases ninety feet apart."

In 1845 Cartwright, then twenty-five, joined some friends in a meadow beside a pond in what is now known as the Murray Hill section of Manhattan. He had a chart in hand. Red Smith, the columnist, says the dimensions of the baseball field Cartwright laid out that day may have been determined by the size of the meadow, or perhaps Cartwright just stepped off thirty paces and said, "This seems about right." But Smith also says:

> Ninety feet between bases represents man's closest approach to absolute truth. The world's fastest man cannot run to first base ahead of a sharply hit ball that is cleanly handled by an infielder; he will get there only half a step too late. Let the fielder juggle the ball for one moment or delay his throw an instant and the runner will be safe. Ninety feet demands perfection. It accurately measures the cunning, speed and finesse of the base stealer against the velocity of a thrown ball. It dictates the placement of infielders. That single dimension makes baseball a fine art—and nobody knows for sure how it came to be.

Alexander Joy Cartwright:
the Aristotle of baseball.

Perhaps baseball players are occasionally inclined to slight the life of the mind. (After being introduced to Ernest Hemingway, Yogi Berra said, "Quite a fella. What does he do?" "He's a writer," said a friend. "Yeah?" said Yogi. "What paper?") But baseball is the sport most satisfying to the mind, perhaps because of its use of space and time.

Other sports are played in a strictly defined space, like a basketball court or football field. However, baseball has what one writer (George Grella) calls "potential for infinity." Even foul balls are in play until they land in the stands, and if you removed the stands, the field of play would extend forever through 360 degrees. The republic, the planet, the *universe* would be an extended baseball field. What a jolly idea.

Even when confined by fences and stands, a baseball field is remarkably large, and there is no clock and no tie game. As Grella says, "Baseball's unique freedom from any external time [means that] the game succeeds in creating a temporary timelessness perfectly appropriate to its richly cyclical nature." In theory, a game could (and in heaven surely all games do) go on forever.

Of course, in this life, all things must end, even the best things: baseball games. But baseball games call to mind the title of a poem by Robert Frost: "Happiness Makes Up in Height for What It Lacks in Length."

THE CASE FOR I.T.
(INEPTITUDE TRANSFER)

May 17, 1979

A jolting conclusion suggests itself: Chicago Cub fans, of whom I am one, are at least symptoms of what ails the West, and may be what ails the West.

This thought broke like thunder when, on opening day, a Cub fan cheerfully said that all the team needed in order to be a winner were "three starting pitchers and an outfielder." The fan was not being witty, as Oscar Wilde was when he described a particular woman as "a peacock in everything but beauty." Rather, that Cub fan, like most of them, fits the description of Lord Halifax, Britain's foreign minister at Munich: "He had an infinite capacity for being trodden on without complaint." But Cub fans are gifted complainers, as I learned when, on the eve of the season (on the *Today* show), I said, approximately, this:

> When the Mets were dreadful, they were cute. When the Red Sox blew the pennant, they had a tragic dignity. But the Cubs are just mediocre, and if they play this season they will just embarrass themselves and their fans. If, however, they flatly refuse to come out of the dugout, they can give the world a shining example of a heroism suited to an age of antiheroes, lowered expectations, tempered hopes and contracted horizons: heroic resignation. A white towel hoisted over the dugout would be a banner to which realists could repair, a symbol of unconditional surrender to undeniable facts.

This thought touched the flaming, tigerish spirit for which Cub fans, unlike their team, are noted. Many fans have communicated with me in simple, austere terms—the philosophic gist being that I am the sort of person who would be much improved by being drawn and quartered.

But Cub fans exemplify the muddiness of mind that made Munich (and Suez, the Department of Energy and other calamities) possible. They fancy themselves idealists, but theirs is a dotty idealism that confuses ecological and athletic criteria. They idealize the team for playing at home on real grass, illuminated by solar energy. An idealist, as H. L. Mencken said, is someone who notes that a rose smells better than a cabbage and concludes that a rose will also make better soup.

But I have received a letter from a Virginia gentleman, whose professional address—on Jefferson Davis Highway—suggests that he should be listened to on the subject of losers. John Nies says that my strategy for the Cubs— unconditional surrender—is "by Washington standards rather barren." He says:

"As Mr. [Joseph] Califano [Secretary of Health, Education and Welfare] will tell you, the situation in which the Cubs find themselves is not of their own making. The basic truth of the matter, at least in Washington, is that failure in *any* enterprise is always someone else's fault. This is the corollary, of course, of the proposition that success is a product of avarice and related vices."

Nies has some suggestions:

First, consider the possibilities of affirmative action. The Cubs' ineptitude is obviously the product of years of neglect. This can be corrected by requiring the Yankees and the Red Sox to accept as starters those Cubs who, because of broken homes or other socioeconomic reasons, have a batting average of less than .100 or who can't throw a ball straight more than five feet. This program, called Ineptitude Transfer (I.T.), if carefully monitored, should be productive.

Next, let us think about whether it is really fair to retire a Cub hitter after three called strikes, which is the same standard used to judge the skills of a Ted Williams or a Reggie Jackson. . . .

It is too much to hope that government will accept the truth taught by competitive sport, and even by uncompetitive sport, such as the Cubs play. The truth is that, as a carpenter once said to William James, "there is very little difference between one man and another; but what little there is, is very important."

A concluding unscientific postscript:

Since my season-opening fit of foul temper, the Cubs have been, if not awesome, at least marginally adequate. This year the June Swoon did not come, as it usually does, in early May, which may, or then again may not, prove something.

Not. The 1979 Cubs finished fifth, eighteen games out of first.

THE 1980 CUBS' STRENGTH: CANDOR

April 6, 1980

SCOTTSDALE (ARIZONA) COMMUNITY COLLEGE TEAMS are called "The Fighting Artichokes." That smarty-pants name, like the cheerleader in an artichoke costume, is drollery intended to de-emphasize athletics.

Training just a bunt away, in Mesa, are fellows who never emphasize athletics: the Chicago Cubs. This will be a National League record-smashing Cubs' season: the 35th in a row without winning a pennant, eclipsing the achievement of the 1916–49 Phillies. So perhaps the Cubs deserve a droller name, like "The Battling Broccoli" or "The Aggressive Asparagus."

But it probably is deflating enough to be named after immature animals. Purdue Boilermakers: visions of biceps and hairy chests. Denver Broncos: kicking. Georgia Tech Yellow Jackets: stinging. Chicago Cubs? Fuzzy, cuddly. And don't give me that a-rose-would-smell-as-sweet-by-any-other-name rigamarole. If roses were called turnips, they wouldn't cost $37.50 a dozen, and people playing hardball shouldn't call themselves Cubs. Still, it once was even worse. In 1890, most of the Cubs' players defected to another league and the manager, Adrian "Cap" Anson, replaced them with youngsters promptly nicknamed "Anson's Orphans."

Today's Cubs manager, Preston Gomez, recently generated this headline: GOMEZ EVALUATES CUBS: NO SPEED, BAD ARMS, LEAKY INFIELD. Candor is the Cubs' only passion. A movie of what Cubs management calls "highlights" of the 1979 season begins with the song from *Annie* about how "tomorrow is always a day away." The first scene is of an outfielder losing a ground ball in his cap. In the next "highlight" the Cubs pulverize Phillies pitchers for 22 runs. And lose, 23–22.

Lowlights, anyone? Last September this story was filed from Pittsburgh by *The Washington Post*'s Tom Boswell, who is what Dante could have been, had medieval Italy had sportswriters:

> The pennant contender's best friend arrived here tonight—the Chicago Cubs. Like a platoon of cavalry coming to the rescue, the Cubbie Bears got to Three Rivers Stadium just in time to hand a game to the Pittsburgh Pirates.
>
> Who says it is easy to field on artificial turf? The Cubs could look mystified on a pool table. . . . [The Cubs' pitcher's] first pitch was lined at shortstop Ivan DeJesus—a judicious choice since DeJesus has twenty-eight errors. . . . The ball struck squarely in his glove and ricocheted into left field as though it had struck a skillet.
>
> [A single to right:] The ball struck right fielder [Larry] Biittner several vicious blows, fell to the turf exhausted. . . . [A single to left:] Dave Kingman charged the dribbling ball. . . . How an almost motionless ball can elude a six-foot-six man nicknamed King Kong has not been determined. But Kingman never touched it.

Today, Cub fans are disappointed about the baseball strike, now threatened for May twenty-third. They are for a strike, of course, but they wish it could start immediately after the first game and extend through September. In that case, they could say their team finished "just a game off the pace."

Today, wherever Cub fans gather, this question is heard: "When is the Sutter trade?" They assume that pitcher Bruce Sutter, the team's athlete, will be traded. Cub fans remember the trade of Lou Brock, about 3,000 hits ago, to the Cardinals. (A Cardinal fan sends me Christmas cards containing not a message of peace but a picture of Brock in his Cubs uniform. When the Russians conquer America, they will recruit concentration camp guards from among Cardinal fans.)

As an athlete, I was a diligent underachiever. I was one of those people who a coach calls "huggers": benchwarmers you keep around "so you can hug 'em after you win, instead of having to hug the guys who play and sweat." Cub fans (and Cub players) suspect that there is something melancholy about sports achievers. Successful athletes compress into such a short span most of life's inevitable trajectory of rise and decline. And what remains, beyond a wisp of reputation?

Last winter *The New York Times* contained a small obituary, datelined Bastrop, Louisiana:

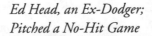

Ed Head, an Ex-Dodger;
Pitched a No-Hit Game

He lived sixty-two years, reared three sons and probably experienced the full range of joys and sorrows. But when he left this life, he was remembered for what he did to the Boston Braves one afternoon in 1946.

And yet, and yet . . .

How many of us will have even an afternoon memorable enough for strangers to mention thirty-four years later?

THE ANSWER IS: RONALD REAGAN. THE QUESTION IS: WHO IS THE ONLY PERSON TO HAVE HELD AMERICA'S TWO MOST DIFFICULT JOBS?

April 12, 1981

DRENCHED IN FLORIDA sunshine, the spring training game was under way and everyone was as bubbly as ginger ale. Everyone, that is, except the Baltimore Orioles' batboy, who had a large lump in his cheek: his first chaw of tobacco. In the fourth inning he turned as green as grass and departed. Spring is a season for manly rites of passage, and in spring, especially, a lad's reach should exceed his grasp.

The next day the batboy was back, and so was the lump. And among the spectators, this columnist with his eight-year-old recalled Rolfe Humphries' poem "Polo Grounds":

> *Time is of the essence. The crowd and players*
> *Are the same age always, but the man in the crowd*
> *Is older every season. Come on, play ball!*

Baseball's soothing continuities were exemplified that day in Florida by the gentleman seated nearby. Jack Dunn works for today's Orioles. His grandfather owned the minor league Orioles and signed a kid off Baltimore's sandlots, a kid named George, last name Ruth.

Today baseball reflects the Stockmanization of life: too much talk about money. David Stockman is supposed to talk about it incessantly, but it is tiresome when sports pages read like releases from the Office of Management and Budget. The Yankees' Dave Winfield hits about .280 and earns a salary the size of the Kemp-Roth tax cut. In 1929, Lefty O'Doul hit .398 with 254 hits—a National League record never surpassed. It earned him a $500 raise. In 1932 he hit "only" .368 and his salary was cut $1,000.

With terrible swiftness players become men in the crowd, older every season, so they should read this 1914 editorial in *Baseball* magazine:

> It is, as a rule, a man's own business how he spends his money. But nevertheless we wish to call attention to the fact that many men do so in a very unwise manner. A very glaring instance of this among baseball players is the recent evil tendency to purchase and maintain automobiles. Put the money away, boys, where it will be safe. You don't need these automobiles. That money will look mighty good later on in life. Think it over, boys.

Baseball recently provided some timely food for thought, a reminder that in spite of the risks, it is still nice to be president, in part because just about anyone you invite will come to lunch. Three days before he was shot, Ronald Reagan lunched with Sandy Koufax, Ernie Banks and some other boys of other summers: baseball immortals. The two most testing jobs in America are president and radio broadcaster for the Chicago Cubs. Reagan has now held both, and at that lunch he blended both jobs.

One table was adorned by a broken-down Yale first baseman (George Bush), a Cardinal first baseman (Stan Musial), a Cub second baseman (Billy Herman) and a Pirate outfielder (Ralph Kiner, who spent, as many players have done, some of his declining seasons with the Cubs). In addition, some relatively new Washington hands got into a genteel rhubarb with an old Washington hand.

Joe Cronin was player-manager of the last Washington Senators team to win a pennant (1933). He is a defender of the American League's sinister Bolshevism that already has inflicted the "designated hitter" on baseball and may, unless checked, produce even worse desecrations.

Paul Volcker, a rangy right-hander from the Federal Reserve Board, told

Stan Coveleski: "Baseball is a worrying thing."

Cronin that the American League's incontinent social experimentation, its restless lust for novelty, is the cause of inflation. Jim Baker, the crafty portsider who is White House chief of staff, is a man of soft but wounding words, and he compared the American League's tinkering with baseball to the Anglican community's tinkering with the Book of Common Prayer. Bush maintained a discreet silence. He may want to run for president someday, and supporters of the designated-hitter rule are, alas, allowed to vote.

Baseball resembles politics. Consider the analysis by Stanley Coveleski, a Cleveland Indians pitcher and philosopher: "The pressure never lets up. Doesn't matter what you did yesterday. That's history. It's tomorrow that counts. So you worry all the time. It never ends. Lord, baseball is a worrying thing."

It isn't for Jonathan Will, who, noting his father's blighted life, has become an Oriole fan. Over the last twenty-two seasons the Orioles have won more games than any other team. For this father, a Cub fan, the worry is:

The Cubs, who last won a pennant in 1945, are entering the thirty-sixth year of their rebuilding effort, and there is the possibility of a player strike. If the Cubs' players withhold their labor, will we be able to tell the difference?

BASEBALL AND SOCIALISM

June 18, 1981

BECAUSE BASEBALL is the institution that most clearly distinguishes life in America from life in the Third World, I almost wish President Reagan would solve the strike by treating the Constitution as recklessly as the owners and players are treating the game.

The owners have some justice but almost no prudence on their side. They want more "compensation" for the ravages, as the owners consider them, of free agency. That is, they want some right to receive a quality player from a team that signs a premier player who has become a free agent.

The players, who are a fierce proletariat, have seen their salaries pulled up by the owners' bidding in the free market for free-agent stars. But the players have been unreasonably uncompromising. A few smart owners and players could quickly reach a compromise less complicated than the infield fly rule.

Then the serious class struggle could begin among the owners. The great American game needs something un-American: socialism. It needs more egalitarian revenue sharing, not as severely egalitarian as the revenue sharing pro football has, but much more sharing than baseball has yet to consider. It will come when, but not before, the "have-not" teams organize and outvote the "haves." If there are twenty-six shoe stores in a town, each owner can aim to drive the others out of business, but the twenty-six baseball owners have a stake in competitive balance.

Edward Bennett Williams is the owner of the Baltimore Orioles and the Cy Young of Washington lawyers (the winningest). He says Reagan should at least pressure the parties into accepting binding arbitration. The White

House replies with a limp non sequitur: "There were also suggestions that he [Reagan] get involved in the coal strike, but he didn't." One trembles for the country when philistines in high places think a baseball strike is merely comparable to a coal strike.

The nation is sentimental about Harry Truman these days, so perhaps Reagan should try something Trumanesque. He could try drafting the players or nationalizing the teams.

Pete Rose has not strained his eyes studying Article II of the Constitution, but he'd get the point if his commander in chief barked, "Pfc. Rose—play ball!" Granted, the only precedent is not encouraging. In 1946, Truman responded to the threat of a railroad strike by seeking a law to draft the workers. The populace, fresh from fighting dictatorships, thought this idea resembled what they had been fighting.

In 1952, the high-spirited Truman tried to prevent a steel strike by ordering his commerce secretary to seize and operate the mills and negotiate a labor settlement. The owners, who did not fancy being turned into government employees by presidential fiat, fought back. The finicky Supreme Court sustained them on the ground that no act of Congress or constitutional provision conferred upon the president the kind of power he was asserting.

However, anyone who has read many modern Supreme Court opinions is well-schooled in result-oriented sophistry, and can suggest how Reagan could rise above conservative principle, slice through due process and seize the baseball teams. Article II says the president "shall take care that the laws be faithfully executed." Dull-witted people construe "laws" to mean merely those passed by Congress. But advanced thinkers understand that law also includes Natural Law. It is not made by legislatures; it is discovered by right reason. It involves, basically, living in the way that is right for human nature. It is often called the will of God.

There have been spirited arguments, not to mention wars, over what God wills. But no one can doubt what He wills for Americans in summer: twenty-six teams playing 162 games. Never mind that twenty-one years ago Natural Law was that sixteen teams should play 154 games. Advanced thinkers know that Natural Law, like constitutional law, is an "evolving, growing" thing.

While the president ponders the responsibilities and opportunities involved in executing Natural Law, there is something baseball people should ponder. Baseball has flourished and fascinated because of intangibles—fragile intangibles. It has had an ambience of ritual matured through long, steady seasons. It has conveyed a marvelous sense of the cumulativeness of life, captured in the richness of baseball statistics. But asterisks are the enemies of this ambience—the asterisks that will now litter the record book, denoting the special circumstances of the summer of 1981, when baseball's spell was broken.

As Thomas Boswell of *The Washington Post* writes, "We are drawn to baseball because, while it may not always teach character, it usually reveals it. And in recent years, that has become the problem." The national pastime has caught the national disease of overreaching—the irresponsible, exploitative and plain dumb abuse of delicate institutions.

BASEBALL AND COMMUNISM

March 28, 1982

WHERE IS TROTSKY, now that we really need him?

I have been done great injury by a malefactor of great wealth, a capitalist pest called CC Assets Distribution Corporation. That is the clanking, officious name for what until recently was called, melodically, the Chicago National League Ball Club.

The Cubs, who have notoriously few athletic assets, invented trickle-down baseball. They acquired aging players (Dizzy Dean, Ralph Kiner) as their careers trickled down to a level suitable for the Cubs, a team forever trickling down in the standings. And now the Cubs' pestilential new management has engaged in a rapacious business practice that makes me think the Russian Revolution treated capitalists about right.

The brutes at the CC Assets Distribution Corporation inform me that they are exercising their right—a *right,* mind you: Is this America or Poland?—to buy back my one share of Cubs stock. Because these robber barons are conscienceless, and because the law is deaf to the voice of justice, I am no longer a baseball owner.

If this is the capitalist system Ronald Reagan wants to save, bring on Wal-

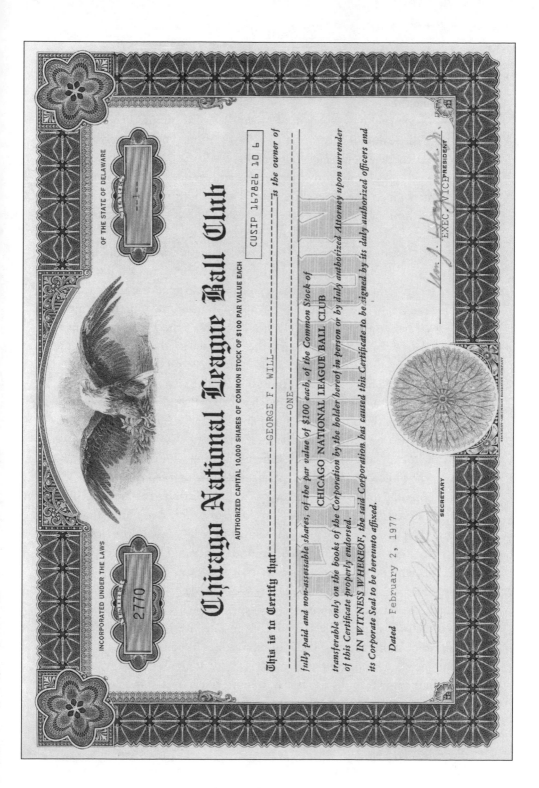

INCORPORATED UNDER THE LAWS

OF THE STATE OF DELAWARE

2770

SHARES

SHARES

1

Chicago National League Ball Club

AUTHORIZED CAPITAL 10,000 SHARES OF COMMON STOCK OF $100 PAR VALUE EACH

CUSIP 167826 10 6

This is to Certify that ——————————GEORGE F. WILL——————————

——————————————ONE——————————————— *is the owner of*

ONE

fully paid and non-assessable shares, of the par value of $100 each, of the Common Stock of

CHICAGO NATIONAL LEAGUE BALL CLUB

transferable only on the books of the Corporation by the holder hereof in person or by duly authorized Attorney upon surrender of this Certificate properly endorsed.

IN WITNESS WHEREOF, *the said Corporation has caused this Certificate to be signed by its duly authorized officers and its Corporate Seal to be hereunto affixed.*

Dated February 2, 1977

SECRETARY

EXEC. VICE PRESIDENT

ter Mondale to destroy it, root and branch. Peremptory letters from faceless financiers; mere money given in exchange for a piece of one's soul—hell must be very like this.

But on a spring day, when all of Nature seems to shout "Play ball!" even Cub fans can enjoy one exquisite baseball pleasure. They can read Thomas Boswell's nifty new book, *How Life Imitates the World Series.*

Sports serve society by providing vivid examples of excellence. So do sports pages when graced by Boswell's byline. He is the thinking person's writer about the thinking person's sport. Like baseball itself, he is graceful, subtle, elegant, inexhaustibly interesting and fun.

Baseball is for all of us who feel as Pete Rose does: "I was raised, but I never did grow up." Boswell is for all who like fine writing. Baseball, like Pericles' Athens (or any other good society), is simultaneously democratic and aristocratic: Anyone can enjoy it, but the more you apply yourself, the more you enjoy it.

Boswell has applied himself. His father works at the Library of Congress and one day he smuggled his son into the closed stacks, to the sacred precincts of deck twenty-nine, and said: "Okay. Here is every book on baseball ever written. Don't go blind." Heaven must be very like that.

Bill Veeck, who, like me, is a former baseball owner, thinks it is to baseball's credit that when the times were out of joint, baseball was out of step: "The sixties was a time for grunts or screams. . . . The sports that fitted the times were football, hockey and mugging." One of Boswell's (and my) pinups, Earl Weaver, the philosopher-king who manages the Baltimore Orioles, says: "This ain't a football game. We do this every day." An Orioles coach says: "In this game it's never going to be third-down-and-one. You don't hit off tackle in baseball, and you can't play the game with your teeth gritted. Muscles are fine. But this is a game of relaxation, conditioned reflex and mental alertness."

That is why Boswell says a good team depends on "the ability to achieve a blend of intensity and underlying serenity which, in daily life, we might call mental health. . . . Baseball is to our everyday experience what poetry often is to common speech—a slightly elevated and concentrated form." Boswell, an English major from Amherst, says, "Each team's season is like a traditional nineteenth century novel, a heaping up of detail and incident about one large family."

Yes, but some teams' seasons call to mind Dickens' *Great Expectations,* an eventful progress toward a happy ending. The Cubs' seasons are Dostoyevskian—*Crime and Punishment* and *The House of the Dead*—full of angst and gnashing teeth. It is the Karamazov family at play.

But the CC Assets Distribution Corporation, a.k.a. the Cubs team, is about to erupt from the dugout for another crack at life without a safety net. Recently (since the days when fans drove to the park in Hudsons, Packards, Studebakers and Nashes—since 1946) the Cubs have had two problems: They put too few runs on the scoreboard and the other guys put too many. So what has the new management announced that it is improving? The scoreboard.

Management recently chastised the players: "The Cubs have gained the reputation of being somewhat laissez-faire in their approach to work." Laissez-faire? At Wrigley Field, they handle words the way they handle ground balls.

THE EARL

October 7, 1982

Baltimore—Baltimore's Orioles wound up one brick shy of a load this season. After 161 games—about 1,500 innings—they and Milwaukee's Brewers were in a dead heat. Milwaukee won the 162nd game. It is said, although it is hard to believe, that there are persons who think 162 games are sufficient. But Orioles baseball is a case study of something the nation should study year-round: craftsmanship.

In the last twenty-six seasons the Orioles have the best won-lost record in baseball. When you realize that twenty-nine years ago the Orioles were the St. Louis Browns, you feel renewed faith in America as the land of upward mobility.

The builder of this dynasty is a man who once said of a pitcher, "I gave Mike Cuellar more chances than my first wife." Earl Weaver, the source of this and other utterances of pith and moment, retired last Sunday, for the nonce. Weaver's passions are well-known. (He once got tossed out of a game during the exchange of lineup cards.) But his contemplative, calculating side enabled his Orioles teams to finish first or second in thirteen of fifteen seasons. If Americans made automobiles the way Weaver makes teams, Tokyo would be clogged with Chevrolets.

The secret of Oriole magic is the mundane: attention to detail. Do the dull things right so the extraordinary things will not be required too often. Not that Weaver's "big bang" theory of baseball makes for dullness. He believes in

Earl Weaver: "I gave Mike Cuellar more chances than my first wife."

three-run home runs—"one swing, then trot"—because he knows that in most games the winning team scores more runs in one inning than the loser does in nine innings.

Thomas Boswell, the world's preeminent Weaverologist, quotes the great man saying: "Smart managing is dumb. The three-run homer you trade for in the winter will always beat brains." It is the license of genius to deprecate genius. Weaver's full testament, as collated by his Boswell, includes this:

> A manager's job is to select the best players for what he wants done. A manager wins games in December. He tries not to lose them in July. You win pennants in the off-season when you build your team with trades or free agents. They're not all great players; but they can all do something.

When was the last time you encountered such lucidity from an American in high office? What Weaver is talking about, and what he exemplifies better than the Supreme Court does, is a quality hard to define, but everywhere indispensable and always recognizable. It is not intelligence, which is plentiful, but judgment, which is scarce.

However, if you thirst for a more high-tech approach, the Orioles have that, too. Ray Miller, the pitching coach, says his research reveals something strange: "There ain't a left-hander in the world that can run a straight line. It's the gravitational pull on the Earth's axis that gets 'em." Boswell reports that when Miller had his minor league pitchers run sprints, he lined the left-handers up on a hill to balance their gravitational field, or he put them on the right-hand side of the line. "If you don't," Miller explained, "they'll wipe out your whole line."

The question for social scientists is: Why does brawny Baltimore have such a relationship with this brainy ball club? Perhaps it is because Baltimore is just the right size and sort of American city. It is lumpy with ethnic groups. Its social fabric is not smooth worsted; it is rich, rough, complex tweed. The Orioles do for Baltimore what the space program did for America: The team is what all have in common.

Or perhaps the point is that Baltimore is a port, so people eat lots of fish, which, as Jeeves always reminded Bertram Wooster, is brain food, just the stuff for Jeeves' hero (Spinoza) and mine (Weaver). Whatever the reason, the team fits the town, as no team could fit a city the size of New York or Los Angeles.

As the Orioles' radio announcers signed off until spring, one of them gave an unself-conscious and almost unurban pep talk. It expressed the way baseball has twined its silken fetters around this city, and in doing so, has made it more of a community. He said approximately this: "I know there are lots of sad kids out there who won't feel like eating tonight. But the good Lord wanted Milwaukee to win, and there is always next year, so, kids, dry your eyes and drink your milk."

So that's what I did.

THE PYTHAGORAS
OF WINCHESTER, KANSAS

April 7, 1983

BILL JAMES LIVES as a solitary genius in Winchester, Kansas. Well, not quite solitary. He has, he says, a wife to neglect. Does she, too, like baseball? "She does now," he says tersely. All James does—I'm not criticizing; he does enough—is compile, each year, *The Bill James Baseball Abstract,* the most important scientific treatise since Newton's *Principia.*

More than anyone since Pythagoras (he, too, thought that the essence of everything could be expressed arithmetically), James believes in numbers. He also believes in looking at evidence.

For example, in 1981 careless persons said the Yankees had an "incredible" won-lost record, 51–3, in games in which they led going into the eighth inning. But James found that the average record for American League teams leading after seven innings was 49–5. The Cleveland Indians, part of baseball's Third World, were 42–3. And James found that the Yankees' remarkable won-lost record was 0–41 when they were behind after seven.

'Round the clock and through the calendar, James sees things no one else sees, and disproves things that "everyone" knows are true. Next time conversation flags at a cocktail party, say: "In 1982, the Indians made sixty-one fewer double plays than their opponents, and no other team in the league had a differential of more than thirty-one. The Twins were the only team that had a losing record even in games when they scored a run in the eighth inning." If people do not burst into applause, you are at the wrong cocktail party.

Two moral imperatives are: Be as intelligent as you can be at whatever you are doing, and savor the sweetness of life. James does both by marinating himself in the mathematics of baseball. Baseball statistics gave many of us our first sense of mastery, our first (and for some of us our last) sense of what it feels like to really understand something, and to know more about something than our parents do.

Baseball people are Pythagoreans, but there are limits in life to what can be quantified. I began to suspect that I was heading for the wrong profession when, as a graduate student at Princeton, preparing to become a professor of political science, I opened a scholarly article on "The Judicial Philosophy of Justice Robert Jackson" and found a mass of equations and graphs. Part of baseball's charm is the illusion it offers that life can be completely reduced to numbers. But how would you like it, reader, if every day from coast to coast newspapers printed a box score of your accomplishments and errors at work the previous day?

Mathematics now has proven what clear-thinking moralists always hoped would be true: The American League's designated-hitter rule, America's worst mistake since electing President Buchanan, is a deserved affliction to its perpetrators. *Sports Illustrated*'s Jim Kaplan, a prophet who will not be without honor in his country while I draw breath, notes that for the first time the National League has won four consecutive World Series with four different teams. Also, the National League has won nineteen of the last twenty All-Star Games. Some MIT mathematicians told

Bill James pondering some new application of Fibonacci numbers to baseball statistics.

Kaplan that the odds against such a result between equals is 23,800 to 1, so Kaplan concludes the leagues are not equals.

Writing with a judgmental tone not heard since the Old Testament prophets were cataloging the shortcomings of the Israelites, Kaplan says to the American League: Your failures are the wages of sin, and the DH is sin. True, Kaplan cites other factors that contribute to National League superiority, such as better farm systems and fewer small parks that encourage mindless, swing-for-the-fences baseball. But the DH also has made American League managers dumber: "Because pitchers don't bat in the American League, managers have tended to leave them in the games when they are losing. As a result, there has been less thinking, less strategy, less managing." With the DH, teams lust incontinently for a big inning, so there is less aggressive scrambling for runs. Sloth. Sin.

I have warned Ronald Reagan: He will be judged by whether he rids the nation of the DH. He has not lifted a finger, preferring to squander his time on lesser matters, like arms control. I am remaining uncommitted regarding the 1984 election until I hear where Senator Alan Cranston stands on the DH.

However, God gave us baseball so that we should not have to think about missiles or the money supply all the time. An old man once said that if he could get through March, he usually found he lived 'til the end of the year. Old man, wherever you are: We made it.

Ancient Greece Got It Right

October 11, 1983

BALTIMORE—Like the fellow in the Bible who tried to reason with the deaf adder and did not get to first base, I have been told that at forty-two I should grow up. I see no merit in this suggestion, but have agreed to think about something other than baseball during the wasteland that stretches like the Sahara between the World Series and spring training.

Before that long night descends, let me note that the Baltimore Orioles, with the best record in baseball during the last twenty-seven years, are one of two American institutions of consistent excellence. The other is the telephone company. The government is fiddling with that, so the Orioles may soon have cornered the market on quality.

Considering the way some less-than-excellent players are paid today, Joe DiMaggio has a point when he says that if he were negotiating a contract with Yankees owner George Steinbrenner, he would be able to say, "George, you and I are about to become partners." Oh, for the days of innocence when the Pirates' Honus Wagner, the greatest shortstop ever, rejected a salary offer of $2,000 by declaring: "I won't play for a penny less than fifteen hundred dollars." (An NFL running back had a problem with those numbers this year when he said his goal was to gain 1,500 yards or 2,000 yards, "whichever comes first.")

Amazingly, the beauty of baseball is not apparent to everyone. Some critics say baseball is just another opiate of the masses, another of the distractions that American society produces so prolifically, diverting attention from the class struggle or the Iowa caucuses. But not all distractions are created equal. Some numb the mind (alcohol, the Iowa caucuses). Others engage the mind (baseball).

Besides, reasonable people want to be distracted from the world's horrors, which sometimes include a baseball team. When Miró's avant-garde sculpture *Chicago* was unveiled in that city, a lady with a lived-in face

Willie Stargell: At play.

was asked if she liked it. "Yeah," she said, "it keeps me from thinking about the Cubs."

It is said that baseball is "only a game." Yes, and the Grand Canyon is only a hole in Arizona. Proof of the genius of ancient Greece is that it understood baseball's future importance. Greek philosophers considered sport a religious and civic—in a word, a moral—undertaking. Sport, they said, is morally serious because mankind's noblest aim is the loving contemplation of worthy things, such as beauty and courage. By witnessing physical grace, the soul comes to understand and love beauty. Seeing persons compete courageously and fairly helps emancipate the individual by educating his passions.

Professional sports can be a melancholy business because an athlete's career compresses so much of life's trajectory into a short span. But as the Pirates' Willie Stargell said, "The umpires always say 'Play ball.' They don't say 'Work ball.'" That is why once when Stargell was boarding another 3 A.M. plane after a night game, he said: "I'm not crying; I asked to be a ballplayer."

Besides, baseball players are less subject than most athletes to the cruelty of the calendar. Look at the Phillies. They are balm to the spirits of middle-aged men. The leadoff batter is forty, the next batter is forty-two, the star pitcher is thirty-eight.* They have between them sixty-one years in Major League Baseball. (Let us leave to philosophers the question of whether the pinball game the Phillies play on that plastic carpet is really baseball.)

Tom Boswell notes that such longevity, although not normal, is not unheard of. Henry Aaron and Warren Spahn got better after they turned thirty-five. Aaron hit 245 home runs after thirty-five; Spahn won 20 or more games seven times, 180 in all after thirty-five. As Boswell says, no other team sport is so fascinated with the process of aging as baseball, perhaps because none of our other sports are based on skill and timing rather than brute force. No other sport has so many ten- and fifteen- and even twenty-year careers.

Great sporting events are unifying events for the communities directly involved. For the nation they are exceptions to what sometimes seems to be a rule that our shared experiences are either sad, such as the assassination of President Kennedy, or divisive, such as the firing of General MacArthur. And the World Series occurs four times as frequently as the Iowa caucuses. What a wonderful country America is.

*They are Joe Morgan, Pete Rose and Steve Carlton.

SPEAKING STENGELESE

March 29, 1984

THE BIBLE, which devout baseball fans consider the *Baseball America* of religion, counsels patience. But what did Job and other supposed sufferers know of the interminable cultural drought of the baseball off-season? My patience is exhausted—with the deficit, the Mondale administration (no point waiting on that one) and all sports that are not baseball.

Jefferson's tombstone lists three achievements: author of the Declaration of Independence and of Virginia's statute for religious freedom, and father of the University of Virginia. Not bad, but not a patch on what my tombstone will announce: Here lies the holder of the major league record for distance sprinted to a league championship series game—Paris to Chicago in October 1983, for a game that started at 2:20 A.M. Paris time.

I planned to use the winter to hone a new argument against the American League's designated-hitter rule. The argument was to be that the rule is a middle-class entitlement program (it entitles some men to play extra years) and hence is partly to blame for the federal deficit. But Baltimore's DH, Ken Singleton, is one of Nature's gentlemen, and helps the Orioles win, so a theory I favor must yield to a fact I love. I support the DH until Singleton retires. That is creative principledness. I learned it in Washington.

Since winter began—since the last out of last year's World Series, in a Sunday dusk in Philadelphia—there has been nothing to do except pout about the rottenness of a universe in which the regular season is just 162 games long. Pout, and study useful facts, such as:

There is no nonpitcher in the Hall of Fame named "Bob." To "dial 8" means to hit a home run. (Get it? On hotel telephones you dial 8 to get long distance.) Only one player's last name is also the name of the capital of a Mediterranean island republic (Steve Nicosia). Aurelio Lopez is the only pitcher in history whose first name contains all five vowels. Ed Figueroa is the only pitcher in history whose last name contains . . .

Never mind. The last days of deprivation, before the great getting-up morning of April 2, have been softened by the arrival of Robert Creamer's biography *Stengel: His Life and Times*. The story is a reminder of how young America is. Casey Stengel, who died in 1975 at age eighty-five, was a twenty-year-old ballplayer when his fellow Missourian, Mark Twain, died. Twain could have written this exchange:

STENGEL: "I won't trade my left fielder."
SPORTSWRITER: "Who's your left fielder?"
STENGEL: "I don't know, but if it isn't him, I'll keep him anyway."

If you disregard the (I guess) sexism, you cannot deny the beauty of this Stengel utterance: "What about the shortstop Rizzuto who got nothing but daughters but throws out the left-handed hitters in the double play?"

After managing the mighty Yankees, Stengel became the first manager of the Mets, who in their first season (1962) lost 120 games. Creamer says the Mets were an early manifestation of the 1960s counterculture, a harbinger of the long hair, short skirts and loud music. The Mets certainly were ghastly and that did, come to think about it, make them emblematic of the sixties. Stengel ("He is a remarkable catch, that Canzoneri. He is the only defensive catcher who can't catch.") was just the fellow to lead them beneath his banner: "They say you can't do it, but sometimes that isn't always true." Once as a Met batter was going to the plate, Stengel pointed to the foul lines and said: "Do you know what them lines are for? They are there to hit the ball on, and those other ball-

Casey: "They say you can't do it, but sometimes that isn't always true."

players are all out there in the middle." That is explaining a subtle sport with Middlewestern concision.

Baseball, like Stengel's long life of peaks and valleys, is like spring itself. It illustrates regeneration, resurrection and life's second chances. Forty years ago, when all able-bodied young men were fighting to make the world safe for baseball, the St. Louis Browns, for the first and last time (you can look it up), won the American League pennant. The Browns had long been, and soon were again, a byword for futility, and in 1954, in the most blessed journey since the Israelites left Egypt for the Promised Land, the Browns moved to Baltimore, land of crabs and coleslaw, which beats milk and honey.

There, Studebaker became General Motors: The Orioles became a dynasty. They have baseball's best won-lost record over the last twenty-eight seasons. And there, on Monday, after the World Championship flag is raised, winter will end with the last eight words of the national anthem, which are, as every real American knows, ". . . and the home of the brave play ball."

BASEBALL IN
THE UNMITIGATED CITY

August 13, 1984

REAL MEN DON'T EAT QUICHE? Real Chicagoans won't even eat veal. Red meat rare, please. Big-shouldered, wheat-stacking Chicago fancies itself hairy-chested. But it has a baseball team that has been a byword for wimpishness. However, the Cubs now are back and standing tall. Their fans—gosh, how many there suddenly are—are sitting atop the world on a pink cloud with rainbows draped over their shoulders. The rest of you had better brace yourselves for a spate of sociology. To understand the peculiar fervor of Cub fans you must understand Chicago's temperament.

Sparky Anderson and Saul
Bellow. The Nobel Prize
winner is below.

Chicago accommodates high culture (it has perhaps America's finest university, finest symphony, finest novelist and finest art museum) but does not wallow in it. One Cubs broadcaster once said on the air to another, "I picked up the *Sun-Times* this morning and saw Sparky Anderson's [then manager of the Cincinnati Reds] picture on the front page. I wondered, what's Sparky done to get his picture on the front page? It turns out it wasn't Sparky at all. It was a writer named Saul Bellow who won the Nobel Prize."

Bellow, the novelist, is one of my pinups (my only pinup who cannot hit behind the runner). He moved back to Chicago from New York, in part because of Chicago's healthily relaxed attitude about the literati. Chicago writers are not expected to declaim about everything under the sun. Joseph Epstein, a man of letters living in the Chicago area, notes that when Susan Sontag gave a speech in New York announcing her recent discovery that communism is a bad thing, she caused a stir. It is inconceivable that Bellow would utter such a banality, or that anyone in Chicago would notice if he did.

Chicago takes life neat: no ice, no water. One mayor told his machine, truthfully, "I'll do any damned thing you boys want me to do"—a thought often thought but ne'er so well expressed. When someone asked a judge to require Sally Rand to wear something beneath the two ostrich-feather fans that she (a mediocre dancer but a great entrepreneur) had bought on credit, the judge snorted, "Some people would like to put pants on horses." This was an opaque but very Chicago-like contribution to jurisprudence, which in Chicago has some built-in elastic. Chicagoans used to carry $10 bills folded with their driver's licenses to settle matters when they were stopped for speeding. That is why Mort Sahl called the Outer Drive "the last outpost of collective bargaining."

Chicago, wrote Nelson Algren, "has grown great on bone-deep grudges." The deepest are against New York, and not just because of decaying New York's insufferable snootiness about thriving Chicago. There also is the atrocity of September 8, 1969, the low point of a low decade. I don't want to beat a dead horse to death but Tommie Agee was out at the plate that night.

The Cubs were in New York playing the Mets, a parvenu outfit that did not exist until 1962. The 1969 Cubs led the pack until a September swoon, the crucial moment of which was the first game of the two-game series the Mets swept. The Mets won it 3–2 when Agee scored from second on a single by a dinky .218 hitter. At least the umpire said he scored. I say the umpire's scandalous decision was the beginning of Watergate. The image of Agee scoring—a summation of all the insults visited on Chicago by New York—is burned on every Cub fan's mental retina. The wound will not heal until there is mighty vengeance from the Midwest, perhaps this year.

Baseball is heaven's gift to struggling mortals, but has meant more thorns than roses for Chicago. The other team, the White Sox, has won only four pennants in eighty-three seasons. The 1919 "Black Sox" took a dive in the World Series. The 1906 "hitless wonders" had an anemic batting average of .230 but still managed to win the series, beating—who else?—the Cubs. It has been said that the test of a vocation is love of the drudgery it involves. Being a Cub fan is a vocation because the memory of man runneth not to a time when rooting for the Cubs was not mostly drudgery.

Today's Cubs are a tribute not to husbandry but to entrepreneurship. Few of this team's players were grown down on the Cubs' farm teams. Most were traded for by Dallas Green, an executive with the breezy eloquence of the Wife of Bath and the administrative flair of Lady Macbeth. Such wheeling and dealing strikes some purists as the summit of crassness, but this is a Republican era, so sharp practices are without moral taint.

A theory, contentedly expounded by the comfortable, is that suffering makes people spiritual. (John Wesley wrote to his sister Patty: "I believe the death of your children is a great instance of the goodness of God toward you. You have often mentioned to me how much of your time they took up! Now that time is restored to you . . . you have nothing to do but serve the Lord.") To those who say that passing through a fiery furnace is good for one's soul—that we learn in suffering what we teach in song—I say: One can have too much soul.

Real Cub fans are 99.44 percent scar tissue. A fast start by the Cubs causes them no palpitations. They know that feints are traditionally followed by faints. But now it is August and, wonder of wonders, the team is still in the thick of things. Dull despair has yielded to flaming hope, which is building like steam in a pressure cooker. And true Cub fans are as mean as are most winners who are unaccustomed to winning: They are busy repelling late-boarders from their gravy train.

Remember, this year baseball is politics carried on by other means. And in America, politics is most bitter when what is at issue is status. The Cubs are William Jennings Bryan, a prairie uprising against highfalutin Eastern pluto-crats wearing spats, the Mets and Phillies. "Arise ye prisoners of starvation!"—that is the Cubs' anthem.

Chicago, wrote Algren, is "an October sort of city even in spring." The numbed nerves of Cub fans are sensing the possibility that this year it could be spring—resurrection, regeneration—in October.

BASEBALL BY THE (ELIAS) BOOK

April 11, 1985

BALTIMORE—You know the feeling you get watching the steamier Greek tragedies, when dynasties are falling and sons are marrying their mothers and everyone is behaving badly and you are thinking: Really, things cannot go on like this. That is how March makes proper Americans feel. Life is vain, the world is a moral void, the universe is an empty shell. Then proper Americans look toward April, the horizon where the sun will rise. The sun is baseball.

Baltimore is the best place to watch the sunrise. I will explain why, after dealing with this disagreeable business: Peter Ueberroth must go. His reign as baseball commissioner is already six months old and the wicked designated-hitter rule has not been repealed. Worse—infinitely so—he is talking about taking an opinion poll on the subject. The mind reels. The thought occurs: "Death, where is thy sting?"

Who needs polls to discover if Michelangelo is superior to Andy Warhol? Some judgments should be beyond the reach of majorities. Democracy has, I suppose, its place, but in baseball? Perhaps public opinion must influence government. But baseball should not be a plaything of that turbulent, hydra-headed monster, the mob. Do we submit theories of astrophysics to referenda? Surely even in an open society there are closed questions, and this is one: Should baseball be desecrated by the DH rule, which allows degenerate, footballesque specialization?

If Ueberroth's baseball Bolshevism is the bad news, the good news is that our can-do country has gone and done it. It has produced a baseball book that almost contains all the information citizens ought to be required to master before being allowed to vote. The book is *The 1985 Elias Baseball Analyst.*

Do you have a Gibbonesque fascination with declines and falls? The book reveals that the 1984 White Sox were only the eighth team in fifty years to suffer a decline of 150 percentage points in their won-lost record compared with the preceding season. In 1984 Cleveland extended to twenty-four its record for the most consecutive seasons (excluding the 1981 strike season) finishing more than fourteen games behind the league or division leader. Before the 1984 Milwaukee Brewers did it, the last team to go in just two years from the best record in the league to the worst was during the Johnson administration. The time before that, Woodrow Wilson was in his first term.

AccDecSyn (Accelerated Decline Syndrome) exists when three criteria are satisfied: a team wins ten fewer games in season X than in season X minus one; it had a losing record in X minus one; it had a winning record in X minus two. The 1984 Giants suffered AccDecSyn.

But enough about incompetence. Let's go to Baltimore, where last Monday the Orioles began what will be their eighteenth consecutive season over the .500 mark. Only the 1926–64 Yankees have done better, and no team has a better winning percentage (.565) over the last twenty-nine seasons. Why are they so good? You can look it up in the Elias book.

It says Cal Ripken, the O's shortstop, has baseball's best on-base average (.452) when leading off an inning. With the opening game tied in the eighth inning on Monday, Ripken led off and got on base. Next came Eddie Murray. The book says that last year he batted .459, with a .838 slugging average, in late-inning pressure situations with runners on base. On Monday he drove in Ripken with a home run. As Murray began his regal, relaxed lope around the bases (Prince Charles could take lessons from Murray about the business of kingly bearing), baseball's magical mix of science and serendipity was on display.

A 162-game season is, like life, a study in cumulation. Things tend to even out, and talent tells. Ripken and Murray are gods, but there are lots of lesser but useful talents, and in a town like Baltimore, where they make good steel and sausage and baseball, they know how to make use of scraps. Who led the American League last year in the percentage of runners driven in from third with fewer than two outs? Elias knows: Jim Dwyer, Baltimore.

Past performances give rise to averages, on which managers calculate probabilities about future performance. The more you study, the less surprised you are. But no matter how hard you study, you still are surprised agreeably often, and the surprises that come to the studious are especially delicious. This is true in baseball and in the lesser stuff that is the rest of life.

The Answer Is Harry Chiti.
The Question Is . . .

April 15, 1985

It HAS BEEN SAID that baseball is to the United States what revolutions are to Latin America, a safety valve for letting off steam. I think baseball is more serious than any Latin American revolution. But, then, I am a serious fan.

How serious? I like *Sports Illustrated*'s baseball issue even more than its swimsuit issue. I would sell my soul for the thrill of hearing a manager say of me what Joe DiMaggio's manager said when asked if DiMaggio could bunt. The manager said he didn't know and "I'll never find out, either." The last words my four-year-old daughter hears at night are ". . . it's one, two, three strikes you're out at the old ball game." (On the "as the twig is bent" principle, my parenting involves the use of "Take Me Out to the Ball Game" as a lullaby.) I have one son who even knows the names of first-base coaches. That is like knowing the name of the secretary of commerce. I have told my other son that if he can hit a slider when he is sixteen he can quit school. I believe in incentives, and in Rogers Hornsby, who said: "Don't read, it'll hurt your eyes." So much for my credentials, OK? Now, listen up. The Japanese have gone too far.

I am not talking, as everyone else is, about how crummy the Japanese are being about American exports. I am talking about a Japanese export, another electronic gadget. It is a sonar system that beeps to warn an outfielder chasing a fly ball that he is approaching the fence. My objection is not that the technology is Japanese. My nationalism stops short of that of the Cubs' pitcher who, when asked if he threw spitballs or otherwise violated the rule against doctoring the ball with foreign substances, replied: "I don't put any foreign substance on the baseball. Everything I use on it is from the good ole U.S.A." My objection to talking fences is not patriotic but aesthetic.

The thought of beeping fences intrudes jarringly on April, a month of buds and box scores. The philosopher in us is consoled by the thought that, although ours is an age of dizzying flux, baseball retains a healthy Luddite hostility to modernity. But already some degenerate teams are using infernal machines, rather than honest manual labor with a fungo bat, to propel balls for fielding practice. And now beeping fences? If this craving for high-tech baseball does not abate, baseball will become as bad as—this is harsh, but it must be said—football.

The fact that football fans have coarse characters and frayed moral fibers cannot be a matter of mere chance. The explanation has something to do with the fact that football combines two of the worst features of American life: It is violence punctuated by committee meetings (huddles). The coarsening effect of football on its fans also has something to do with football's lunatic fascination with technology. The coaches stalk the sidelines wired up like astronauts so they can talk to the assistant coaches with whom they have spent the previous six days doing computer analysis of game films. The NFL is even considering "helmet radios" so that quarterbacks calling plays at the line of scrimmage can be heard clearly by receivers.

Baseball's emphasis is not on machinery, it is on mind, although some players modestly deny this. Bill Lee, Red Sox pitcher, said: "When cerebral processes enter into sports, you start screwing up. It's like the Constitution, which says separate church and state. You have to separate mind and body." Not true. Baseball's emphasis on mind accounts for its fine sense of moral nuance, as in the batter who, after being brushed back by a pitch, said: "They shouldn't throw at me. I'm the father of five or six kids."

Mind, in the form of mastery of facts, is also required of baseball fans. Martin Nolan, who edits the editorial page of *The Boston Globe* but is not otherwise dangerous, is a typical fan. The highlight of his life was when he walked into a saloon and answered that day's sports trivia question: Name the only player active when Ruth hit his last home run and Aaron hit his first (Phil Cavaretta). Heinie Groh boasted that he held the record among non-Yankee, non-switch-hitting third basemen for playing in the most World Series with the largest number of different teams. Ah, but somewhere out in this broad land there is a young, right-handed, non-switch-hitting third baseman with visions of the glory that will be his when he breaks Groh's record. As baseball folks say (stop me if you've heard this), records are made to be broken. Or, as Yogi Berra wired Johnny Bench when Bench broke Yogi's career record for home runs by a catcher, "I always thought the record would stand until it was broken."

One baseball scholar whose mind may have snapped assures me that Harry

Chiti, who was a catcher, sort of, holds this record: He is the only player ever traded for himself. Detroit traded him to the Mets for cash and a player to be named later. The Mets looked him over and designated him the player to be named later. Chiti was, of course, an ex-Cub. Before the Cubs attained their current grandeur, Cubness was the subject of a quiz compiled by a sadist and sent to masochists like me: 1. What Cubs slugger dislocated his shoulder carrying his suitcase down to the hotel lobby? 2. Why was it bad that Cubs pitcher Bill Hands recorded fourteen straight strikeouts? 3. What Cubs batter holds the major league record for leaving the most runners stranded on base in a nine-inning game?

Harry Chiti, the only player ever traded for himself.

4. What Cubs right fielder, trying to throw a runner out at the plate, beaned the batboy? 5. Cubs catcher Cuno Barragan hit a homer in his first major league at bat. How many did he hit in his career? 6. The Cubs once set a major league record by scoring five times in the bottom of the eleventh inning. Who won? 7. The Cubs once blew a 13–2 lead and lost on a home run. Who hit it? 8. The Cubs scored twenty-two runs and lost on a home run. Who hit it? You could look it up. But you only need to look below.

Answers: 1. Dave Kingman; 2. He did it as a batter; 3. Glenn Beckert, 12; 4. Mike Vail; 5. One; 6. The Mets, who scored six in the top of the inning; 7 and 8. Mike Schmidt.

The Nation's Failings
in the National Pastime

August 11, 1985

Harry Caray, the Chicago Cubs broadcaster, recently received a letter from a glutton for punishment. The letter came from a fellow in the Soviet Union who says he picks up telecasts of Cub games on an illegal satellite dish. Condemned by wanton fate to live in the Soviet Union, he turns to the Cubs to assuage his suffering. Imagine his consternation when even that peculiar consolation was threatened by a strike.

President Reagan reveres Calvin Coolidge, but missed this moment for militant Coolidge-ism. Coolidge's career was made when, as governor of Massachusetts, he stopped a Boston police strike on the grounds that there is no right to strike against the public interest. Actually, both sides in baseball's struggle have a right to make a horrid hash of things and the fact that they are doing so proves the national pastime partakes of the national tendency to clothe naked self-interest in the fine silk of philosophy.

The basic truth of baseball is the basic fact of political life: Life is unfair, but the unfairness is not irreducible. Baseball is like the Third World (although not, of course, in per-capita earnings). Except that the collective label "Third World" suggests more similarity than actually exists between the member nations. Think of the Los Angeles Dodgers as Saudi Arabia, and the Montreal Expos as Bangladesh. The different sizes, affluence and traditions of major league markets give certain teams advantages (larger attendance and broadcasting revenues) that must be at least partially compensated for if competitive balance is to be maintained.

Baseball suffers from a surfeit of political philosophy. Many owners and players are, in different circumstances, eager to profess selective worship of "free enterprise." Never mind that owners and players derive much of their incomes from a highly regulated industry, television. Never mind that

70

most teams play in ballparks built by taxpayers and rented cheaply as a subsidy.

Never mind that any sports league depends on competitive balance, which depends on cooperation, which in other industries would constitute conspiracy in restraint of trade. Exemption from laws forbidding such cooperation constitutes yet another subsidy for this semisocialized industry in which wealthy owners and wealthy players conduct a class struggle in the language of "free enterprise."

For years the owners fought to prevent a free market in talent—to deny players the right to sell their services to the highest bidders. When free agency began, owners made two false predictions: that players would move much more often than before, and that a few teams in the big markets would buy all the top talent and dominate baseball.

But Bill James, baseball's Spinoza, says in his newsletter that player migrations are not much more frantic than usual during the last eight decades. Yes, only three Phillies remain from the 1980 championship team, which scattered unusually quickly. But five years after the 1959 White Sox won a pennant—before free agency—only two players from the 1959 team remained.

Furthermore, in the last ten seasons forty division championships have been won. Of the twenty-six teams, nineteen have won at least one. The nine teams that have won two or more division championships include five from the smaller markets (Baltimore, Cincinnati, Kansas City, Pittsburgh, Oakland—combined, fourteen championships in ten years).

The danger the owners did not predict was dumb owners. Irrational bidding for free agents has had a ruinous upward ratchet-effect on all salaries, and bad business decisions have hurt otherwise sound franchises (Texas, Cincinnati, Cleveland). Baseball is a meritocracy: Attendance varies directly and quickly with artistry. Cincinnati's attendance declined from 2.6 million in 1976 to 1.2 million in 1983 as the team declined. The team with the best won-lost record in baseball during the last quarter-century plays in Baltimore, where intelligent entrepreneurship has compensated for demographic disadvantages.

The national pastime has some of the national failings. Its businessmen do not practice the business virtues as well as they praise them. Owners and players are so loquacious in the language of rights, there is only an attenuated sense of collective responsibility for the continuity of the institution. Continuity requires (conservatives, take note) strong central government. But baseball's sense of governance is Italian, which means tenuous. Baseball should show that the vigorous assertion of rights is compatible with a collective sense of responsibility for an institution that should be passed in good health to coming generations.

THE WORK
OF LOUISVILLE'S FATHERS

April 6, 1986

LOUISVILLE, KENTUCKY—I don't want to wax mystical and metaphysical about this, but . . .

Actually, I do want to wax. If an American boy can't get all worked up about a genuine "powerized" Louisville Slugger baseball bat, what use is the First Amendment's guarantee of the free exercise of religion?

When Thomas Aquinas was ginning up proofs of God's existence, he neglected to mention the ash tree. It is the source of the Louisville Slugger, and hence is conclusive evidence that a kindly Mind superintends the universe.

The Big Bang got the universe rolling and produced among the celestial clutter one planet, Earth, enveloped in an atmosphere that causes rain to patter on Pennsylvania ridgetops where ash trees grow. They grow surrounded by other trees that protect the ash trees from wind-twisting, and that forced the ash trees to grow straight toward sunlight. The result is wood with the perfect strength required for the musical "crack!" that is the sound the cosmos makes each spring when it clears its throat and says, "We made it through another winter."

'Tis spring and a young man's fancy lightly turns to thoughts of . . . well, to that, too, but also to baseball and its instruments. Baseballs are made in Haiti and many gloves are made in the Orient, but the bats that put people on the path to Cooperstown are made, one at a time, where you would expect, in mid-America.

The craft of baseball bats:
A lathe operator at Hillerich & Bradsby's "Slugger Park."

Wood lathes at Hillerich & Bradsby's "Slugger Park" plant take just eight seconds to make a bat for the masses. But craftsmen—the junior member of the workforce has seventeen years seniority—take longer to make bats for major leaguers. The bat-makers must take care. Ted Williams once returned a batch of bats because the grips did not feel right. They were found to be 5/1,000th of an inch wrong.

Hillerich & Bradsby charges $12 for each big leaguer's bat, and loses about $13 on the deal. The company does it for the prestige. It must have been relieved when Orlando Cepeda retired. He used to discard a bat after getting a hit. His reasoning (in which I find no flaw) was that there are only so many hits in a bat; you cannot tell how many there are in a bat; and he did not want to risk using a bat from which all the hits had been taken. (My father, although he used to teach logic, does not understand that, or this: It is dreadful to win a spring training game, because a team is only going to win so many games in a year and why waste one in Florida?)

The production of real bats here has declined because of a monstrous development—the popularity of aluminum bats. Hillerich & Bradsby makes such ersatz Sluggers, but commits that unnatural act in southern California, a region of novelties and regrets.

Colleges, those incubators of heresies, use aluminum bats for a grotesque reason: They last longer. Institutions of higher learning should understand that immortality is not a virtue in things that should not exist at all. Because metal bats are livelier than wooden bats, they distort the college game. Scoring soars, 200-minute games become common and some teams—yes, teams—have batting averages over .350. (In 1979, Wichita State batted .384.) Aluminum bats in the big leagues would produce every fan's ultimate nightmare: a blizzard of asterisks in the record book, denoting records set after baseball became subservient to the science of metallurgy.

People who will not recognize tradition as a sufficient argument should bow to aesthetic as well as scientific considerations. When aluminum hits cowhide, the sound is as grating as fingernails scraping a blackboard. If the sound of the aluminum bat were a food, it would be lima beans. Imagine a balmy summer evening, the portable radio on the front porch emitting the soft cicada-like sizzle of crowd noise. The announcer says: "Here's the pitch— and the runner is off at the ping of the bat!" "Ping"? The prosecution rests.

A. Ray Smith never rests. Louisville, like Renaissance Florence, is not especially large but is immoderately drenched with fine art, which in Louisville includes baseball. A. Ray (to know him for five minutes is to be on a first-name—well, initial and first-name—basis) is the reason God made Oklahoma, where he did well in what Oklahomans call the oil bidness. Now he is doing good in Kentucky, giving the community baseball.

A. Ray, an ebullient fellow, has not got the word from French philosophers who say that angst is the right response to the twentieth century. It is hard to get the hang of existential despair when your Triple A Louisville Redbirds recently drew 1,062,000 fans, more than five major league teams. A few of those fans probably were craftsmen from Slugger Park who came to the ballpark to see their handiwork put to work. Imagine, working amidst ash chips, which smell better than bacon in the morning. It is enough to make a boy wax poetical: I think that I shall never see a tree as lovely as what folks here make from some of them.

RING LARDNER,
CALL YOUR OFFICE

April 14, 1986

JADED PEOPLE who think life has lost its tang should perk up and pay attention to Mike Smith. He is a fireballing fireman who wants to hurl starboard-side heat for the Big Red Machine. . . . Sorry. In spring I sometimes slip out of English and speak American. Let's start over.

Smith is a right-handed relief pitcher who spent the spring trying to make the Cincinnati Reds. He was cut just before the Reds headed north. That's too bad, because Smith is a fountain of what teammates call Smittyisms. He once asked a waitress to put some neutrons on his salad. (Croutons? Close enough.) Checking out of a hotel, he said he wanted to pay his accidentals. Who has not had some of those in hotels? He says his coat is warm because it has good installation. He says: "I've been healthy my whole career except for nagging injuries the last few years." (He is just twenty-five.) Given the choice between returning from a game by car or bus he chose the bus, because, although it might be less comfortable, it would be quicker: "It's got bigger tires."

Ring Lardner, call your office. A character has wandered out of your pages and into the Reds' bullpen in Yankee Stadium. You may say Smith sounds like Yogi Berra (who said about playing outfield: "It gets late early out here"). But Yogi has set the record straight: "I really didn't say everything I said." Smith sounds sort of like Kansas City's Dan Quisenberry, who may be evidence that life on the knife-edge of danger makes relief pitchers odd. Quisenberry says the best thing about baseball is "there's no homework." Nah, the best thing about baseball is that its pace allows, and its nuances demand, deep thinking.

Of course, there can be too much of that. Baseball has been blemished by stories of drug abuse, but a case can be made that one team has been hurt by a virulent outbreak of religiosity. The decline of the Baltimore Orioles' pitching has coincided with some of the Birds' pitchers becoming born again.

Mike Smith: Yogi Berra for a new generation.

Instead of swapping lore about opposition batters they are discussing Scripture. Religion is fine in its place, but whatever became of the red-white-and-blue principle of a wall of separation between church and dugout?

Granted, it takes all kinds to make the world of baseball. It takes the Royals' Buddy Biancalana, who in eighty-one games had more errors (10) than RBIs (6). And it takes the Red Sox's human hitting machine, who constantly generates the Latest Incredible Wade Boggs Statistic, such as: In 1985 Boggs popped up only three times in 653 at bats, only once in fair territory. One hundred and twenty-four of his 240 hits came with two strikes. He swung at and missed only one first pitch.

Ever since the Big Bang, the universe has been expanding, and zillions of new stars and other stuff have been forming from the dust. The number of things to know about is increasing much faster than our ability to know them. That is true of baseball, too. The stuff of baseball, its crystalline essence, is statistics. Baseball is generating statistics faster than any fan can master them. Of course everyone knows that the Cleveland Indians drew

11,502 on Fan Appreciation Day and that of Pete Rose's first 4,192 hits, 29 came off pitchers who later became dentists. But the really rarefied air of high scholarship is the realm of an elite few, such as Al Kermisch.

The Florida sun has tanned Kermisch as brown as the skin portion of an infield after it has been hosed. Spring training, where Kermisch frets over the Orioles, is his only respite from the rigors of research in the Library of Congress, where he studies old box scores. When Kermisch, seventy-one, retired after twenty-three years in the Army, he started doing full-time what he had done intermittently while stationed at the Pentagon. And now he holds the major league record for most time spent with the library's microfilm machines. The fruits of his labor are sweet. For example, before Kermisch, the world was sunk in darkness, believing that a player for the 1898 Phillies was the first player to hit a home run in his first time at bat. Kermisch restored Reason to its throne by documenting that two other players did it in 1887—and on the same day.

Kermisch is a SABRite, a member of the Society for American Baseball Research, which publishes the world's most learned periodical, *The Baseball Research Journal.* Readers have learned from him the saga of Emil Batch, who is not a household name but should be. At the Polo Grounds on September 16, 1904, Batch, who had joined the Brooklyn club that month, hit home runs off two future Hall of Fame pitchers, Christy Mathewson and Joe "Iron Man" McGinnity, who that season were compiling records of 33–12 and 35–8, respectively. Batch played only three more seasons and hit only five more home runs, but he was king for a day, which is more than most of us can say. Thanks to Kermisch, we who have never tasted glory can savor Batch's moment.

Some people do not savor baseball, they suffer it. Consider the case of Edward Bennett Williams, Washington's premier lawyer and the owner of the Orioles. On this cool Miami night the O's are going to storm from behind to wax the Mets, but in the early going things are not going well. The Mets are hitting the ball hard and deep, sometimes off the wall, and even when the ball is caught Williams, one of Nature's pessimists, is not pleased. He sees in everything portents of a season in which the O's will lose 162 games.

Suddenly, on a three-balls, no-strikes count Gary Carter, the Mets' slugging catcher, is fooled and squibs a soft semi-pop-up that falls like a feather into the Oriole third baseman's glove. Is Williams pleased? Hardly.

"Contumacious!" he thunders, smarting from the indignity of someone swinging at his pitcher's 3-0 pitch. "No respect," he says. "We lawyers say someone is contumacious when they show so little respect. We've got nothing.

Nothing." Williams, who holds the major league record for deriving distress from baseball, has rounded into midseason form. It is time to head north.

LA PLATA'S
CHEERFULNESS QUOTIENT

August 4, 1986

LA PLATA, MARYLAND—To get here from Washington, you drive about an hour southeast, until you strike America. In that village of a few thousand souls, folks raise tobacco and soybeans and children. And a bumper crop of pickup trucks. Tonight a covey of pickups is backed up to the outside of the center-field fence at American Legion Field, where the local heroes—Southern Charles County Little League All-Stars—are lying in wait for some city slickers from the D.C. Metropolitan Police Boys and Girls Club. A clash of cultures as well as athletes, right? Wrong. What is going on here is childhood and other pleasures that illustrate the continuities and common denominators of American life.

There are, of course, particularities of places. The pickups are being used for what is known, even in the toniest circles, as tailgating. But La Plata tailgating is not what is done with Volvo station wagons at the Yale-Harvard game, where the Perrier flows like water, washing down pâté. La Platans are knocking back RC Cherry Cola and getting outside of hot dogs. Americans scarf down 50 million hot dogs on an average summer day. Trivia time: At which place are the most hot dogs consumed in a year? A particular ballpark? No, 2 million at O'Hare Airport. But at American Legion Field the ladies sweltering in the cinder-block concession stand are doing their level best to keep La Plata hot on the heels of O'Hare.

The first game this evening was broadcast on the local radio station but by

Lining one out in La Plata.

the time the nightcap begins at 8:30 P.M. the station is off the air. This is a good community to grow up in: The children are playing later than the radio station. Tonight the clay of the all-skin infield looks mustard yellow under the lights, which are enveloped in a swirling snow of moths. The boys go through pregame rituals of being introduced and reciting the Little League pledge that addresses all the large questions of life (God, country, law, sportsmanship). The national anthem is sung. ("No more of this Memorex stuff," says the PA announcer. "Live tonight.") The singer is a man of strong voice and even stronger opinions. He says La Plata should have a taste of the anthem's tangy fourth stanza. Dispensing with the dawn's-early-light business, he begins: "Oh! thus be it ever, when freemen shall stand/Between their loved home and the war's desolation!"

A baseball game is necessary to lighten things up after any stanza of our somber anthem, and any boy worth his salt knows all the game's liturgical moves. He taps his bat against his shoes to knock the dirt out of his spikes—the dirt that would be in the spikes if his shoes had spikes. If he is a pitcher he only half-wears his warm-up jacket, draping it over his shoulder and putting his pitching arm in a sleeve—not that a twelve-year-old arm needs such pampering. It is all part of our national manner. At the culminating moment of my misspent youth I helped an East Berliner escape through the wall. He was going to stroll in a U.S. military uniform past the East German police. I told him I would teach him to walk like an American, meaning the gait of a relief pitcher ambling in from the bullpen. He was a natural. Now he lives in West Germany.

As is occasionally the case when ten-, eleven-, and twelve-year-old boys start flinging a baseball around, the game this night has more ardor than artistry. In the big leagues there is a lively argument about whether the ball is livelier than it was last year. Home runs are flying off the bats of some unlikely players and out of parks at an unusual clip. (The manufacturer concisely denies any change: "Same cows, same standards." Yes, Virginia, the old horsehide isn't horsehide anymore. It has been cowhide for years.) In La Plata each team had one of those ragged innings Little Leaguers occasionally have, when the ball suddenly seems livelier because of the way it is bouncing off infielders' gloves.

The city boys won the six-inning game, 13–10. A major league outfielder, who did not talk like one, once said: "To a pitcher, a base hit is the perfect example of negative feedback." There was a lot of such feedback this night. But the game was brisk and orderly and all the boys had fun, thanks to four middle-aged men who had put in full days at work and then donned black trousers and blue shirts and black caps and umpired the night away. They are nice symbols of a nice fact: The American habit of pitching in is alive and well.

In 1981, when tax rates were cut and thus the tax benefit of charitable giving declined, people predicted a sharp decline in charitable giving. What happened? Giving increased more than 50 percent in four years. Economic facts, such as an increase of disposable income, help explain this. But volunteerism, the giving of time, also increased. That suggests, agreeably, that community spirit is not primarily a matter of economic calculation. It varies a lot with society's Cheerfulness Quotient. La Plata's CQ is high.

Joseph Epstein has written that growing up is often understood to be a misery, and that insecurity, angst, midlife crises and decay are said to be the fates of grown-ups. Therefore, "We can figure on roughly thirty-five to forty minutes of enjoyment in a normal life span." The players and spectators at La Plata's American Legion Field used up their shares, and about four other persons' shares, in one night. Epstein notes that happiness can be barely described, let alone analyzed, whereas unhappiness can be analyzed to a fare-thee-well. Besides, unhappiness implies criticism of the world. This is why intellectuals are so happy when they are miserable. Epstein wrote this in an essay titled "The Crime of a Happy Childhood." That title describes La Plata's only crime wave.

It is, of course, a journalist's duty to dwell on bad news, but the only bad news from La Plata is that all the fun the children are having bodes ill for American literature. Hemingway said the first requisite for a writer is an unhappy childhood. The world of letters will have to fend for itself, looking for no help from the boys who spend their summers on American Legion Field.

THE DH:
ON THE OTHER HAND . . .

October 23, 1986

FIDELITY TO CONSERVATIVE PHILOSOPHY occasionally requires minor course corrections, and small perfecting amendments to policies touching civilization's core values. Consider, for example, baseball's designated-hitter rule, and the scandal of the laughing umpire.

Hitherto I have described the designated-hitter rule as evidence that the West is and deserves to be in irreversible decline, and as the blackest blot on the Republic since the Dred Scott decision. My adjusted conviction is: The DH may be a thing of beauty graven on the heart of mankind by the finger of God.

Since 1973 the American League has allowed a DH, who almost always bats for the pitcher. Because the National League did not adopt that rule, the designated hitter was permitted in the World Series only every other year. This year Peter Ueberroth, baseball's commissioner, made a Solomonic decision: The DH would be permitted in games played in the American League team's park. However, the first game was played in the National League team's park (Mets' Shea Stadium), so the Red Sox pitcher, Bruce Hurst, had to bat. It was his first at bat in eons. The spectacle was so ludicrous that the home plate umpire laughed.

Think about that. Umpires are carved from granite and stuffed with

The first game of the 1986 World Series: Bruce Hurst's third "serious strikeout."

microchips. They are supposed to be dispassionate dispensers of Pure Justice, icy islands of emotionless calculation. In short, umpires should be natural Republicans—dead to human feelings. But not even an umpire can be stolid when Hurst is at bat.

Having struck out his first two trips to the plate, on his trip toward his third strikeout Hurst said defiantly: "I'm serious!" And the umpire cracked up. Nothing that causes such a collapse of decorum can be in the national interest. It is time to think the unthinkable: Perhaps the DH serves conservative values.

Conservatism's categorical imperative is: tradition. Its central principle is: "All improvements are for the worse." And: "Any change at any time for any reason is appalling." The three arguments against the DH are: Tradition opposes it, logic forbids it and it is anti-intellectual because it diminishes strategy. All three arguments fail.

Tradition? The National League, which fancies itself too highfalutinly traditionalist for the DH, plays pinball "baseball" on plastic rugs spread on concrete in cavernous, antiseptic new stadiums in Houston, Cincinnati, Philadelphia, Pittsburgh, Montreal and St. Louis. Besides, by now the DH has lengthening tradition, so conservatives have their traditional problem: If longevity sanctifies, the DH (like, say, the Warren Court's Miranda decision) is semisanctified.

The logic-chopping argument against the DH is given by Professor Dwight Gooden, pitcher and part-time logician: "The DH is a tenth player. Softball has ten players. Baseball has nine players." This attempt to win the argument about the DH by semantic fiat fails because . . . well, if the Constitution is what the Supreme Court says it is, baseball is whatever the rules say it is. Within reason. Up to a point.

My argument here makes me queasy, so I will tiptoe off the thin ice and deal with the notion that the DH diminishes strategy. The theory is that when pitchers must bat, managers must be Aristotles, deciding when to remove pitchers for pinch hitters, or when to have pitchers bunt. But it is disproportionate to preserve choices, which often are obvious, at the cost of having pitchers—one-ninth of the batting order—cause umpires to be convulsed with merriment.

On the other hand, of the two arguments for the DH, one—the argument from democracy—shocks conservative sensibilities. The democracy argument is: The DH increases offense and the people like offense, ergo . . .

Ergo schmergo. Democracy is fine in its place, but baseball, like religion and other important things protected by the Bill of Rights, should be beyond the reach of majorities, not blown about by the whims of the unwashed.

The real case for the DH is this: It represents the triumph of evidence over ideology. The anti-DH ideology is that there should be no specialization in baseball, no division of labor—everyone should play "the whole game." That theory is slain by this fact: Most pitchers only go through the motions at bat.

The DH is a way of facing that fact. It says: Only serious batters shall bat. Without the DH, every ninth batter is unserious. A pitcher hitting is like the shortstop pitching. Baseball does not expect an unserious pitcher—say, the shortstop—to pitch to one of every nine batters on the opposing team.

Conservatism abhors novelties (such as the DH) but deplores things (such as pitchers at bat) that cause lapses from decorum (such as laughter) by authority figures (such as umpires). Conservatism is a demanding mistress and is giving me a migraine.

BLUE-COLLAR GOVERNMENT

March 29, 1987

LAKELAND, FLORIDA—In the glamorous world of the big leagues, you usually can find in the bowels of the ballpark ninety minutes before game time a middle-aged man sitting in long underwear with his hands covered with mud from the Delaware River. Welcome to the blue-collar world of the men whose collars really are blue—the umpires, baseball's judicial branch.

The man with the mud will be umpiring home plate that day. During the season, sixty baseballs (fewer here at spring training) are rubbed with mud—only the Delaware stuff will do—to remove the cowhide's slickness. The long underwear spares umpires the discomfort of itchy dust and the inelegance of sweat-stained trousers. Umpires understand, as de Gaulle did, that dignity sustains authority.

In 1914, Christy Mathewson, the pitcher, said, "Many fans look upon an umpire as a sort of necessary evil to the luxury of baseball, like the odor that follows an automobile." Such fans should imagine what life would be like without the likes of Richie Garcia and Durwood Merrill, two of the American League's finest.

Umpires' compensation and benefits have markedly improved in recent years.

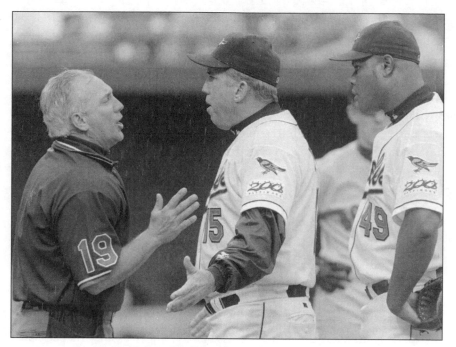

Richie Garcia: "Call 'em fast and walk away tough."

In 1998 a first-year umpire earns a base salary of $75,000 a year. An umpire in his thirtieth season earns $225,000. Every November 1 every umpire gets a $20,000 annual bonus, paid from baseball's pot of postseason revenues. Umpires get $5,000 for working the All-Star Game, $12,500 for a Division Series, $15,000 for a League Championship Series and $17,500 for the World Series. In addition, each of the fifteen crew chiefs (eight in the American League, seven in the National) get an extra $7,500 a year. All umpires get thirty-one vacation days during the season—one week early in the season, two weeks between Memorial Day and Labor Day, one week in September, plus three additional days somewhere along the line, and the All-Star break. That is not a lot of time off, considering that for umpires there are no home games.

A senior umpire who does a lot of postseason work can earn maybe half as much as a mediocre utility infielder. The infielder's mediocrity is apparent. Umpires aspire to unnoticed excellence.

It is said that umpires are expected to be perfect on opening day and improve all season. So they, too, need spring training for an essential element of their craft: timing.

Garcia, forty-four, came to umpiring from Key West and the Marine Corps. The corps was good training for a vocation that an umpire once summarized in seven words: "Call 'em fast and walk away tough." Garcia is a compact man with a spring in his step and baseball on his brain: On off-days, he watches televised baseball games.

Like the best baseball people, if he is awake he is working. He studies box scores to be aware of what hitters are hot, what pitchers are wild, what fielders are making errors. The night before working home plate, he begins thinking about tomorrow's starting pitchers: their moves to first, their tendency to balk, their mix of pitches.

Merrill, forty-seven, a bear of a man from Oklahoma, via Hooks, Texas, was a burned-out high-school football coach at twenty-eight, so he became an umpire. Studies show that umpires endure stress levels not much lower than those of air-traffic controllers, big-city policemen, inner-city teachers and Texas high-school football coaches. Umpires endure the stress in quest of a perfection so unobtrusive it is invisible to 50,000 people.

The key to excellence, says Merrill, is "angle and position": being in the best position to make the difficult calls such as swipe tags and trapped balls. There is another ingredient: confidence.

When Babe Ruth was called out on strikes by umpire Babe Pinelli, Ruth made a populist argument, inferring weight from raw numbers: "There's forty thousand people here who know that last one was a ball, tomato head!" Pinelli replied with the assurance of John Marshall: "Maybe so, but mine is the only opinion that counts." As Garcia tells young umpires and every parent should tell every young person, "Just because they're yelling at you doesn't mean you are wrong."

Umpires are islands of exemption from the litigiousness of American life. As has been said, if someone gets three strikes on you, the best lawyer can't get you off.

Long ago, the ethic of umpiring was put pristinely by umpire Bill Guthrie: "Der ain't no close plays, me lad; dey is either dis or dat." De jure, perhaps, but de facto it can be a little different. Strict construction of baseball's rules, as of the Constitution, leaves room for judicial interpretation.

"Anybody can see high and low," says Merrill. "It is 'in and out' that is umpiring." The saying "Good umpires are pitchers' umpires" means that good umpires are not afraid to call strikes. Their calling borderline pitches strikes makes pitchers more confident and batters more aggressive. That is, good umpiring makes good baseball, a fact from which a large lesson flows.

The business of umpiring is to regulate striving, to turn it from chaos into ordered competition, thereby enabling excellence to prevail over cruder qualities. Umpiring is, in a word, government, and it is very valuable, a fact some of today's "conservatives" should consider.

Section 9.01(a) of the baseball rule book says: "The umpires shall be responsible for the conduct of the game. . . ." Some of us, emerging parched from the desert of the off-season, think there is no nobler responsibility.

THE FUSE THAT LIT
THE FIRE

April 13, 1987

SECOND BASE IS not for the fainthearted. On a double play the second baseman making the pivot has his back to the base runner who is barreling in from first with disruption on his mind. Jackie Robinson was a second baseman.

He also was a dream maker when, forty years ago, he took the field for the Dodgers on opening day at Ebbets Field against the Boston Braves. Robinson's first major league game was the most important event in the emancipation of black Americans since the Civil War. He is one of the two most important blacks in American history; he was the fuse that lit the fire. In 1944, eleven years before Rosa Parks refused to move to the back of a Montgomery bus, Lieutenant Robinson was court-martialed for insisting—successfully—that Fort Hood, Texas, adhere to Army orders desegregating buses. He was a lieutenant only because when he was excluded from Officer Candidate School he protested through another black at Fort Riley, Kansas—Joe Louis.

The athletic successes of Louis and Jesse Owens in the 1930s (Robinson's brother Mack finished second to Owens in the 200-meter dash in Berlin) made the absence of blacks in baseball glaring. Then the war in which blacks fell fighting Hitlerism nurtured the idea that anyone who could cross Omaha Beach should also be eligible to cross major league foul lines. Also, commercial considerations mingled with the ethical. Until the war three-quarters of all blacks lived in the South, and all sixteen major league teams were in the North. War production drew blacks north to the bleachers.

As Jules Tygiel makes clear in his splendid book *Baseball's Great Experiment: Jackie Robinson and His Legacy*, Robinson was a physical and moral miracle. He probably was not even the best player in the Negro leagues but may have been the greatest all-around athlete in American history. At UCLA he lettered in football (11 yards a carry in his junior year), basketball (led the conference in scoring), track (NCAA broad-jump champion) and baseball. He won championships in golf and swimming and was a fine tennis player. But it was his temperament that made him perfect for the task the Dodgers' Branch Rickey set for him.

Robinson was an alloy of fire and ice, a fierce competitor who in 1947 had to leash his pride and smother his resentment, channeling his passion into baseball performance. Baseball requires a delicate equipoise that combines the relaxation required for success over a (then) 154-game season and the intense concentration involved in hitting a rocketing round ball with a round bat—and, when in the field, tensing in anticipation on at least 120 pitches every game. Robinson had to excel at the most difficult game under the most difficult of conditions. With the attention of black America focused on his every at bat, he succeeded, in spite of excruciating tension and execrable abuse.

He became the perfect model for black Americans, and for white Americans, too. His style of play was everything that blacks were then rarely allowed to be—confident, aggressive, dashing, aristocratic. In a 1947 game with the arch-rival Giants, with the score tied and one out, Robinson doubled. When he tagged and went to third on a flyout, a Giant official complained: "That's bush stuff. With two outs he's just as valuable on second as he is on third. What's he going to do now—steal home, I suppose?" On the next pitch he did. Some called him uppity.

More called him exciting. In 1946 a war-weary nation welcomed the ballplayers home by setting a new major league attendance record. In 1947, thanks to Robinson, the record was smashed. Most called him admirable. By the end of 1947 a poll ranked him the second most admired American man, behind Bing Crosby. He certainly was a bargain. His 1947 salary was the major league minimum—$5,000, less than a third of what some of today's stars make per at bat.

Jackie says goodbye: His final exit from the Ebbets Field clubhouse,
January 7, 1957.

Three Dodgers protested Robinson's presence. Rickey got rid of them. When in June 1947 Bill Veeck, owner of the Indians, made Larry Doby the first black in the American League, he took Doby to the clubhouse. Three players refused to shake Doby's hand. Veeck traded them. And remember the grace of Joe Gordon, the Indians' infielder. Tygiel says that in one of Doby's first games he struck out swinging wildly on three pitches. Gordon, the next batter, who normally hit that particular pitcher, fanned on three pitches, probably deliberately, then went and sat next to Doby in the dugout. Tygiel says that it is arguable that Doby more than Robinson spurred the search for black players. Robinson was an athletic prodigy. Doby represented a larger class of the merely—merely!—talented blacks.

"Like plastics and penicillin," wrote a commentator midway through 1947, "it seems like Jackie is here to stay." Robinson played through 1956. Like a comet he flared brilliantly and burned out quickly. Afflicted by diabetes and heart disease, he died in 1972 at fifty-three. But what he began demonstrated the wonderful plasticity of American life. By the end of 1953, seven National Leaguers had won Rookie of the Year awards: six, including the last five, went to blacks. In the American League blacks won *The Sporting News* Rookie of the Year award in 1951 and Player of the Year award in 1952. In 1953, in Jacksonville, Florida, where a few years earlier the park had been closed to prevent Robinson from playing, attendance rose 135 percent as Floridians flocked to see the nineteen-year-old Henry Aaron. A fan in Shreveport, Louisiana, hollered at the local manager, "When you gonna get yourself some niggers so we can win some ball games?" When Doby accidentally spiked a white shortstop, the violence expected to follow such an incident did not happen. *The Sporting News* headline was: NEGRO SPIKES WHITE RIVAL— AND THAT'S THE WHOLE STORY.

All teams were not integrated until 1959, when the Red Sox fielded a black. But by September 1948 Robinson had exercised an American's most sacred First Amendment right, arguing with an umpire so vehemently that he got ejected. In 1947 Robinson broke in playing first base. A rival gashed him badly, high on his calf, while crossing the base. The spiking seemed deliberate. Robinson neither left the game nor retaliated—then. But a few years later, when Robinson was settled at second base, the spiker came sliding in. Robinson tagged him high and hard, removing a few teeth. Call that an emancipation proclamation.

Perhaps the Players
are Livelier

July 16, 1987

OAKLAND—When baseball's best practitioners assembled here for All-Star festivities, not all thoughts were festive. Some brows were furrowed in puzzlement, some eyebrows were elevated by suspicion and some lips were pursed in disapproval about the fact that baseballs are being hit over fences at a record rate.

Many a cynic with a flair for *le mot juste* says the ball has been "juiced." This is a base canard, but one that illustrates the American tendency to explain puzzlements in terms of conspiracies or technology or, as in the current case, both.

Cynics say: In the 1920s the ball was made livelier to rescue baseball from the "Black Sox" scandal. Baseball recently got a black eye from drugs, and fans love home runs, therefore . . .

Not so fast. True, home runs are crowd pleasers. As a morose owner (Clark Griffith of the Washington Senators) once said: "Fans like home runs and we have assembled a pitching staff to please our fans." But the homer-glut, properly understood, illustrates the inadequacy of explanations that involve a single cause or a malevolent motive.

The sudden disequilibrium between hitting and pitching does have something to do with a new technology—the aluminum bat used by high schools and colleges to save money. Wood bats break, but aluminum bats demoralize pitchers by making George Bretts out of banjo hitters. It is harder to get a fastball by the faster, livelier aluminum bats. Even a jammed hitter often dumps the ball over the infield. So pitchers, including youngsters whose arms are still developing, rely on breaking, sinking pitches that wear out arms.

In the 1960s, pitchers such as Juan Marichal and Bob Gibson (both of whom also had terrific fastballs) showed that pitching low is the ticket to

Cooperstown. Umpires call what is thrown, and they began to make the strike zone lower and smaller. Today a pitch above the belt is usually a ball. This trend was intensified when American League plate umpires quit wearing the cumbersome "mattress" chest protectors that required them to stand almost erect behind the catcher. Now they, like National League umpires, wear chest protectors under their shirts and crouch next to the catchers on the

Mark McGwire, "a redwood that wandered over to Oakland from Muir Woods."

inside corner of the plate. This, too, has pulled the strike zone down, encouraging those sinking pitches that take a toll on arms.

Furthermore, pitching in organized baseball, meaning the professional leagues, is declining because disorganized baseball, meaning what kids do, is becoming too organized. Strong arms are developed by years of throwing the way the American child was meant to throw—from sunup to sundown. But today's busy children are schlepped hither and yon in station wagons, play a few innings of baseball, and then are whisked on to other, needless to say, lesser activities (soccer practice, science clubs, etc.).

When pitching gets strong, batters get relief: The pitching mound was lowered in 1968. When pitching gets bad, batters get greedy. Strikeouts also are up this year, because more batters are swinging away with two strikes on them, trying to reach the bleachers and the big contracts.

The cynics who want a special prosecutor appointed to dissect the ball make much of the fact that rookie Mark McGwire, the Oakland Athletics' man-child, has hit 33 home runs by the All-Star break. (The full-season record for a rookie is 38.) But look at him. Take an afternoon and walk around him. He is a growing boy of twenty-three and at 6 feet 5 and 220 pounds he looks like a redwood that wandered over to Oakland from Muir Woods.

When his teammate Jose Canseco, last year's Rookie of the Year, came to Oakland, the team had to send out for a uniform that would accommodate his biceps. Lively ball? These guys could hit rice pudding 400 feet. Human beings are becoming bigger (perhaps antibiotics are the explanation) and hitters are helping evolution along by using weight training.

A "juiced" ball may have been used in the early 1930s to draw crowds during the Depression. In the 1970s, such a ball was used briefly in spring training, until it became clear that pitchers were going to be decapitated by line drives. But today the single-cause crowd that explains home runs in terms of a doctored ball should remember Einstein's (or was it Boswell's; it is hard to keep those two straight) axiom: Explanations should be as simple as possible—but not any simpler.

SYSTEMS EQUILIBRATE. REALLY.

February 21, 1988

COOPERSTOWN, NEW YORK—There now. Warm your chapped hands in the glow of that dateline. This village, to which baseball addicts trek for a February fix, is a place to ponder something not frequently noticeable in the modern age: progress.

Human beings seem to take morose pleasure from believing that once there was a Golden Age peopled by heroes and demigods, an age of greatness long lost and irrecoverable. But actually things are better than ever, at least in baseball, which is what matters most. And the reason for the improvement says something heartening about Life.

The Hall of Fame, a shrine to baseball's "immortals," is located here because of a sweet myth that is—as most myths are—impervious to evidence. The myth is that Abner Doubleday invented baseball here in 1839 in Farmer Phinney's pasture. The 150th anniversary of that nonevent will be tumultuously celebrated next year. It has been said that the only thing Doubleday started was the Civil War, and even that assigns him too grand a role. He was a Union officer at Fort Sumter, but the Southerners fired first.

However, the Hall is here, so grown men come here to gaze wide-eyed at Mel Ott's luggage tag, Christy Mathewson's checkers set and the shoes worn in 1975 by the player who scored baseball's millionth run. Here the words describing a Babe Ruth exhibit speak of "the might of his smite as he hit balls out of sight." And here we can take pleasure from this paradox: The reason some of today's statistics are less spectacular than yesterday's is because baseball generally is superior to what it was. Do not take my word for it, take that of Harvard's Stephen Jay Gould.

Gould teaches biology, geology and the history of science. His special interest is evolutionary processes. As a student of life's long-term trends, he

94

EDWIN DONALD SNIDER
"DUKE"
BROOKLYN N.L., LOS ANGELES N.L.,
NEW YORK N.L., SAN FRANCISCO N.L.,
1947 - 1964
HIT 407 CAREER HOME RUNS AND TIED N.L.
RECORD WITH 40 OR MORE ROUND-TRIPPERS
FIVE YEARS IN A ROW, 1953-1957. BATTED .300
OR BETTER SEVEN TIMES IN COMPILING .295
LIFETIME AVERAGE. TOPPED LEAGUE IN SLUG-
ING PCT. TWICE AND TOTAL BASES THREE TIMES.
FIRST TO HIT FOUR HOMERS IN A WORLD SERIES
TWICE -- IN 1952 AND 1955. SET N.L.
RECORD FOR SERIES HOMERS (11).

"There he is!": Duke Snider.

has pondered the extinction of the .400 hitter (none since 1941) and he concludes that the cause is not, as you had feared, "entropic homogeneity." Rather, the reason is that systems equilibrate as they improve.

While the highest averages have declined, the average batting average has remained remarkably stable over time. It was around .260 in the 1870s and is about that today. But the highest averages have declined because narrowing variation is a general property of systems undergoing refinement.

Variations in batting averages—the gap between the highest averages and the leagues' averages—shrink as improvements in play eliminate many inadequacies of the majority of pitchers and fielders. Today's "just average" player is better than yesterday's. Major league players meet, Gould says, in competition "too finely honed toward perfection to permit the extremes of achievement that characterized a more casual age."

As baseball has been sharpened—every pitch, swing and hit is charted—its range of tolerance has narrowed, its boundaries have been drawn in and its rough edges smoothed. As Gould says, Wee Willie Keeler could "hit 'em where they ain't" (to the tune of .432 in 1897) partly because "they"—the fielders—were not where they should have been. They did not know better. Today's players play as hard as the old-timers did, and know much more.

In 1987 San Diego's Tony Gwynn hit "only" .370 because average play has improved so much that there are fewer opportunities for geniuses like Gwynn to exploit (in Gould's phrase) "suboptimality in others." The "play" in playing professional baseball is, Gould says, gone. Baseball has become a science in this sense: It reemphasizes repetitive precision in the execution of its component actions. That is why variation decreases at both ends, with the highest and lowest averages edging toward the league average. Standard deviations (take a deep breath: the square root of the sum of the squares of all individual averages minus the major league average, divided by the total number of players) are narrowed by progress.

That is a thought to chew on here at the Shortstop, one of those little restaurants where Formica goes to retire and a grilled cheese and vanilla malt sets you back $2.65. Nourished, you can savor this February scene:

A father with a wife and three children in tow zigzags through the Hall's hall containing the bronze plaques celebrating the achievements of each immortal. "There he is!" exclaims Father when he finds the object of his quest—the plaque honoring Duke Snider, a Dodger. The children show signs of having heard their fill from Father on the subject of Snider's superiority to all who have come since, and the wife is wondering if the marriage vow concerning "for better, for worse" covered this, but Father is lost in reveries about olden days when giants strode the Earth.

SKILL, AND "MERE" WILL

April 11, 1988

CAL RIPKEN SR., manager of Baltimore's Orioles, smokes Lucky Strikes and drinks Schlitz beer. The Luckies are not filtered and the Schlitz is not "light." He is a bandy-legged former minor league catcher who looks like something whittled from an old fungo bat. His home is in Aberdeen, Maryland, site of the U.S. Army Proving Ground, where tanks and such things are tested for toughness. Aberdeen's principal export is Ripkens, two of whom, Cal Jr., twenty-seven, and brother Bill, twenty-three, play shortstop and second base, respectively, for Father. Barring an act of God, sometime in June, in the season's seventy-third game, Cal Jr. will become especially emblematic of the great virtue of the sport of the long season—constancy. He will play in his 1,000th consecutive game.

Still far over the horizon is one of baseball's most durable records, Lou Gehrig's 2,130 consecutive games. But Ripken could break that in June 1994, when he will be thirty-three, two years younger than Gehrig was when disease stopped him. To those who say he needs a day off, he replies that he has many (too many, his tone suggests; Ripkens consider the season unconscionably short) between October and April, so his streak is really a series of 162-game streaks. But a positive argument for continuing the streak speaks to the problem of maintaining the intensity necessary for high performance throughout a long season in the sport with the highest ratio of mental-to-physical demands.

The authors of the most important book published since Gutenberg—*The Elias Baseball Analyst,* of course—disparage streaks such as Ripken's.

Ripken Family Portrait: Bill, Cal Sr., and Cal Jr.

Homer nods and the *Elias* authors err. They distinguish between records that reflect skill and records, such as consecutive-game streaks, that reflect mere will. But that is too stark a distinction. Natural gifts, however great, and skills, however sharply honed, still must be summoned to application by strength of will. The summons is not easy on a muggy August night in Cleveland when neither team is in the hunt for a pennant. Skills must be willed into action by an intensity that does not well up spontaneously. Such intensity must be cultivated. For some players, such as Ripken, playing every day is part of an ongoing mental preparation.

On the other edge of the continent, in San Diego, another craftsman is giving tutorials in constancy. Tony Gwynn toils in right field and relative obscurity for the San Diego Padres. They used to be conspicuous for the frightful yellow-and-brown uniforms that made them look like tacos. Now they wear sedate pinstripes and the brown of refried beans. But San Diego is boxed in by Los Angeles, ocean, desert and Mexico, which explains why Gwynn, a genius, gets so little attention. Last year he batted .370, the best

National League average since Stan Musial's .376 in 1948. Gwynn never went more than eight at bats without a hit. If in the same number of at bats he had garnered just eighteen more hits—approximately one every ten days—he would be the most famous athlete in America because he would have been the first .400 hitter since Ted Williams in 1941. Gwynn, who seems to remember every pitch thrown to him, probably can remember eighteen close calls or great catches made against him last year.

Rogers Hornsby, who batted .358 over twenty-three seasons, avoided eyestrain by refusing to look out a train window or at a movie. This season Gwynn will carry his movies around with him. Outside his house sits a large satellite dish. Inside there are five VCRs and one MVW—most valuable wife. Alicia helps record and edit Padres and other National League games for Tony to study. And now he has a portable VCR to take on the road. So on the afternoon before facing, say, Rick Sutcliffe at Wrigley Field that night (yes, night at Wrigley: The world turns), Gwynn will study Sutcliffe's pitches to him in previous at bats, and Sutcliffe's move to first base.

Gwynn has been known to show up at a social event with a batting glove hanging out of his hip pocket, having stopped on the way for some swings. He is one of baseball's most cheerful as well as hardest-working stars, but I have seen him momentarily miserable. On the Padres' bench two hours before a spring training game in Phoenix, he found himself incapable of doing something a ballplayer must sometimes do: sit. Although he was in uniform, he had sutures in his hand from minor surgery and could not play that day. He fidgeted and finally bolted to the clubhouse, away from the unendurable sight of others preparing to do what he lives to do: work.

A player-philosopher has made much of the fact that umpires holler "Play ball!" not "Work ball!" But baseball is hard work and the best players, like Gwynn and Ripken, have a work ethic grounded in their elemental urge to compete, constantly. Players who excel in the self-contained world of the sport of the long season know something. It is something universally important. It is that God is indeed in the details and that if you solve all the little problems there are no big problems. Gwynn, Ripken and others at the peak of this particular profession are there because they have cultivated a kind of concentration unknown to most people.

Everybody knows—who is this "everybody"?—that Ripken is too big (6 feet 4 and 225 pounds) to play shortstop, a position frequently played by small or willowy fellows with nicknames like Rabbit (Maranville), Pee Wee (Reese), Scooter (Rizzuto) and Slats (Marion). But the memory of man runneth not to the last time Ripken missed infield practice. He is constantly pondering the little things—where to play this batter when that pitcher has a particular ball-and-strike count. He has been an All-Star shortstop four consecutive times. A lot of teams were skeptical about Gwynn because he was a shaky outfielder. Last season he won his second Gold Glove.

The season that begins this week and will not end until the nip is back in the air will offer many lessons about the rewards of diligence. If every American worked the way Ripken and Gwynn do, America would have so few problems we could all go to more games. So study them. That utilitarian reason for going to games is offered to you if you are the sort of person for whom pleasure is an insufficient reason to take yourself out to the park.

"THE MOMENT'S OVER"

July 14, 1988

WHAT IS THIS summer's most entertaining movie for grown-ups about? Everything. *Bull Durham* is about baseball and love, and what else is there?

Yes, there are other things, such as presidential politics and Roger Rabbit. But baseball, properly practiced and appreciated, is a form and object of love, and thus touches, at least tangentially, all of life's great themes.

One such theme is the dignity of honest mediocrity, even in the unforgiving meritocracy of professional sports. Another is the necessity—indeed, the obligation—for special discipline on the part of the especially gifted.

In olden days, most baseball movies went like this. Boy meets baseball and falls in love. Then boy meets girl and inexplicably (one grand passion should suffice) falls in love yet again. The girl's role is to sit in the bleachers beneath a broad-brimmed hat and look anxious in his adversity and adoring in his inevitable triumph over it.

Bull Durham is different in two particulars, one of which is the girl, who is decidedly no girl. The other is the ballplayer, who is no Lou Gehrig. He is not the Pride of the Yankees, or even of the Durham Bulls.

Annie is more than thirty summers old, but is a fetching sight wearing a short off-the-shoulder dress and, as accessories, batting gloves. She pitches Whitman and Blake to students of English at a community college and also at one ballplayer each season. "A guy will listen to anything if he thinks it's fore-play," she says from considerable experience.

Annie, the thinking person's theist—"I believe in the Church of Base-ball"—takes one player as her lover each season but is not, by her lights, promiscuous: "I am, within the framework of a baseball season, monoga-mous." Furthermore, "I'd never sleep with a player hitting under .250 unless he had a lot of RBIs or was a great glove man up the middle. A woman's got to have standards."

But the real keeper of standards, which is the movie's moral theme, is Crash Davis, a journeyman catcher. He once made it to the major leagues, but only for a cup of coffee. Now, in his twelfth minor league season, he is brought to Durham to teach baseball's craftsmanship to a promising but unpolished pitcher, Ebby Calvin "Nuke" LaLoosh.

When Annie asks Crash, in effect, to compete with Nuke for the privilege of being her lover for a season, he walks away, saying: "I'm not interested in a woman who is interested in that boy." In terms of physical skills, Crash is not much. But in terms of character, he is the keeper of the flame of craftsman-ship. While Annie teaches Nuke about, well, life, Crash teaches him that his million-dollar arm does not mean he can get by with a five-cent brain.

In baseball, concentration is required of everyone. Alas, Nuke is a male bimbo, an airhead who even has to be tutored by Crash in the clichés that comprise the basic interview. ("We've gotta play 'em one day at a time. . . . I just wanna give it my best shot.") When Nuke asks why Crash dislikes him, Crash says: " 'Cause you don't respect yourself, which is your problem, but you don't respect the game—and that's my problem."

Nuke has no idea how much hard work is required to achieve excellence, even when Nature has given great talent. It has been said that the difference between the major and minor leagues is just a matter of "inches and consis-tency." That is essentially true of the difference between excellence and mere adequacy in poetry or surgery or anything else.

When Nuke bounces into the dugout after one good inning, there's this exchange:

NUKE: "I was good, eh?"

CRASH: "Your fastball was up and your curveball was hanging. In the Show [major leagues], they woulda ripped you."

NUKE: "Can't you let me enjoy the moment?"

CRASH: "The moment's over."

Crash has learned the essential lesson of life: Nothing lasts. Everything must be achieved anew—on the next pitch, the next at bat, in the next game, the next season.

Remember back when you would fuel up for a Saturday matinee with Jujyfruits and watch a baseball movie? The protagonist, invariably a paragon of physical prowess and moral virtue, would be begged by some boy to perform a heroic deed, and would sweetly promise to do so and would promptly deliver. But in *Bull Durham* there is the following exchange—the most satisfying moment in the history of movies:

BATBOY: "Get a hit, Crash."

CRASH: "Shut up."

Then Crash strikes out. And grown-ups in the audience sigh contentedly. They have sat through their fill of syrupy sports movies that are sweet enough to give a viewer diabetes. When Crash says, "Shut up," and strikes out, a grown-up thinks, happily: "Now I've seen everything!"

Which, as I said, is what the movie is about.

LET THERE BE LIGHTS

August 15, 1988

WHAT IS WRONG with this picture? Nothing. But bitter controversy swirls around the things that cast the shadow on the grass in the picture. The picture is of Wrigley Field, where the Chicago Cubs have played daytime baseball since 1916. The shadow is cast by light standards. There will be night games at Wrigley. "The horror, the horror," say shocked "purists." But their position is pure malarkey.

Playing some night games will enhance something that can stand a bushel and a peck of enhancing—the Cubs' competitiveness. The Cubs will play fewer games in the sauna of Midwestern summer afternoons. They will have less difficulty adjusting to the sharp difference between their home and away schedules.

Real baseball purists want to see the game played well. That consideration seems decidedly secondary to many Cub fans who natter on . . . and on . . . and on about the Wrigley Field ambience, gestalt, "experience," etc. While they are waxing poetic and semitheological about the sunshine (which can be found elsewhere) and the democracy of the bleachers (a democracy of, by and for the people privileged enough to skip work in the afternoon), the Cubs are getting waxed by better teams. Too many Cub fans seem to think that, leaving aside the mundane business of batting and pitching and fielding, the Cubs are, morally, a cut above the other twenty-five major league teams. Such fans think of the Cubs as baseball's Williamsburg, a cute, quaint artifact for historic preservation. They say lights are horrid because the Cubs are custodians of sacred tradition.

What's wrong with this picture?

In 1913, when Churchill was a young first lord of the Admiralty, some stuffy men accused him of traducing the traditions of the British Navy. "And what are they?" replied Churchill. "They are rum, sodomy and the lash." Wrigley Field's most conspicuous tradition is mediocre baseball. The Cubs have not won a pennant since 1945, the year the Dow Jones high was 195, *Carousel* opened on Broadway and a hit song was "On the Atchison, Topeka and the Sante Fe." The song was about passenger trains. The Cubs have not won a World Series since 1908, two years before Mark Twain died. The Cubs are now in the eightieth year of their rebuilding effort. If—when—they fail to win the pennant this year, they will break a record previously held by the St. Louis Browns: the longest span (forty-three years) without winning a league championship. In the seasons 1946 through 1987 the Cubs won 3,033 games and lost 3,567, putting them 534 games below .500 for that period. As this is written, they are below .500 this season. They could go undefeated in the 1989, 1990 and 1991 seasons and still be below .500 for the postwar era. Real Cub fans should say of tradition, "Enough already."

I will wager dollars against doughnuts that 99 44/100th percent of all the "baseball purists" who have worked themselves into a tizzy about Wrigley's lights are not even serious fans. They are dime store aesthetes cultivating a pose of curmudgeonliness, confusing that with a delicate sensibility. As they rhapsodize about Wrigley Field, untroubled by the aesthetic shortcomings of the baseball played there, they sound like those fishermen who say it is not catching fish that matters, it is the lapping of the water against the boat and the murmuring of the breeze in the pines—the ambience, gestalt, experience, etc. Fiddlesticks. People satisfied with fishless fishing will not catch fish and are not real fishermen. People satisfied with the Wrigley Field experience— see them swoon about the ivy on the outfield walls—should be as serious about baseball as they are about botany.

When next you see a Cub fan theatrically suffering the vapors at the mere mention of being deprived of day baseball eighteen times a year (that is the night-game limit until the year 2002) ask that fan to answer, under oath, this question: How often do you actually go to Wrigley Field to savor the ambience, gestalt, experience, etc.? Remember this: Baseball fans, like fishermen, fib. For example, you cannot swing a cat by the tail anywhere in America without conking on the head someone who swears that he or she spent his or her formative years in Brooklyn's Ebbets Field and that the cup of joy was forever dashed from his or her lips when the Dodgers went west. But if all the sentimentalists who say these things had really passed through the Ebbets

Field turnstiles a tenth as often as they say, the Dodgers would still be in Brooklyn.

There have been night games in Major League Baseball since 1935. Fifty-three years constitutes a considerable tradition in an institution only 112 years old (the National League, "the senior circuit," was founded in 1876). And were it not for Pearl Harbor, the Cubs today would be in their fifth decade of night baseball. Material for light standards had been bought and was donated to the war effort.

There is today too much aestheticization of judgments. Dukakis is "Zorba the clerk." Bush is a preppie. But peace and prosperity are at stake. The point of politics is good government, not the display of charm. And the point of a baseball team is good baseball, not inferior play somehow redeemed by a pretty setting. Part of the Cubs' problem may be that too many Cub fans have an attitude problem. They are too devoted to the wrong thing. Let there be lights.

Good Character, Not Good Chemistry

October 2, 1988

Sport is play, but play has a serious side. Competition can be elevating for participants and spectators. Thus the integrity of sport is a civic concern. And it is important to say precisely why what Ben Johnson did was wrong.

Runners at the highest levels of competition comprise a small community. They know all that is possible regarding enhancement of performance. And they know what is permissible. Johnson used steroids surreptitiously and in defiance of clear rules that are constantly reiterated. However, Johnson and many others involved in the intense pursuit of competitive edge may not really understand the reasons for the rules he broke.

Legs have 40 percent of the body's muscle mass. Steroids build muscle mass as well as hasten healing. Johnson's legs exploded him to victory by a margin of 13/100ths of a second. Did steroids make the difference? Hard to say. What has to be said is why using substances constitutes cheating.

When judging a performance-enhancing technique or technology, the crucial criterion is: Does it improve performance without devaluing it? Begin by considering precisely the value drained away by cheating, then decide if use of steroids constitutes cheating.

Last year, A. Bartlett Giamatti, baseball's next commissioner, flexed his mental muscles regarding disciplinary action against a pitcher who was caught using sandpaper to scuff balls, thereby giving pitches more pronounced movements. Giamatti, who was then president of the National League, noted that most disciplinary cases involve impulsive violence, which is less morally grave than cheating. Such acts of violence, although intolerable, spring from the nature of physical contests between aggressive competitors. Such violence is a reprehensible extension of the physical exertion that is integral to the contest. Rules try to contain, not expunge, violent effort.

But cheating derives not from excessive, impulsive zeal in the heat of competition. As Giamatti puts it, cheating has no organic origin in the act of playing, and cheating devalues any contest designed to declare a winner among participants playing under identical rules and conditions. Toward cheating, the proper policy is zero tolerance.

Now, advances in training and sports medicine (medicine broadly defined, which reaches beyond prevention or treatment of injuries) make problematic the idea, central to sport, of competitors competing on an even footing. Nowadays there can be significant inequalities regarding techniques of training and nutrition.

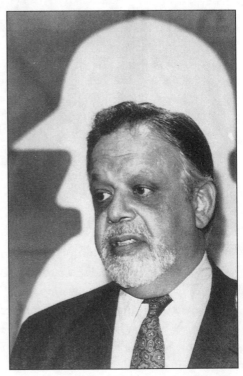

A. Bartlett Giamatti, beginning his brief tenure as commissioner of baseball

Intensity in training should be rewarded with success in competition. But intense training should involve enhancing one's powers by methods (e.g., weight training) or materials (eat your spinach) that enhance the body's normal functioning. It is one thing to take vitamins, another thing to take a drug that facilitates abnormal growth (or makes a competitor abnormally aggressive).

An athlete steps over the line separating legitimate from illegitimate preparation for competition when he seeks advantage from radical intrusions into his body. A radical intrusion is one that does not enhance normal functioning but rather causes the body to behave abnormally. Illegitimate interventions cause an athlete to perform not unusually well—every athlete's aim—but unnaturally well.

Steroids are dangerous to the user's health. Even if an athlete is willing to run the risk, his competitors should not have to run it in order to compete. That is a sufficient reason for proscribing them. But even if steroids and other performance-enhancing drugs were risk-free, there would still be sufficient reasons for cleansing sport of them.

Drugs that make sport exotic make it less exemplary. Sport becomes less of a shared activity. It becomes less a drama of people performing well than a spectacle of bodies chemically propelled.

Athletes who seek a competitive edge through chemical advantage do not just overvalue winning; they misunderstand why winning is properly valued. It is properly valued as the reward for, and evidence of, praiseworthy attributes. They include the lonely submission to an exacting training regimen, and the mental mastery of pressure, pain and exhaustion.

In short, sport is valued not only because it builds character but because it puts on display, and crowns with glory, for the elevation of spectators as well as participants, attributes we associate with good character. Good character, not good chemistry.

A society's recreation is charged with moral significance. Sport would be debased, and with it a society that takes sport seriously, if sport did not strictly forbid things that blur the distinction between the triumph of character and the triumph of pharmacology.

A Mosaic of Memories

October 1988

In 1903 America was feeling its oats. There was a young Rough Rider in the White House and his energy, ebullience and optimism were infectious. The future seemed as bright as Teddy Roosevelt's toothy smile. Henry Ford rounded up $100,000 that year and founded the Ford Motor Company, and the first transcontinental automobile trip was accomplished in just sixty-five days. And baseball, like the rest of the country, was revving up for a good time. In 1903 one of the great enduring traditions of American life began: the World Series.

Eighty-five years have gone by in a blink. Time flies when you're having fun.

In the nineteenth century there were baseball playoffs called the World Series. For example, in 1887 the St. Louis Browns lost to the Detroit Wolverines in a fifteen-game series. Two years later the New York Giants won a nine-game series against a team with a memorable name—the Brooklyn Bridegrooms. But it was not until 1903, in the full flush of confidence that came with the new century, that the World Series as we know it was born.

The name World Series is as characteristic of our country as, well, baseball itself. *World* Series? In 1903 baseball was played very little outside the United States and Major League Baseball extended only from Boston to St. Louis. So why the *World* Series? Well, why not? That is how we Americans talk because that is how we think: BIG. Remember, the first American Congress met in Philadelphia in 1774, when most Americans lived along the Atlantic coast of an unexplored continent. And what did these rambunctious Americans call their Congress? The *Continental* Congress. Again, we Americans think big. That is why we accomplish big things. Our national exuberance is expressed by the very name of the World Series.

Our national attention is riveted by the World Series more than any other regular event besides the Super Bowl, which actually is about eight hours of

A tradition begins: The 1903 World Series.

advertisements and folderol with a football game lost somewhere in the froth. For four or five or six or seven October days, America resonates with World Series sounds. From living rooms and workshops and taverns to fishermen at sea and farmers alone on their tractors, the baseball season in its splendid crescendo supplies background music to American life.

For those of us who grew up in the 1950s, the sound of Mel Allen and the Gillette Blue Blade jingle ("To look sharp, and be on the ball . . .") were aspects of autumn's tang. They were as much a part of autumn as the smell of burning leaves, back when burning leaves was permitted and raking leaves was a boy's duty—a duty lightened by the presence of a portable radio pouring forth the World Series play-by-play.

In recent years the Series has been played at night. That is all right, for several reasons. More people are able to enjoy it. And school-age kids no longer have to concoct those transparent lies we told to wriggle our way out of school during the Series. ("My grandmother died. . . . The school bus was hijacked. . . . My other grandmother died. . . . I am allergic to arithmetic in October. . . . Would you believe another grandmother died?")

We are a busy, bustling, pell-mell people. We are preoccupied with our personal or local concerns. However, certain great events bring us together by focusing our attention on a single subject. Often these are somber events. Many Americans remember, as though it were yesterday, exactly what they were doing the moment they heard about the attack on Pearl Harbor, or the death of Franklin Roosevelt, or the assassination of John Kennedy. However, there also are many moments of intensely shared pleasures—*continental* pleasures. The World Series regularly supplies such moments.

Many of us can remember exactly what we were doing (in my case, what high-school class I was skipping) on October 8, 1956, when the Dodgers' Dale Mitchell took a called third strike to end Don Larsen's perfect game. Now jump four years ahead, to October 1960. Do you remember what you were doing—or what you were supposed to be doing—when the Pirates' Bill Mazeroski broke Yankee hearts with a ninth-inning shot over the left-field wall in old Forbes Field?

Over the years we savor the memories of Series heroes. And one of the special delights of doing so is that some of the heroes were only October heroes. Some of our most vivid memories have been provided by players who were, for a fleeting moment, made larger than life by being in the brilliant World Series spotlight.

One of the most electrifying moments in World Series history involved a mediocre second baseman catching a dinky pop-up. It was Billy Martin's catch of Jackie Robinson's windblown pop in 1952. The Yankees took a 4–2 lead in the top of the seventh inning of the seventh game, but the Dodgers loaded the bases in the bottom half. There were two out and the runners were off at the crack of Robinson's bat. First baseman Joe Collins lost the ball in the sun. For a stunning moment, forever frozen in fans' memories, it seemed that the tying runs might score on a ball barely hit past the pitcher's mound. Then Martin materialized to grab the ball just before it touched the infield grass.

Do you remember Dusty Rhodes? Cleveland Indian fans wish they could forget him. In 1954 the Indians won 111 games—an American League record that still stands—and they did that when the season was just 154 games long. But they were swept in four games by the New York Giants, with Rhodes doing much damage.

In seven seasons Dusty played in nearly 600 major league games and got just 300 hits. However, four of those hits (together with seven RBIs) came in six at bats in the 1954 Series. Two of the hits were home runs. Rhodes had the indispensable ingredient for a great pinch hitter—supreme confidence. With the game on the line and Rhodes on the bench, Giants manager Leo Durocher would hear Rhodes' Alabama accent: "What are ya waitin' on, Skip? Ah'm your man." He certainly was Durocher's man in October 1954.

In the World Series, as in less exalted spheres of life, little things can mean a lot. We all know, from hard experiences, how many bad bounces there are in our daily lives. We know how easily things can go wrong from simple bad luck. More than once the course of a World Series has been altered by bad bounces and other mundane mishaps.

In the seventh game of the 1924 Series at Washington's Griffith Stadium, John McGraw's Giants were leading the Senators, 3–1, going into the bottom of the eighth. Then Lady Luck jilted the Giants. The Senators scored two runs when a grounder off the bat of player-manager Bucky Harris took a bad bounce over the head of the Giants' third baseman, Fred Lindstrom. With the game tied and the Series on the line in the bottom of the twelfth, Washing-

Giants Willie Mays and Dusty Rhodes celebrate after winning the first game
of the 1954 Series, behind Rhodes' 3-run homer and Mays' running catch
of Vic Wertz' 450-foot drive.

ton's catcher, Muddy Ruel, led off. He lifted a lazy pop foul. Giants catcher Hank Gowdy tossed aside his mask—but not far enough. He stepped in the mask, his foot got stuck, he staggered after the ball and it fell to earth. So did the Giants. Ruel promptly doubled. He scored and the Senators had their first—and, it turned out, their last—World Series championship.

The most famous World Series bad bounce came in perhaps the only World Series game more exciting than that 1924 Giants-Senators contest. It came in the seventh game of the 1960 Yankees-Pirates Series. In that Series the Yankees set a slew of offensive records. They compiled a team batting average of .338, and a .528 slugging percentage. They raked Pirates pitchers for 91 hits, 27 of them for extra bases. They outscored the Pirates 55 to 27. And they lost the Series.

Why? Well, yes, of course, Mazeroski hit that bases-empty home run in the bottom of the ninth. But Mazeroski's run would not have won the game if the Pirates had not scored five in the eighth. In that inning the leadoff man singled. The next batter hit a tailor-made double-play ball to Yankee shortstop Tony Kubek. It took a wicked hop and struck him in the throat, knocking him out of the game. Suddenly, instead of none on and two outs there were two on and no outs. The Pirates were on their way to a flag.

Yes, bad bounces and journeymen players, as well as dazzling plays and Hall of Famers, make up the mosaic of memories that surround the World Series. Since 1903, baseball, like the country in which it was born, has been getting better and better. And eighty-five years later, baseball is increasingly an international enjoyment. Major League Baseball has expanded in North America to include two great Canadian cities, and baseball has been immeasurably enriched by players from countries south of the United States. Today baseball is an Olympic sport, played around the world, and the World Series is seen and heard around the globe. Broadcasts of baseball have spread the October story of baseball's climactic contests in many languages to many millions of fans far away. Now, baseball's greatest event is truly a *World* Series.

PLAY BAIL!

October 6, 1988

THE SECOND PITCH Ed Cicotte of the White Sox threw in the first game of the 1919 World Series hit Cincinnati's leadoff man. New York gamblers got the signal: The Series was fixed. Today, in a political season that mocks the idea of progress, a season loud with lamentations about sleaze in Washington and sharp practices on Wall Street, it is well to revisit an era when America was really raw.

The era is accessible through the movie *Eight Men Out,* based on Eliot Asinof's book of that title, about the Black Sox scandal. There are two fine novels on that subject, Harry Stein's *Hoopla* and W. P. Kinsella's *Shoeless Joe,* which is being made into a movie. Who, half a century from now, will write novels and make movies about Watergate? As many as today are interested in the Teapot Dome scandal. But when scandal touched baseball, it touched a national nerve.

The Black Sox scandal involved two timeless themes of art: love and regret. In that instance, it was love of vocation and regret about losing it. The most poignant figure was Shoeless Joe Jackson, the illiterate natural who compiled the third-highest lifetime batting average in history and who was so reflexively great that even when throwing the Series he could not stop himself from hitting .375 and setting a Series record with twelve hits.

The scandal is a window in a dank basement of American history. In 1919, Americans were feeling morally admirable, if they did say so themselves, and they did. They had been on the winning side in "the war to end war." The fixed Series occurred three months before the beginning of a misadventure in moralism, Prohibition.

But gambling was as American as the gold rush—the dream of quick riches—and when the government closed racetracks during the war, gamblers turned to baseball, which then was America's biggest entertainment industry.

Hotel lobbies where teams stayed teemed with gamblers. "Hippodroming" was the nineteenth-century word for throwing games, and in postwar America there was a new brazenness by gamblers.

On September 10, 1920, various Wall Street brokerage houses received "flashes" on their news wires: Babe Ruth and some teammates had been injured in an accident en route to Cleveland. Quickly the odds on that game changed, and the gamblers—the source of the lie—cleaned up.

The White Sox conspirators assumed they would get away with their plot because they assumed, almost certainly correctly, that other major leaguers had gotten away with fixes. In response to the scandal, the team owners, frightened about the possible devaluation of their franchises, rushed out and bought some virtue in the person of a federal judge to serve as baseball's first commissioner.

Kenesaw Mountain Landis, with his shock of white hair over craggy features and his mail-slot mouth, looked like a statue of Integrity Alerted, just as Harding, elected in 1920, looked like a president. Landis was a tobacco-chewing bourbon drinker who would hand out stiff sentences to people who violated Prohibition. He had a knack for self-dramatizing publicity. He fined

Kenesaw Mountain Landis:
A man happy in his work.

Standard Oil of Indiana $29,240,000 in a rebate case (the Supreme Court overturned him) and tried to extradite Kaiser Wilhelm on a murder charge because a Chicagoan died when a German submarine sank the *Lusitania.*

Landis barred from baseball eight Sox players, including one who merely knew about the conspiracy but did not report it. It was rough justice. Nothing happened to the gamblers, and some of the players were guilty primarily of stupidity and succumbing to peer pressure. Most of them were cheated out of most of the money gamblers had promised to them, and only one player made much ($35,000). But roughness can make justice effective. Baseball's gambling problems were cured.

The 1920s, the dawn of broadcasting and hence of hoopla, washed away memories of the scandal. Those years were the Golden Age of American sport—Babe Ruth, Jack Dempsey, Gene Tunney, Red Grange, Knute Rockne, Bobby Jones, Bill Tilden, Man o' War.

From Wall Street to Main Street, and including both ends of Pennsylvania Avenue, America back then—when a U.S. senator appeared in advertisements endorsing Lucky Strike cigarettes—was immeasurably less scrupulous about standards of behavior than it is today. Baseball put its house in order because of the Black Sox. Ten years later, the crash ushered in a new age of regulation of financial institutions. And various scandals, before and after Watergate, have produced refinements (and some overrefinements) in rules about comportment in the corridors of power.

Civilization advances by fits and starts, often stimulated by shocked sensibilities. As another baseball season comes to a climax, it is well to consider how far we have come in the sixty-eight years since Chicago children began their sandlot games with the cry "Play bail!"

REVENGE OF THE ECTOMORPHS

October 10, 1988

Baseball pitchers are the only oppressed minority the Supreme Court cannot help. Many of them are physically disadvantaged. Tom Boswell says, "Hitters are mesomorphs, pitchers are ectomorphs." Rendering that thought into the vulgate, Boswell says that in a locker room pitchers look like the guys the others beat up. (Only a pitcher would have a name like Orel Leonard Hershiser IV.) And baseball's rulers are forever picking on pitchers, revising the rules to prevent pitchers from prospering too much. "They have never made a rule that helps the pitcher," says Hershiser. He is basically right about the trend since the nineteenth century, when pitchers were grudgingly allowed to throw overhand.

Twenty years ago baseball even sliced the mound from 15 to 10 inches to help hitters. The poor dears had been reduced to jelly by the bombardments of 1968. But last week a blade of a lad, who wears thick glasses when punching his pitching notes into his laptop computer, finished a flawless September, pitching his 59th consecutive scoreless inning. Hershiser eclipsed the streaks of four Hall of Famers, Carl Hubbell (45 1/3), Bob Gibson (47), Walter Johnson (55 2/3) and Don Drysdale (58). Not bad for a boy born with spina bifida, who was cut from his high school and college teams.

Sports are generally fun and frequently inspiriting but last week the sports pages were dominated by stories about the debasement of competition by drugs. Thus too little notice was given to Hershiser's stunning achievement, which is comparable to Joe DiMaggio's 56-game hitting streak of 1941. Hershiser popped a record Drysdale set in 1968, the year pitchers were rampant. The American League batting title was won that year with an anemic .301 average. There were 748 fewer home runs than in 1966. There were 4 no-hitters and 17 one-hitters. Seven times pitchers struck out 15 or more in a game. There were 339 shutouts. The National League had 44 1–0 games. The Tigers' Denny McLain won 31 games. The Cardinals' Bob Gibson started 34 games, completed 28, gave up just 1.12 runs per 9 innings and struck out 268 in 304 innings. One month after Drysdale's streak, Gibson saw a 47-inning scoreless streak ended when he yielded a run on a wild pitch. He immediately ran off another 23 scoreless innings, so he went 70 innings without any hitter getting an RBI.

Horrified, baseball's rulers lowered the mound, and other changes have been made to succor hitters. Sure, batting against big league pitching is still no day at the beach. The pitching rubber is 60 feet 6 inches from home plate. A pitcher releases the ball about 55 feet from the plate. A 90-mph fastball gets there in .41 of a second. An 80-mph curve loiters, taking .09 of a second longer. But pitchers have little margin for error—the plate is just 17 inches wide—and the margin has been contracting. Umpires have been shrinking the strike zone and hitters have been becoming bigger, so pitchers increasingly find themselves behind in the count to confident mesomorphs. Hitters have thrown enough tantrums to enlist umpires in their campaign to prevent pitchers from backing hitters off the plate by throwing inside.

It is under this post-1968 adversity that Hershiser has done something arguably more difficult than what DiMaggio did. DiMaggio had to hit one pitch safely in 56 consecutive games. Hershiser threw around 700 pitches to around 220 batters without allowing any of them to advance 360 feet. His task was complicated by his team's four errors behind him during the streak. And in the 59th inning he had to get four outs: A batter struck out on a wild pitch that bounced and he reached first base before the catcher caught up with the ball.

Stand Hershiser next to his unshaven teammate Kirk Gibson, the untamed football player, and Hershiser looks as feeble as a columnist. But stand him on the mound and he is undiluted intensity. He hits enough bat-

Orel Hershiser of the Dodgers finishes his 59th consecutive scoreless inning.

ters to prove that he is not too nice to claim the inside corner of the plate. Does he go to the mound planning to pitch a complete game? "A perfect game," he replies. "If they get a hit, I am throwing a one-hitter. If they get a walk, it's my last walk. I deal with perfection to the point that is logical to conceive it. History is history, the future is perfect."

But in the future there always lurks something that can never be wholly subdued by talent: luck. Any protracted achievement like Hershiser's illustrates the satisfying mixture of skill and luck in the most satisfying of sports. Baseball, with its long, leveling season, is the severest meritocracy among sports: There is ample time for talent to tell. Yet luck plays an unexpungeable part. A pitcher can pitch brilliantly and get beaten by poorly hit balls dribbling past or blooping over infielders. A pitcher can pitch poorly and get away with it when line drives are rocketed right at infielders and long flies are run down by panting outfielders.

Good luck goes into any streak. Twice in the 56 games DiMaggio benefited from close calls by official scorers on hits that could have been called errors. Twice he got dinky hits—a catchable fly fell untouched, a full swing produced a slow roller to an infield pulled back. But as Stephen Jay Gould argues, the inevitable role of luck in no way diminishes DiMaggio's achievement. Gould, a Harvard scientist, says that long streaks necessarily are products of skill and luck. Great athletes have a higher probability of success than normal athletes have in any instance—any at bat, any inning pitched. A streak is a series of discrete events occurring with the probability that is characteristic for the particular player. That probability is leavened by luck.

Single instances of success can be all luck. With the score tied in the first game of the 1954 World Series between the Giants and Indians, the Giants brought in Don Liddle to pitch with two runners on. The Indians' batter crushed a Liddle pitch 460 feet to the deepest part of the deepest center field in baseball, where only Superman could catch it. Superman did. Willie Mays made his famous over-the-shoulder catch. Liddle was immediately yanked. He strode into the dugout, put down his glove and said, "Well, I got *my* man." Liddle was lucky. Hershiser has got 177 men out without anyone scoring and his streak will resume in April. For how long? Talent, leavened by luck, will tell.

PETE ROSE'S CHROMOSOMES

April 2, 1989

SARASOTA, FLORIDA—Baseball, sport of the long season and strong oral tradition, tells of the time when the Cincinnati Reds' plane hit severe turbulence and Pete Rose said to a teammate: "We're going down. We're going down and I have a .300 lifetime average to take with me. Do you?" The teammate's response, which could reasonably have been homicide, is not recorded.

As this is being written, while teams break camp and head for hard work, Rose's infractions, if any, regarding rules about gambling, have not been revealed. No such infractions are unserious. However, some good facets of Rose have been revealed through the seasons.

Rose has baseball in his chromosomes. Tell him Lindbergh flew the Atlantic in 1927 and he responds, "The year Ruth hit sixty." To you, 1941 means Pearl Harbor. To Rose, 1941 means DiMaggio hitting in 56 consecutive games and Williams hitting .406. A statistician once tried to stump Rose with this arcane question: What active player has the highest ratio of flyouts to groundouts? Rose replied, "Easy. Gary Redus." Rose was right.

"The trick," said Casey Stengel, "is growing up without growing old."

"I was raised," Rose once said, "but I never grew up."

"All games," says Tom Boswell, "offer an alternative reality," and baseball, with its relentless schedule and statistical richness, particularly appeals to the fanatical personality. But Rose the man-child has an adult understanding of the ethic of sport.

He was last the focus of national attention four seasons ago in his quest for his 4,192nd hit to break Ty Cobb's career record. Boswell, in his new collection of baseball essays, *The Heart of the Order*, remembers the Sunday in Chicago that began with Rose two hits shy of Cobb's 4,191. That night the Reds would head home for a sold-out series where he would break the record.

Pete Rose, September 11, 1985: Hit number 4,192.

Player-manager Rose was not going to play that Sunday because the Cubs had scheduled a left-handed pitcher. But the left-hander got hurt, was replaced by a right-hander, and Rose immediately wrote himself into the lineup. By the fifth inning he had tied Cobb with two hits.

In the ninth inning the score was tied, no outs, Reds runners on first and second, Rose at bat. He could sacrifice the runners over to second and third, saving The Hit for the home folks. But Dave Parker, a slugger, was on deck. If Rose sacrificed, the Cubs would walk Parker with first base open. So Rose calculated, reasonably, that the Reds would have a slightly better chance of winning if he tried for a hit.

He failed. To get a hit, that is. But he succeeded brilliantly at showing, as Boswell says, the meaning of the phrases "integrity of the sport" and "best interests of the game."

Boswell rightly notes that Rose, like Cobb, is not a balanced personality. But Cobb was a hideous cauldron of anger, competing with ugly ferocity. Rose combined cheerfulness and a competitiveness that burned with a hard, gemlike flame. He competed simultaneously against the other team and his own high standards.

Sport can produce self-absorption, and a moral sense that is sharp only because, like a knife blade, it is very narrow. This leads some stars to a sense of exemption from the restraints which normal people must respect. Rose may not have resisted the temptation of living beyond restraints.

But one reason for participating in sports is to become better—better at the sport and in the soul. Acquisition of particular skills leads to appreciation of all skills. To learn a sport is to learn what mastery means, even if you fall far short of mastery. Playing a sport, and appreciating the play of a Rose, is an apprenticeship in craftsmanship.

Becoming better at something is called self-improvement, a term with two meanings. It means improving one's self, one's character, one's core identity. It also means an unavoidable loneliness, getting better by oneself, in submission to severe self-judgments, in the aloneness of private determination, under the lash of the necessity to satisfy one's demanding self. Sport can be an exacting and elevating school.

So:

In a restaurant near Wrigley Field there is this sign: "Any employee wishing to miss work because of death or serious illness please notify the office by 11 A.M. on the day of the game." In that spirit, the teachers of Victoria and Jon Will are hereby notified that, because of an annual April emergency, Victoria and Jon must be in Baltimore Monday afternoon. But Geoffrey Will will be in school, drawn by love of learning (that's a joke, son) and baseball practice.

LIVING ON THE LIP OF A VOLCANO

April 10, 1989

JIM GOTT'S TEAMMATES on the Pittsburgh Pirates said his earned run average going into a spring training game last week—estimates ranged from 11.20 to 14.40—sounded like an AM radio station. It didn't get better when Texas Rangers batters gave Pirates outfielders a workout. Gott was not shocked by this proof that Nature is indeed red in tooth and claw. All relief pitchers are hard-core realists. Gott is the kind of reliever called a "closer." His job is defined by one of baseball's best features: There is no clock. To win, you have to get the final outs. They are the hardest to get and are Gott's specialty.

Starting pitchers are the sport's surgeons, the dashing stars of the drama. Relief pitchers are those embattled people who cope with crises in emergency rooms. When managers reach for the dugout phone to ring the bullpen, they should dial 911. Relievers like Gott generally get into games when the games are getting out of hand. The Book of Job, the relief pitcher's Bible, gets it right: Man is born unto trouble as the sparks fly upward.

Bart Giamatti is baseball's seventh commissioner and the first to say that the word "paradise" comes from an ancient Persian word meaning an enclosed park or green place, and ballparks exist because humanity has "a vestigial memory of an enclosed green space as a place of freedom and play." Freedom? Play? Bart has not seen a park through the eyes of a relief pitcher. It is work going to the mound with runners on base, the game on the line and a large man 60 feet 6 inches away waving a menacing bat.

Gott is good at his work. Last year he was second in the National League in "saves," a term too technical to define in any magazine other than *Scientific American*. Suffice it to say that 34 times Gott entered games with Pirate leads in danger and snuffed out the danger to achieve a save. He appeared in 67 games, which is a lot, and pitched 77 1/3 innings, which is not. Closers succeed or fail quickly.

Like many relievers, Gott has only one gear: adrenaline overdrive. He is a pupil of the Pirates' wise and witty pitching coach, Ray Miller, a man of many convictions, all of them firm. Miller's mantra is: "Work fast, throw strikes, change speeds." Gott doesn't change speeds much. An 83-mph curveball gets to the plate faster than you can say "curveball," but Gott can crank his fastball up to 97 mph. If you can do that, and are asked to do it for only an inning or so at a time, don't get cute, throw heat.

Spring training is primarily a time for pitchers to get their arms tuned up. Miller isn't worried about Gott's ERA because power pitchers take a while to get the pop on their fastballs. They have to be careful getting there. To be a pitcher is to abuse your arm for a living. Throwing a ball overhand is an unnatural motion, which is why so few do it with consistent success for long. (Can

Adrenaline overdrive:
Pirate pitcher Jim Gott.

you name the only two pitchers with winning records in every season of the 1980s? See below.) It is often a small step (or a small muscle tear) "from Cy Young to sayonara." Starting pitchers are eager to have long careers in this era of large salaries, so they are lucky to live in the age of relief pitchers.

Historian Bruce Catton once said that if someone from McKinley's era were brought back and seated in a ballpark "he would see nothing that was not completely familiar." Well, one thing, the game is the same, but real relievers—people who make their livings putting out fires—used to be rare. The 1904 Red Sox pitchers had 148 complete games in a 154-game season. The 1905 Cubs had 133 complete games. Of Christy Mathewson's 561 decisions (373 wins, 188 losses), 435 were complete games. The percentage of complete games in the National League in the nine decades of this century are: 72.7, 63.4, 50, 44.3, 41.6, 32.8, 27.2, 22.5 and in the 1980s just 13.3.

What has happened since September 7, 1908, when Walter Johnson shut out New York for the third time in four days? OK, Johnson was perhaps the best pitcher ever. But what has happened since May 1, 1920, when Brooklyn and Boston played a 26-inning 1–1 tie and both starting pitchers, neither of them notable, went the distance? Well, yes, a lot has happened—wars, revolutions, stuff like that—but most important, there has been a decline in the strength of ballplayers' arms. Or so say many smart people, including Miller.

Miller says that back when the world had its priorities right, the best athletes were drawn to baseball and the best of them (Miller, a pitcher, is prejudiced) were sent to the mound. The biggest kids became pitchers and baseball became the center of their lives. They played for hours in pastures, when most boys grew up a line drive's distance from pastures, or in vacant city lots when there still were some. Nowadays kids spend hours—hours that could be better spent strengthening their arms by throwing—in cars being hauled from one overorganized activity to another.

Miller says there also is "overcoaching" of young people. They are learning to throw curveballs, knuckleballs, all sorts of things when the emphasis should be on throwing hard and often. Then there is another modern pestilence—aluminum bats. It is hard to throw fastballs past them, so breaking balls are favored. Finally, Miller, like most of us over forty, sees national decline in the decline of fastballs among the young. "It's a statement on society. Everybody is looking for the easy way out. You can't find a big, strong kid who wants to throw year-round, who will stand out in the yard and throw rocks and knock cans down, just making himself bigger and stronger and throw better."

Gott, twenty-nine, is a man after Miller's heart. He is 6 feet 4 and 220 pounds, a throwback to the era of no-damned-nonsense-about-nuances. He was recruited by big-time college football programs but saw the sinfulness of jeopardizing a baseball career. He has the reckless, contagious ebullience of someone who actually likes living for six straight months on the lip of a volcano. The only regrettable thing about Gott and other closers is that they cause games to end. But between now and late October, there is always tomorrow.

The answer is: Jack Morris and John Tudor.

PETE ROSE AND HIS FRIENDS

June 29, 1989

Lₐₛₜ ʏᴇᴀʀ Tᴏᴍᴍʏ Jᴏʜɴ, then a Yankees pitcher, set a modern record by making three errors on one play. Judge Norbert Nadel has made five errors while butchering what should have been a routine play.

Nadel, an elected judge in Pete Rose's hometown, made a dumb decision. He began from a foolish premise. Then he committed the very offense—a prejudgment—that he accuses baseball's commissioner of committing. Nadel mistakenly assumed that his judicial ukase is justified if Commissioner A. Bartlett Giamatti actually is by now less than open-minded about Rose. And Nadel compounded the confusion by continuing to keep secret the report on Rose's activities.

America's judiciary has an awful itch to bring every facet of life under its supervision. The itch is so widespread that any person with a problem that an itchy judge might alleviate can hope to hit upon a judge who will try to do so. Rose, a fine contact hitter, did just that.

Nadel has prejudged Giamatti, declaring him prejudiced and imposing upon him the burden of proving himself innocent. Nadel cited no case law in which a court has interfered with the commissioner in the exercise of his duties. Nadel cited no law of any sort.

Government action is not involved in the Rose case, so constitutional due-process requirements do not pertain. The only contractual rights involved are the commissioner's rights, rights that Rose and everyone else acknowledges when signing the standard player's contract. Perhaps Nadel accepts the prevalent premise that any judicial fiat in the name of "fairness" is justified.

Baseball's traditional, tested procedures were going forward and Rose did not like the destination he anticipated. So he attacked the process. Nadel was agitated by Giamatti's letter to another judge, endorsing the truthfulness of one of Rose's accusers.

But even without that letter, Rose probably would have attacked the process, and Nadel probably would have supported him, on the ground that baseball's commissioner is in such cases both investigator and adjudicator. However, that is not a novelty. The Federal Trade Commission and Securities and Exchange Commission have a similar combination of functions.

If Giamatti has erred, it has been in the spirit of fairness. He has tried too hard to be fair. After receiving the 225-page report on Rose's activities, Giamatti gave the report to Rose and his lawyers and gave them thirty days to interview and depose witnesses. They contacted only one; they interviewed none. Instead, they sought the evisceration of the office of commissioner.

The office was created in the wake of the 1919 Black Sox scandal to do what it has done brilliantly: protect baseball's integrity. If Nadel succeeds in insinuating himself (and hundreds of imitators) into baseball's disciplinary procedures, the commissioner's core function—discipline—will be rendered permanently problematic. Yet another American institution will have been broken to the saddle of supervision by nanny government. The insidious permeation of life by politics and state power will have advanced.

Courts have refused to intervene when asked to do so by owners who wanted to block commissioners who have, in effect, seized the owners' property. In 1931, the first commissioner, Judge Kenesaw Mountain Landis, declared a St. Louis Brown a free agent in a dispute with the Browns' owner, Phil Ball. In 1976, Bowie Kuhn blocked Charles Finley, owner of the Oakland Athletics, from selling three players for $3.5 million. Kuhn did so under the broad grant of power to act "in the best interests of baseball."

As this is written, news organizations are seeking the Rose report that the commissioner has offered to release and that Rose has not tried to suppress. No one knows why Nadel has kept it secret. Explaining his actions is not Nadel's strength.

The author of the report, a Washington attorney, interviewed eighty people. Rose has read the report and he knows the truth about his activities. Hence he knows if the report is assailable. Soon we will all know about the law-enforcement officer who says Rose's fingerprints are on betting slips, and the handwriting expert who says Rose's printing is on such slips, and the nine people who say they witnessed Rose's gambling activities, and the telephone records and canceled checks allegedly involving gambling.

Has there been an extraordinary conspiracy against Rose? Or has there been an incredible concatenation of coincidences and accidents that have piled up what looks like, but is not, evidence of gambling in violation of baseball's rules? Not likely. What is likely is that he violated those rules a lot and for a long time and now has compounded his offense by lying about it and attacking the governance of baseball.

So, no plea bargaining. Rose is a tough guy seeking justice, not mercy. More than 4,000 times he has walked into clubhouses where the rules are posted. Bet on baseball, you "shall be" suspended for a year. Bet on your team, you "shall be" permanently ineligible. Shall be, not may be.

If he is innocent on both counts, he still should be suspended for a year. Denny McLain was suspended for ninety days in 1970 and Leo Durocher for a year in 1947 for associating with gamblers.

Rose now says: Don't believe my former associates who are accusing me—they are criminals. Precisely the point.

A Pʀᴏꜰᴇssɪᴏɴᴀʟ Cᴀᴛᴄʜᴇʀ

October 5, 1989

Tᴏʀᴏɴᴛᴏ—Concision and simplicity can be elements of eloquence, as Jamie Quirk showed when he said, "I'm a professional catcher." Those words, in context, revealed one reason why it is right for grown-ups to play, and care about, baseball games.

With one out in the eighth inning of their 160th game, the Baltimore Orioles were leading the Toronto Blue Jays 1–0 and were five outs from tying them for first place in the American League East. But a Blue Jay runner was on third. The Orioles pitcher was a rookie who has, as baseball people say, a knee-buckling curve. Quirk called for a curve low and away. It was too much of both. It went in the dirt, bounced to the screen, the runner scored. The Blue Jays won in the eleventh.

The official scorer called it a wild pitch. Quirk called it a passed ball: "A major league catcher has to block that ball. . . . I should have blocked it. . . .

I'm a professional catcher." Maybe he should have, maybe not. Two things are certain. One is that America would be immeasurably improved if more Americans—teachers, workers, journalists, everyone—had Quirk's exacting standards of craftsmanship and accountability. The other is that Quirk, who will be thirty-five this month, did a manly thing in trying to block blame from reaching a twenty-two-year-old pitcher.

In the hours before D-Day, General Eisenhower drafted a statement to be issued if the invasion failed. First he wrote: "Our landings in the Cherbourg-Havre area have failed to gain a satisfactory foothold and the troops have been withdrawn." But then he struck the last six words and wrote instead: ". . . and I have withdrawn the troops." By replacing the passive with the first-person-singular pronoun, Eisenhower stepped up to the pitch: He took responsibility. Quirk was like Ike.

Quirk is, in baseball's evocative language, a journeyman. His travels took him to the Royals, Brewers, Royals again, Cardinals, White Sox, Indians, Royals yet again, Yankees and Athletics before he arrived in Baltimore in midseason, in time to vivify the axiom that sport reveals as well as builds character. He may not be back in Baltimore next year, but he is a nice emblem of this year.

A professional at his job: Jamie Quirk.

After beginning the 1988 season with a record 21 consecutive losses and going on to lose 107, the Orioles in 1989 relied heavily on hungry rookies and some veterans who had been given up on by other teams. (Quirk had been released nine times.) The 1989 Orioles, who were in the hunt in the last weekend of the season, are called "overachievers." Meaning what? They achieved more than they were "supposed" to? Who are these supposers who lay down the law about other people's limits?

Baseball teams often reflect their cities. The Cubs have the edgy insecurity of the Second City. The Mets and Yankees are pure New York: chaos leavened by recriminations. Baltimore is just a nice town built around basics—a harbor, some manufacturing. After 1988, the Orioles rebuilt around baseball's basics, speed and defense.

Frank Robinson—Hall of Famer, 1989 Manager of the Year (surely) and all-star aphorist—says: "Speed comes to the ballpark every day. The three-run home run does not." Speed serves defense, which improves pitching: Pitchers become aggressive, putting the ball in the strike zone, counting on fleet fielders to catch it.

Defense is baseball's underappreciated (by fans, not baseball people) dimension. Players spend more time with leather on their hands than with wood in their hands. The 1989 Orioles were the second team in history to have fewer than ninety errors. Their fielding percentage (.98602) was the best ever.

"When you've been around seven or eight years," said Cal Ripken, the shortstop, during this his eighth season, "you might think twice about making a diving catch on gravel and sliding into the wall. But at this stage of our young players' development, they don't think about it."

Ripken is not exactly Methuselah. He will be twenty-nine on opening day 1990, which is awfully far away. Today, baseball, the sport that combines, better than any other, team play and personal accountability, is coming to its autumn crescendo, beyond which stretches . . .

Jonathan Yardley says there are only two seasons, baseball season and The Void. When, toward the end of this season, George Bush was asked who he thought would win the American League East, he said, "I've given up on the Rangers." Good thinking. The Rangers are in the AL West.

Mr. President, read Baltimore's lips: The 1990 AL East champions open at home, forty miles from your front porch, April 2, the end of The Void.

The 1990 Lockout:
No Hits, Many Errors

March 26, 1990

Rube Waddell, the Philadelphia Athletics' Hall of Fame pitcher, liked to eat crackers in bed. A nuisance only for Mrs. Waddell? Nope. In olden times the Athletics, when on the road, slept two to a bed. Waddell's roommate made Connie Mack, the manager and owner, put an anticracker clause in Waddell's contract.

Today conditions are rather better for players. And for owners, too, because the players, having radically improved their lot, have made baseball a better product. So this year, what spoiled spring for the national pastime? Two national blessings did—prosperity, and the freedom to fight over how it should be divvied up. There also was obduracy arising from old animosities between players and owners, and a failure all around to appreciate baseball's special vulnerability, which arises from the importance to it of continuity.

For a century, until 1975, players were chattel, without bargaining power. For example, in 1929 the Phillies' Lefty O'Doul batted a blistering .398, collecting 254 hits, still a National League record. It earned him a $500 raise. In 1930 he hit "only" .368 and his salary was cut $1,000. Today O'Doul would own Philadelphia. When free agency came to baseball, the owners, most of them confirmed Cassandras, predicted an end to competitive balance because rich teams and big markets would buy up the best of players. Score that prediction an error.

In the ten years between 1978 and 1987, for the first time ever, ten different teams won the World Series. In the fourteen seasons with free agency, twelve different teams have won the Series, sixteen have made it to the Series and only three (Mariners, Indians, Rangers) have failed to win division titles. And before free agency? The Yankees finished first twenty-six times in thirty-nine consecutive winning seasons (1926–64). Between 1903 and 1964 there

Lefty O'Doul, former Phillie.

were sixty-one World Series and a New York team was in thirty-nine of them. In thirteen Series, both teams were from New York.

Competitive balance has coincided with a competitive market for players, whose salaries have risen tenfold since 1975. Has this made team ownership a hardship? Hardly. The Orioles, bought in 1979 for $12 million, were sold in 1988 for $70 million. The Mariners, who in their thirteen years of existence have never had a winning season, were bought last year for $80 million. The Yankees, bought in 1973 for $10 million, might fetch twenty-five times that today. Such appreciation of assets is not a mere result of the playful whims of rich hobbyists. The market is reflecting the potential for real economic returns. And now CBS will pay $270 million for sixteen regular-season games, the league championship playoffs and the World Series each of the next four seasons—about $130,000 per out. Given the economic value of which the players are the primary creators, it is misplaced moralism to deplore their large salaries.

At this moment of conspicuous prosperity, the owners launched an assault on the players' hard-won rights. On the eve of the lockout, Ron Darling of the Mets said, "Let me get this straight. The owners are about to shut down baseball when it's more prosperous than it's ever been, and the players are the ones who have to get their urine tested?" The owners do have a serious worry—the disparities of teams' wealth deriving from differences in urban markets. Those disparities have been exacerbated by the increased importance of local broadcasting revenues.

When twenty-six textile manufacturers compete, each wants to grind the others to dust. When twenty-six teams compete, each wants to win, but to do so in a league made exciting by competitive balance. In the 1980s, the small-market teams did well. Two World Championship flags fluttered in Los

Angeles and one in New York, but others flew in Philadelphia, St. Louis, Baltimore, Detroit, Kansas City, Minnesota and Oakland.

Competitive balance may now become endangered by disparities of local broadcasting revenues. The Yankees get more than $60 million. The teams in the three smallest markets—Kansas City, Milwaukee, Minnesota—each receive less than $3 million. But instead of trying to control costs by fighting bloody battles to suppress players' earnings, the owners might better fight among themselves about revenue sharing. Now that labor troubles have produced baseball's seventh disruption in eighteen years, owners should reconcile themselves to the players' emancipation and bargaining power.

Disruptions fray and eventually may sever the cords of affection that bind fans and communities to the sport of the long season and long historical continuity. No other sport is so steeped in its own traditions. But baseball is currently crippled by its weak institutional memory. Only six teams, three in each league (Dodgers, Cardinals, Expos; Angels, Royals, Brewers), have had the same ownership for at least twenty years. Subtract those six and the average tenure of the other twenty owners—fourteen of whom arrived in the 1980s—is just seven and a half years. That is two years less than the average career of an established (at least two years' service) player.

The players' union is still too suffused with the spirit of its former leader, Marvin Miller, who says: "Baseball fans shouldn't take themselves so seriously. They're merely consumers. And sport's consumers are no more important than any other consumer. If there's no baseball this year the fans shouldn't be any more upset than they would be if they bought a car and didn't have it delivered on time. Baseball fans should stop exaggerating their own importance." Let me count the ways that is foolish.

It is the institution of baseball that the fans take seriously and consider important to the spirits as well as the economies of communities. And it is dumb for the players' union to encourage the fans, who are the source of the players' salaries, to think of baseball as analogous to a consumer durable—a purchase that can be put off with no emotional loss or other cost.

A baseball man once noted that the day Custer lost at Little Bighorn, the Chicago White Stockings beat the Cincinnati Red Stockings 3–2, and both teams wore knickers and still do. Baseball has many continuities. But the owners and the union, in their brutal self-absorption and self-indulgent animosities, may one day wake up and find that fans who once said "Take me out to the ball game" are saying instead "I don't care if I ever get back" to the ballpark.

THE PRODIGY

April 8, 1990

Van Meter, Iowa, has 747 residents and no traffic light. In the 1940s it had about 300 residents and was a good place to grow up, listening to a Des Moines sportscaster named Dutch Reagan and watching trains rumble west carrying beams from Indiana steel mills, the beams bearing banners proclaiming their destination: "The Golden Gate Bridge, San Francisco." One Van Meter boy was bound for glory, and got a fistful of it fifty years ago this week on Chicago's South Side.

Correct thinkers think—know—that "baseball trivia" is an oxymoron: Nothing about baseball is trivial. But connoisseurs of, shall we say, arcana adore this question: Name the occasion when every player on a major league team had precisely the same batting average before and after the game. It was April 16, 1940, when Bob Feller of the Cleveland Indians pitched a no-hitter against the White Sox on opening day. All the White Sox were batting .000 before and after the game.

Feller, a baseball prodigy, was a major leaguer before he was old enough to shave, the only major leaguer who returned to his hotel to do high-school homework. On July 6, 1936, after his junior year and four months before his eighteenth birthday, he pitched for the Indians in an exhibition game against the St. Louis Cardinals. His first pitch was a called strike. The batter turned to the catcher and said, "Let me out of here in one piece." The batter had just seen—sort of—the fastball that later would cause a batter (Hall of Fame wit and pitcher Lefty Gomez) to say, after taking a called third strike with his bat on his shoulder, "That one sounded a little low."

In September 1936, before returning to high school for his senior year, the seventeen-year-old "phenom" broke the American League single-game record and tied Dizzy Dean's major league record by striking out seventeen Philadelphia Athletics, thereby—now *here* is a record that will not soon be broken—

132

becoming the only pitcher ever to achieve as many strikeouts in a game as he was years old. This and the rest of Feller's career, recounted in his memoir *Now Pitching: Bob Feller* (with Bill Gilbert), illustrates the axiom, "As the twig is bent . . ."

In the movie *Field of Dreams* (and the novel on which it is based, W. P. Kinsella's *Shoeless Joe*), an Iowa farmer and baseball fanatic hears a voice from the sky say, "If you build it, he will come." The farmer inexplicably but correctly intuits this message to mean that if he builds a ballpark, Shoeless Joe Jackson will return from the dead.

The farmer does, and Joe does, saying, "This must be heaven." The farmer says, "No. It's Iowa."

No, *this* is Iowa: Bob Feller's father, a farmer, built his son a ballpark—felled trees, leveled a pasture, erected bleachers. He even switched other fields from corn to wheat because wheat took less time to harvest, leaving more time for baseball.

(Fathers. In Commerce, Oklahoma, at dusk after days in the zinc mines, a father makes a switch-hitter of the boy he named after his hero, Tigers catcher Mickey Cochrane. The father is Mutt Mantle.)

Feller, with Ted Williams and Joe DiMaggio (they were twenty, twenty-one and twenty-four respectively in 1939), was part of baseball's golden trio on the eve of the war that was to consume what could have been their most productive years. After Pearl Harbor, Feller immediately enlisted in the Navy, chafed under a stateside assignment with a physical-fitness program, then became chief of an antiaircraft gun crew on the battleship USS *Alabama,* which had a population about six times that of Van Meter. In two years, the

A major leaguer before he was old enough to shave: Bob Feller.

Alabama steamed 175,000 miles and won eight battle stars for participating in eight Pacific landings.

Feller won 100 games at a younger age than anyone else ever has. He had 107 when he enlisted, at an age when Cy Young, baseball's winningest pitcher (511), had won none and Walter Johnson, the second winningest (417), had just 57. The war probably cost Feller at least 100 wins. Even so, he had more "low hit" games (15–3 no-hitters and 12 one-hitters) than anyone else until passed by the Rangers' Nolan Ryan (16–5 no-hitters and 11 one-hitters). Ryan has had 192 more starts than Feller had.

What is he proudest of? Probably having been on his ship off Saipan when U.S. forces shot down 400 enemy aircraft. And he has something else to treasure. Ted Williams, baseball's best pure hitter, ever, said of Feller:

> That was the test. Three days before he pitched, I would start thinking about Robert Feller, Bob Feller. I'd sit in my room thinking and seeing him, thinking about him all the time. . . . Allie Reynolds of the Yankees was tough and I might think of him for about two hours before a game, but Robert Feller, I'd think about him for three days.

That is a compliment as elegant as Williams' swing.

GEORGE STEINBRENNER: AN ACQUIRED TASTE

August 6, 1990

THIS SUMMER a suburban Washington dinner theater is putting on the 1955 musical *Damn Yankees*. At first I thought, "What fun, I'll take the children." Then, pulling myself up from the time warp, I had second thoughts. The children would not get it—would not understand the role

Damned Yankee George Steinbrenner resigns from management of the team, August 20, 1990.

played by the Yankees. The evening would just confirm them further in their view that their father is a fossil.

You may dimly remember the *Damn Yankees* story. It is Faust for the modern age. The protagonist is a middle-aged, unathletic but ardent fan of the Washington Senators. (Remember your ancient history, from back when the saying was, "Washington—first in war, first in peace and last in the American League.") The fan sells his soul to the Devil for one sensational season as a major league player—a perfectly reasonable transaction, I think. In that season he (I am leaving out a lot) leads the Senators to victory. Over whom? Who else? That irresistible force, the Leviathan of the diamond, that Cadillac (another anachronism; today we would say Mercedes) of major league franchises. The Senators beat the perennially mighty and therefore universally detested Yankees.

That was then, this is now. Then Whitey Ford was pitching and Yogi Berra was catching and Mickey Mantle was belting the ball out of Yankee Stadium's ZIP code (oops, that was pre–ZIP codes) and the memory of man ranneth not to when the Yankees were other than awesome. Now the Yankees are the worst team in baseball. Look to your nonlaurels, Atlanta Braves—the Bronx Bumblers have captured baseball's booby prize. And the Yankees' owner, George Steinbrenner, is the worst problem on the plate of the commissioner of baseball, Fay Vincent, who must think the Devil is plaguing him.

An earthquake messed with Vincent's first World Series, a lockout delayed his first opening day, it rained on his first All-Star Game, and this summer he has the migraine-inducing duty of sifting through Steinbrenner's wonderfully imaginative and glaringly incompatible and completely unconvincing stories about why he gave $40,000 to an unsavory character who gambles. Steinbrenner is almost certainly innocent of gambling. And that about exhausts his innocence.

Steinbrenner is, shall we say, an acquired taste. He can be charming when his interests are not engaged and he is dealing with people not in his employ. The rest of the time, which means most of the time, he is hard to take in even small doses. Vincent, having engaged Steinbrenner in long discussions about rules and laws and ethics, must wince when he reads the title of the book his predecessor, Bart Giamatti, wrote about Americans and their games: *Take Time for Paradise*. If this is paradise, Adam and Eve were smart to get themselves expelled.

Steinbrenner is a bore and a buccaneer, overflowing with the animal spirits that fuel capitalism in its rawer forms. Such spirits sometimes seek additional outlets in the ownership of sports franchises. Vincent is a gentleman and a scholar.

He is a graduate of Yale Law School. (Pete Rose on Vincent: "He's an intellectual from Yale, but he's very intelligent.") It is said that the study of law sharpens the mind by narrowing it. However, Vincent is a voracious reader. Trying to find a biography he has not read is like naming, say, the St. Louis Cardinals catcher in 1912: It is possible, but requires research. (By the way, the Cardinals catcher was Ivey Wingo.) Vincent carefully measures the words he selects to explain his measured responses to problems. In his delicacy and disdain for flamboyance baseball's eighth commissioner is utterly unlike the first.

The commissioner's office is one of those institutions that is (in Emerson's words) the lengthening shadow of man. The man was Kenesaw Mountain Landis, a Chicagoan who has the visage of an Old Testament prophet who has looked around and is not amused by what he has seen. Landis was a judge, an egomaniacal and grandstanding judge, but he was just what baseball needed in its hour of maximum need—the aftermath of the Black Sox scandal, the fixed World Series of 1919. Eight players, some more dumb than dishonest, were banned from baseball for life; nothing happened to the gamblers. Then baseball picked itself up, dusted itself off, built Yankee Stadium, put Babe Ruth on center stage and rollicked through the 1920s.

Landis became (with assists from Ruth and the lively ball) baseball's savior seventy years ago. From the owners he extracted an extraordinary empowerment for his office. A commissioner may (note well: may, not must; it is a right, not a duty) take remedial measures against any "act, transaction or practice" that is "not in the best interests" of baseball. That clause is a huge grant of discretion. Like any such grant, it is a mixed blessing for the recipient.

The commissioner's power is unconstrained, other than by the commissioner's prudence. And it is unappealable, unless the commissioner acts more capriciously than any commissioner ever has. The sweep of the "best interests" clause generates pressure to use the power. The pressure often comes from people impatient to use fiats to cut through complex problems, sweeping like a scythe through procedural niceties. Nothing matches the impatience of a baseball fan fed up with his team's owner. No one is as fed up as Yankee fans are.

The remedies available to the commissioner acting in baseball's best interests run all the way up the escalation ladder to the expulsion of an owner from the ranks of ownership. But this power is like a nuclear weapon. Its only satisfactory role is as a deterrent. Using it today probably would involve unacceptable collateral damage in the form of endless litigation.

Consider another analogy, from constitutional law. The "best interests" clause of baseball's constitution resembles the "equal protection" and "due process" clauses of the Constitution. A willful judge can do almost anything in the name of those clauses if he is indifferent to the damage done to the texture of the law and the stature of his office. But a judicious judge will exercise self-restraint. He will be a strict constructionist because judicial power is best preserved by being used reluctantly and economically.

Baseball's "best interests" clause has been invoked some seventy times in seventy years. It has been used to suspend a manager (the Dodgers' Leo Durocher in 1947, for consorting with gamblers). It has been used to bar two retired stars, Mickey Mantle and Willie Mays, from any contact with baseball as long as they were employed at an Atlantic City casino. It was used in 1976 to stop an owner, Charles Finley of the Athletics, from conducting a fire sale of players, a sale that would have instantly degraded the franchise. (Finley was furious about the coming of free agency. Blocking the sale did not prevent

Finley from wrecking his team. The law has limits. The Athletics have risen from the ruins, several times. Nothing is forever, not even ruination.)

Now, would it be in baseball's best interests were Steinbrenner to sell the Yankees? Hey, ask me a hard one. Baseball is a game of inches but this is not a close call. Of course Steinbrenner is bad for baseball's grandest franchise, and hence for the game. But that fact does not entail the conclusion that Vincent should hurl Steinbrenner into outer darkness forever. A mere monetary fine would be derisory; permanent expulsion would be disproportionate; a substantial suspension—say, through 1991—would be about right.

Steinbrenner's sins are manifold and manifest. There is the scarlet sin of his transaction with the gambler. And there are scores of mundane sins of stupidity which have reduced the Yankees to rubble. No one of these sins seems to warrant the nuclear weapon of forcing him to sell, however much that might make Vincent the toast of the Bronx (and, truth be told, of Steinbrenner's fellow owners). But there are precedents that should make Steinbrenner nervous, and it is in baseball's best interests that he should be nervous.

In 1943 the owner of the Phillies was forced to sell his team because he bet on games. In 1953 the owner of the Cardinals was forced to sell because he was convicted of tax evasion. But back then a franchise was an economic entity akin to a corner candy store. Today it is more like Neiman Marcus. A difference in degree becomes a difference in kind. To force one of today's owners to sell, even at a fair market price (the Yankees would bring at least $200 million), might trigger judicial sympathy for any Steinbrenner claim that he was being deprived of property without due process. Courts traditionally have been wary about intervening in the internal governance of private associations, but in the current climate of judicial hubris, a judge can almost always be found who will try to fine-tune any controversy.

(Here is a pretty judicial pickle. Imagine trying to assemble an impartial jury of New Yorkers to hear Steinbrenner's case. "Tell the court, Mr. Prospective Juror, do you have any strong opinions about the owner who masterminded the trade of Fred McGriff from the Yankees to the Blue Jays in exchange for a couple of no-names? Stop snarling, Prospective Juror.")

It is baseball's double misfortune that Steinbrenner is not just an owner, but the owner of the Yankees. Damn them to your heart's content, they have been important to the game's health.

From 1926 through 1964 they had thirty-nine consecutive winning seasons. (The longest current streak is the Blue Jays' seven.) In those thirty-nine years the Yankees finished first twenty-six times. From 1949 through 1958 they won nine pennants. They finished second in 1954, when the Cleveland Indians set a league record with 111 wins in a 154-game schedule. If the Yankees' 103 wins had been, as such a total usually is, enough to win in a walk, the Yankees would have been in ten consecutive World Series.

Competitive balance has been excellent in the last dozen seasons. Balance is better for baseball than the sort of dominance the Yankees enjoyed. Baseball benefits from occasional minidynasties. The Athletics and Reds were such in the 1970s; the Athletics are today. However, it was good for baseball when the most glamorous team, the Yankees, had glamour. To be blunt, Steinbrenner's mismanagement of the Yankees matters much more than the mismanagement of the Braves. The Yankees, the source of so much of baseball's most stirring history—Ruth, Gehrig, DiMaggio, Mantle—are simply irreplaceable as carriers of a tradition that lends derivative glory to teams that compete against them.

Of course, nothing lasts. The ravages of time are lethal, especially when assisted by the ravages of a Steinbrenner. The Yankees were once, it seemed, one of those rare institutions that could not be ruined. Wrong. Such institutions are not merely rare; they are, because there are Steinbrenners, nonexistent. The Yankees had a huge market, a vibrant farm system, a fat treasury, an inspiriting tradition. And yet they were brought low by the ten-thumbed touch of their owner.

Some serious folks from the Harvard Business School have studied the Oakland Athletics' current management. They say it is a model of sound practices. Steinbrenner could serve as the reverse, as baseball's dumb-o-meter: study his decisions, do the opposite, and you will do well. There is no need to rehash here all the talent-squandering trades, the morale-shattering tirades and other madcap misadventures that have made Steinbrenner's regime resemble Mussolini's Italy—despotism tempered by anarchy. Suffice it to say you can cover recent Yankee history with a slew of "E-O" notations—error by the owner.

Baseball is hard to play, and it is extremely difficult to judge baseball talent. Even professionals make misjudgments. (Two of today's players who probably are headed for the Hall of Fame, Roger Clemens and Ryne Sandberg, were not picked in baseball drafts until the twelfth and twentieth rounds, respectively.) Amateurs like Steinbrenner should butt out. Steinbrenner should have been a football owner. The NFL's farm system is run by big universities. And how hard is it, anyway, to judge the beef trust who become linemen? Weigh them, time them, sign them.

But Steinbrenner is not just error-prone, he is an error machine. He is because he lacks an attribute essential for baseball (and, not coincidentally, for democracy): patience. Baseball is an appropriate national pastime for this democratic nation precisely because it both requires and teaches what Americans often lack: patience. (The American prayer: "Lord give me patience—and I want it right now!") Democracy rests on persuasion, which takes time. Democracy involves constant compromising, which means partial failure to get one's way. Democracy is the politics of the half-loaf. And baseball? The best team is going to get beaten about sixty times this year, and is going to be hammered many of those times. Steinbrenner has a football temperament. In the NFL, your team only plays sixteen games, so if it loses three games in the early going, it is rational—well, by football standards—to slit your wrists.

The late Edward Bennett Williams, the Washington attorney who bought the Baltimore Orioles in 1979, had been president of the Washington Redskins. He had a football frame of mind. But after he spent lavishly and futilely on free agents for the Orioles he learned a lesson. "There are," he said, "three things money can't buy—love, happiness and an American League pennant." One cause of Steinbrenner's downfall is that at first he seemed able to buy success. His swashbuckling impatience seemed validated by spending (for Reggie Jackson and Catfish Hunter, especially) that helped produce the 1977 and 1978 Series winners. But baseball is a great leveler, punishing the impatient who throw money rather than intelligence at problems.

(And yet . . . perhaps Steinbrenner should keep control of the Yankees. The Yankees get about $55 million a year in local broadcast revenues. Some other teams get only $5 million or less. Perhaps Steinbrenner's incompetent squandering of his money prevents the Yankees from disrupting the league's balance.)

Steinbrenner will be punished for his association with a gambler. And the shipwreck of the Yankees is condign punishment for Steinbrenner's utter lack of baseball sense. Alas, Yankee fans, too, are being punished. But life is unfair and the commissioner can do nothing about that defect in the universe. Furthermore, he cannot make baseball blunders punishable offenses.

Today baseball is better than ever, on the field and in the front offices. You might not think so, reading the sports pages. Recently they have read like extracts from *The Wall Street Journal*—money, contracts, labor strife—and police blotters—gambling, drugs. But there have always been dumb and coarse owners (and congressmen and senators and journalists and . . .). They have to be lived with, and survived. Steinbrenner will be.

It is said democracy is a splendid thing that the people who run it do their level best to ruin. Baseball is like that. But listen to the levelheadedness of

George Anderson, a.k.a. Sparky, of the Detroits. He says: "We try every way we can do to kill the game, but for some reason, nothing nobody does never hurts it." Still true, so far, but stay tuned.

BASEBALL LIT. 101

Fall 1990

I HAVE READ a bunch of books and written a few. And here I sit in Washington, my desk piled high with political clutter, and in the middle of the clutter sits a pearl past price—a copy of the first book I remember reading. It was published in 1947 when I was six years old. It was written by Garth Garreau, an author not as important as Tolstoy, except to me. The title of his book is *Bat Boy of the Giants*. Look to your laurels, Herman Melville. In my (perhaps warped) mind, *Bat Boy of the Giants* ranks right up there with *Moby Dick* on the list of American classics.

Garreau's book is just a boy's story of a boy's dream come true—his year as batboy for the New York Giants. My copy is tattered but very precious to me because it was a gate through which I passed into a lush, friendly garden, the wonderful world of baseball books. To repay my debt to baseball for all the pleasure it has given me in my forty-eight years I have now planted something in that garden.

I recently completed work ("work"? not really) on a project—my baseball book—that would be any baseball fan's fantasy. The project required me to attend baseball games in eleven major league parks from Canada to California in a single season. I also spent hundreds of hours talking, in clubhouses and dugouts and hotel lobbies and coffee shops, with scores of baseball's most interesting people. They included players, managers, coaches, executives, writers, broadcasters. The result is a book, *Men at Work: The Craft of Baseball*.

One of the arguments I make in the book is that baseball is better than ever.

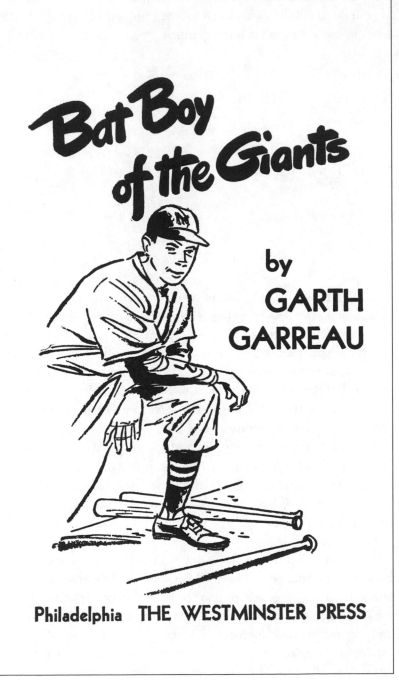

Bat Boy
of the Giants

by
GARTH
GARREAU

Philadelphia THE WESTMINSTER PRESS

"Look to your laurels, Herman Melville": *Bat Boy of the Giants*

And one reason that is true is the presence of men like two members of the Giants' family, two men I interviewed for the book—Roger Craig and Al Rosen.

I spoke with Craig in the restaurant of the Sheraton Hotel in downtown Montreal. I had dinner with Rosen in the restaurant of San Francisco's Campton Place Hotel. (The Campton Place is to hotels what Will Clark is to first basemen: the state of the art.) I came away from both conversations knowing more about baseball and knowing why the Giants are one of baseball's current success stories.

The reason the Giants are winning is that the Giants are thinking. Sounds simple, does it not? It isn't.

Baseball is the sport which most rewards attention to the most minute details—attention by players, managers, executives and fans. I came away from my two-year project convinced that the caliber of major league managers is dramatically improved over what it was a generation ago. I have no doubt that a good manager can be, like a pitcher, a 20-game winner for his team—that what he does, if he does his job right, can mean 20 wins his club otherwise would not get. His job does not begin—nor end—with each day's game. Rather, it involves twelve months of planning for seasons, planning for each series, and each game. And during the game it involves extraordinary *watchfulness,* three hours of intense acquisition of, and instant analysis of, information about the game in progress.

Today's elite of managers who have mastered baseball's watchfulness includes Oakland's Tony La Russa (one of the four principal subjects of my book), St. Louis' Whitey Herzog, Baltimore's Frank Robinson—and certainly San Francisco's Roger Craig.

Roger Craig never won 20 games in a season when he was a pitcher. Indeed, he lost 46 games in two seasons for the ramshackle expansion Mets in the early 1960s. But in 1989 he was a 20-game winner for the Giants.

To talk with Roger Craig about the relentless pace of decision making during a game, pitch by pitch, is to come away both exhilarated and exhausted. One is exhilarated by Craig's mastery of his demanding craft, and exhausted by trying to assimilate all the information he effortlessly assimilates and dispenses.

As Roger Craig would be the first to insist, a manager is only as good as the talent he has to work with. That is why Al Rosen—when I was a young fan, he was one of baseball's premier talents—is a big reason the Giants are now on such a splendid roll.

I live and work in Washington, a single-industry town. The industry is government. The industry is not doing very well. The job of government is to look ahead, over the horizon, to see problems coming while they are still small and to master them before they become big. That also is a general manager's job in baseball. If Washington were run as well as Al Rosen runs the Giants, the federal budget would be balanced and we political columnists could turn our attention, full-time, to something more fun—and more useful—than politics. Such as? Baseball.

I turned some of my attention to writing about baseball, without waiting for the budget to be balanced. Baseball is immortal, but I am not, so I did not want to wait for Washington to do its job as well as the Giants do theirs.

BLAME BURT WILSON

Fall 1990

FOR THE PAST two years I have been enjoying myself shamelessly. I have been combining my vocation, which is writing, with my avocation, which is following baseball. Did I say "following"? The word is too bland. Try: immersing.

The result of my two-year combination of vocation and avocation has now become a book, *Men at Work: The Craft of Baseball*. While I was traveling around doing the research for it, I was frequently asked two questions. One was: How did you come to be such a baseball fan? The second was: What gives you, a political commentator, the right to have so much fun? The short answer to the first question is: Blame Burt Wilson. The short answer to the second question is: More political commentators (and doctors and autoworkers and bankers and, for that matter, politicians) should do what I had the fun of doing. They should see the serious side of baseball, the relentless and successful pursuit of excellence.

I was born, in 1941, in downstate Illinois, in Champaign-Urbana. I spent my formative years, meaning my first eighteen years, being formed, in part, by the late Burt Wilson and other Cubs broadcasters. I would get to Wrigley Field only once, occasionally twice a year. Once was a birthday present. Sometimes a second trip was a prize for selling the required number of subscriptions to a local paper for which I was a paperboy—the *Courier,* now long gone. Aside from those trips, my connection with baseball was radio. It was (this fact may astonish younger people who were raised with—by?—television) enough.

Radio is a medium of the imagination, which is to say a medium that engages the mind.

Chicago Cubs broadcaster Burt Wilson.

And baseball is the sport that most engages the mind. It has a pace, a one-step-at-a-time orderliness (working through a *lineup,* a batting *order*) that demands quick and constant thinking about what has just happened and what will, or at any rate should, happen next. The lesson I learned in my two-year sojourn with baseball is that mind matters: Those teams play best that think best. The thinking begins before the season and below the major league level, and extends to thinking about the decade, the next season, the next game, the next batter, the next pitch.

Those days of my youth, from the late 1940s through the mid-1950s, were, to say no more, not the salad days of the Cubs franchise. And what made my suffering especially acute was the fact that central Illinois was then, as now, badly infested with Cardinal fans. Cardinal fans probably should be allowed to vote, and perhaps even to enjoy most other civil rights, but Cardinal fans were (and probably still are) insufferable.

However, for the downstate Cub fan—who could, after all, have jumped the other way, onto the Cardinal bandwagon—rooting for the Cubs conferred one exquisite pleasure. It enabled him or her to be against the team that the Cardinals radio broadcaster was so obviously, passionately supporting. He was Harry Caray, and he was that hard to take. This was because he so deeply cared for the home team, relishing Cardinal successes and suffering through failures. If you were a Cardinal fan that was fine. If you were not, it was insufferable.

I do not remember life before baseball, and I strongly suspect that, in some metaphysical sense, there *is* no life before baseball. Be that as it may, my two years spent writing *Men at Work* were two years in close contact with baseball's best people. These years convinced me that American life is better because of baseball, and would be better still if more people emulated baseball people.

Baseball is a severe meritocracy, an arena of exacting, unforgiving competition, in which there is a direct correlation between the amount of luck you have and the amount of work you do. Over 162 games it is not luck that matters. What matters is a passion for excellence. Today I live and work in Washington. In recent years there has been considerable anxiety felt there, anxiety about the vigor of America, and about our commitment to excellence. There have been many voices insisting that the nation is suffering from "imperial overstretch"—trying to do too much abroad. I came away from my two years immersed in baseball with quite a different conclusion. I believe that we suffer not from "imperial overstretch" abroad, but from "individual understretch" at home. Too many Americans are not asking enough of themselves, not holding themselves to the kind of exacting standards that baseball enforces on its participants severely.

Few Americans have their daily performance put under the kind of microscope that ballplayers are under from April to October. Few Americans are in the position every ballplayer is in each morning. At breakfast a player can look in the newspaper and see in small type, in the box scores, the merciless mathematics of his job performance of the day before. Maybe if we all were evaluated that way, every day—we who write columns, make cars, create laws, teach school, sell insurance, run banks, lay bricks, whatever—we would do our jobs better.

Perhaps the point should be put this way. One reason we so rarely write "E-4" on our scorecards when the Cubs are in the field is that so many people sit, with pencils poised, prepared to note precisely what Ryne Sandberg does. He is judged every day, and has measured up to that pressure. He does his job so well—better, perhaps, than it has ever been done—because he is pulled to excellence by the demands of close scrutiny, and by pride in performance.

The baseball portion of my life has another dimension that is directly influenced by the formative influence of growing up a Cub fan. I serve on the board of directors of the Baltimore Orioles. If imitation really is the sincerest form of flattery, the Orioles are about to pay the Cubs a lavish compliment. Baltimore (actually, the state of Maryland) is building the Orioles a new park. I do emphatically mean a *park,* not a "stadium." And I actually mean a new-old park.

A baseball *park,* like Wrigley *Field,* is a place for play. A stadium is a site for gladiatorial extravaganzas, such as football. Baltimore's new park, like the Cubs' old one, will be made primarily of steel, with the lightness and airiness that that material, unlike concrete, can give. The park will have the same intimacy that makes fans participants in, rather than mere spectators at, the event.

It is hard to believe, but this is true: Aside from Wrigley Field, the oldest National League park is San Francisco's Candlestick Park.* Candlestick is the wrong kind of park. It is a park in name only. Since being enclosed by seats to accommodate Forty-Niners football crowds, it is a stadium and is spiritually as well as physically cold. It is also in the wrong place. Baltimore's new park will be where baseball belongs, in the heart of a city, just as Wrigley is.

One of the conclusions to which I came while writing *Men at Work* is that baseball today is better than ever. The talent is better, the commitment to excellence is deeper, the element of mind—thoughtfulness; attention to detail—is larger than ever. And another reason for the improvement of baseball is this: Baseball today is learning, rather late, what we in central Illinois knew four decades ago. It is learning not to try to improve on what is already right. Baseball begins with a physical setting, and the Cubs' setting is the best there ever was.

In 1998, the Milwaukee Brewers moved to the National League, and Milwaukee's County Stadium became the league's second oldest stadium. It is soon to be replaced, as is Candlestick, a.k.a. 3-Com Stadium.

In 1990, I published *Men at Work: The Craft of Baseball.* The book was well received. It was on *The New York Times* bestseller list for twenty-five weeks, occupying the top of the list for nineteen, and was the second bestselling nonfiction book of that year. One reason the book found such a large audience is, I think, that it was unsentimental and antiromantic. Although suffused with admiration for its four principal subjects—Tony La Russa, Tony Gwynn, Orel Hershiser and Cal Ripken, Jr.—and for the general professionalism and craftsmanship of most of the men wearing major league uniforms, its theme was that baseball is hard work by grown men. However, Professor Donald Kagan—learned fan, Yale historian and classicist—concluded that my unsentimental and antiromantic treatment of baseball was also antiheroic. His argument against my misunderstanding (as he saw it) of heroism was published in *The Public Interest*, a small but intellectually upscale quarterly usually devoted to questions of public policy. I wrote a response. Here is our exchange.

GEORGE WILL'S BASEBALL— A CONSERVATIVE CRITIQUE

By DONALD KAGAN (*The Public Interest*, Fall 1990)

BASEBALL, more than any other sport, has inspired good writing from important authors and gained serious attention from thoughtful people. From Ring Lardner's ignorant and mean-spirited "busher," Jack Keefe, to Mark Harris' intelligent and warmhearted southpaw, Henry Wiggen, to Bernard Malamud's mythical Arthurian hero, the "natural" Roy Hobbs, writers have used baseball and its players to say something about the world and the people in it. How someone sees the game and its players reveals the kind of person he is and what he values.

My friend Bart Giamatti was a student and explicator of epic poetry before he became president of Yale University, president of baseball's National League and commissioner of baseball. He viewed the game as an epic, whose elements were simple and primordial: A man stood on a hill and hurled a rock at another man, who waited below with a tree trunk in his hands. (Malamud had a similar vision, in which the bat was "like a caveman's ax.") So it must have been from the time of the Stone Age. A dramatically heroic and potentially tragic confrontation stands at the heart of this most poetic game.

From a more classical perspective Giamatti regarded baseball as a kind of Homeric *Odyssey*. The batter is its hero. He begins at home, but his mission is to venture away from it, encountering various unforeseeable dangers. At each station opponents scheme to put him out by strength or skill or guile. Should they succeed, he dies on the bases, defeated. If his own heroic talents are superior, however, he completes the circuit and returns victorious to home, there to be greeted with joy by the friends he left behind. But Giamatti knew the *Iliad*, too, and as a longtime Red Sox fan he believed that the tragic epic best corresponded to baseball; thus he observed that the game "was meant to break your heart."

That is not how George Will sees it. Educated at Connecticut's Trinity College and at Oxford and Princeton, the holder of a doctorate in political theory, a former professor himself and the son of a professor, he has become a Pulitzer Prize–winning columnist and a political commentator on national television, and he has earned a reputation as the most thoughtful and urbane of conservative journalists. His bestselling book *Men at Work* clearly shows his characteristic analytic intelligence, a witty and graceful writing style, a deep knowledge of baseball and its history, and a love for the game and the men who work at it in the major leagues. It is not a book, however, for those who look to the game for the celebration of that heroic greatness that can inspire and elevate the rest of us to admire a natural excellence that we ourselves can achieve only in dreams. His book is not for humanists, poets, or hero-worshipers—but for systems analysts, social scientists and computer programmers.

As we would expect from its author, it is no mere narrative account but makes a powerful argument. Supported by a formidable array of statistics and testimony from current participants, Will rejects the widespread assertion that baseball today is a degenerate perversion of the great game that once was. Critics point to the dilution of talent caused by the expansion from sixteen to twenty-six teams, and to the unseasoned and untutored players who still must learn the rudiments of the game when they are brought too soon to the majors to fill out the added rosters. They complain of the absence of the great dynastic championship teams that we knew in better times, the decline of hitting (the most difficult and most exciting part of the game), the shortage of great players—in short, the mediocrity of baseball today.

Will dismisses these complaints as the usual crabbing of elders almost as old as baseball itself. To him "the national pastime is better than ever in almost every way and is getting better every year." For this conclusion he offers three major reasons:

(1) The games are getting closer. The powerful 1988 American League champion Oakland Athletics scored only 180 runs more than their opponents for a per-game average margin of victory of 1.1 runs. The great Yankees of 1927 had an advantage more than twice that size—2.44 runs—and the Yankees of 1939 defeated their rivals by an average of 2.7 runs per game.

(2) Competition for the championships is becoming more equal. No team

has won the World Series for two consecutive years since the Yankees of 1977 and 1978. Since then there has been tremendous volatility: In the eleven seasons from 1979 through 1989 nine different teams won the American League pennant and seven won in the National League. Compare this with the dynasties that dominated the past: The New York Giants won four pennants in a row from 1921 through 1924; the Brooklyn Dodgers won six out of ten from 1947 through 1956; and the Los Angeles team that has usurped their name won three of four from 1963 through 1966. The greatest dynasty of all, of course, was created by the New York Yankees. From 1921 through 1928 they won six of eight pennants; from 1936 through 1943 they won seven of eight; from 1947 through 1964 they won fifteen of eighteen (winning four consecutive pennants once and five in a row twice during that last stretch).

(3) The culminating reason for the superiority of the modern game is that it is smarter; now, as never before, intelligence is the decisive element in the game.

The very name of his book is ominous for Will's approach to the subject: *Men at Work: The Craft of Baseball.* It is not a game but a *craft;* the participants do not play, they *work.* "Baseball was evolving from lower forms of activity about the time the colonies were evolving into a nation, and baseball became a mode of work—as distinct from a pastime—remarkably soon after the nation got going." The participants succeed at their craft as men do at any other, by means of hard work and intelligent study. Will knows, of course, that baseball players need physical ability and natural talent, but he mentions these as little as possible. In his view baseball has progressed and improved because intelligence and knowledge have come to the fore, aided by advances in technology. Charts, computers and videotapes have made it possible to acquire and organize information better than ever before and therefore to use it more effectively and decisively. "Games are won by a combination of informed aggression and prudence based on information."

As George Orwell once put it, only an intellectual could believe that. This is the fantasy of a smart, skinny kid who desperately wants to believe that brains count more than the speed, power and reckless courage of the big guys who can play, but it is also the dominant message of this book. More puzzling than this bizarre prejudice is Will's defense of the modern game against its detractors. As a conservative, a self-proclaimed Tory, he might be expected to be a *laudator temporis acti,* a praiser of the past even beyond justice. An admirer of a nobler time should look askance at the use of the designated hitter and other specialists who demean the all-roundedness esteemed by both the principle of aristocracy and liberal education.

One need not be a conservative, however, to be appalled by what has happened to baseball. Aesthetically, the decline is evident. Baseball was meant to be played on Nature's green grass in the sunshine. Bart Giamatti liked to point out that "paradise" derives from an Old Persian word that meant "enclosed park or green." Baseball responds to "a vestigial memory of an enclosed green space as a place of freedom or play." For Will, of course, it is a place of work—hard, dangerous and exacting. Most modern baseball fields suit Will's vision better, for they are anything but parks, not to mention paradise. Many of them have replaced the grass with a surface hard as a pool table, whose covering has seams that sometimes come undone. In some of them the sky is shut out, turning the game into an indoor sport, like bowling and roller derby. The fields tend to be uniform and standardized, lacking the delightful peculiarities that real ballparks like Ebbets Field, Griffith Stadium, Crosley Field and the Polo Grounds used to have. The modern stadia seem fake, manufactured, unnatural. They are noisy, distracting and offensive places, where scoreboards ceaselessly blare rock music and show cartoons. They sound military charges, tell the fans when to cheer and produce mechanized rhythmic noise that used to be supplied rarely, spontaneously and at appropriate times by the collision of human palms. Everything possible is done to turn the spectator's attention from the game.

This may well be necessary, because the game has become much more boring. In the 1940s the Yankees began their games at three o'clock in the afternoon, and they were generally over by five. On June 25, 1990, a day picked at random, omitting a twelve-inning game that lasted four hours and fifteen minutes, twelve games were played in the major leagues. The quickest lasted over two and one-half hours, the longest over three and one-half; the average was two hours and forty-three minutes. This is not because there is more scoring today: The highest-scoring team in 1987 averaged 5.5 runs per game; the figure in 1941 was 5.6.

The percentage of elapsed time that involves significant action in a baseball game is always small, but it has become intolerably so. Part of the increased dead time results from a prodigal use of relief pitchers unknown in better days. Much of the rest consists of pitchers holding the ball or throwing to first to limit the running game that is the modern substitute for the most difficult part of the game and its life's blood—hitting. As Ted Williams neatly put it: "When you're coming towards the park and you're two blocks away, and you hear a tremendous cheer, that isn't because someone has thrown a strike. That's because someone has hit the ball." The threat posed by batters who can hit with consistency and power is what gives the game excitement and drama, and what provides the danger that alone makes great pitching and fielding impressive. Baseball was not meant to be a track meet, but the new fields—with their distant fences that make home runs into outs, and their hard surfaces that produce singles out of ordinary ground balls—are turning it into one.

Nor is the argument from equality compelling, for modern baseball is so equal because it is mediocre. The critics' complaints are sound—the quality of play is diminished everywhere, and no team can stock itself with enough talent to establish itself as a dynasty. Instead, an equality of incompetence reigns. The last time great dynasties flourished was the 1950s, when the Yankees dominated the American League and the Dodgers controlled the National League almost as completely, challenged most successfully by an impressive Giants team. This is precisely the period that Will particularly scorns. Home runs, he tells us:

> began to drive out other forms of offense. When home runs became the center of baseball's mental universe, the emphasis shifted away from advancing runners. The new emphasis was on just getting runners on base to wait for lightning to strike. The major league teams of the 1950s were like American automobiles of the 1950s: There was not much variety or subtlety. . . . The stolen base was like the foreign car: It was considered cute and fun and not quite serious, and was not often seen . . .
>
> The wonder is that baseball took such a wrong turn [in] . . . the 1950s. Yes, that was a conservative decade. The Eisenhower years have been characterized as "the bland leading the bland." Bland was fine in politics. . . . But baseball is entertainment and bland entertainment is not fun. . . . It was insufficiently entertaining because it was not sufficiently intelligent.

That is an extraordinary passage to be written by a conservative and a baseball fan. Consider the contempt for "wait[ing] for lightning to strike." That is just what thrilled fans did in the 1920s and 1930s, as they watched the Yankees of Ruth, Gehrig and Lazzeri, waiting for their legendary "five o'clock lightning." Whatever else may be said of American cars of the fifties, they had size and power; the foreign car of the day was the Volkswagen beetle, a tiny simulacrum of an automobile, miserably cramped and powerless.

The fifties were when the first great black players—Jackie Robinson, Willie Mays, Roy Campanella, Don Newcombe, Henry Aaron, Frank Robinson and Ernie Banks—came into their own and raised the quality and excitement of the game to a new level. All the thrills offered by baseball were present in abundance. If you like hitting you could have enjoyed watching Stan Musial, Williams, Aaron, Mays, Duke Snider, Mickey Mantle, Yogi Berra and Roberto Clemente. If pitching is to your taste you could have seen Bob Feller, Warren Spahn, Early Wynn, Whitey Ford and a host of other outstanding hurlers. If defense is what you want, the fifties were graced with such brilliant shortstops as Pee Wee Reese, Phil Rizzuto and Luis Aparicio. Stealing bases, to be sure, was an appropriately minor part of the game, but no one who saw Willie Mays run the bases will ever forget it, and the thrill of watching Jackie Robinson steal home cannot be matched.

In the fifties these great players were not scattered about one or two to a side, as at best they are today, but were often collected in one place to make a great team. At their peak the Dodgers terrified everyone with a lineup that included Robinson, Snider, Campanella, Gil Hodges and Carl Furillo; and the 1951 Yankees could field a team that included Joe DiMaggio, Mantle, Berra and Johnny Mize, who averaged 404 career home runs apiece. Great pitching staffs, with a depth not equaled in our time, were also assembled. The same Yankees had three pitchers (Allie Reynolds, Vic Raschi and Eddie Lopat), each of whom averaged almost eighteen victories a season from 1950 through 1952; in 1953 they were joined by Ford, who won eighteen that year. The Cleveland staff of the same era—which included Feller, Wynn, Bob Lemon and Mike Garcia—was even more impressive.

But even though pitching is generally conceded to be between 75 and 90 percent of the game, these Indians won only one pennant, in 1954, when they won 111 out of the 154 games (162 are played today) to beat out the Yankees, who won "only" 103. The Dodgers and Yankees faced stiff competition in the fifties, and there were tight pennant races. In fact, the 1950s witnessed two of the most thrilling pennant races and the single most miraculous game in the history of baseball. In 1950 the Phillies won the pennant by beating the Dodgers at Ebbets Field on the last day of the season on a tenth-inning home run by Dick Sisler. In 1951 the Giants came from thirteen and a half games behind on August 11 to tie the Dodgers on the last day of the regular season. With the Giants trailing 4–2 in the bottom of the ninth inning of the third and final game of the playoffs, Bobby Thomson hit a three-run homer to win the game. It was the only time ever that the pennant was decided by the last pitch of the regular season.

Why does Will think that such a glorious era was dull? It was a time of heroic greatness and consistent excellence, when dynasties were challenged by other dynasties. The war between the Yankees and Dodgers extended from 1947 through 1956, a decade—the very length of the war between the Greeks and Trojans. It is true that most of the action took place in New York City among the Dodgers, Giants and Yankees, and that Will is devoted to the Chicago Cubs. But in the twelfth century B.C. all the action was at Troy, and you didn't have to root for Troy or Argos or Ithaca to appreciate the show. Of course, the Cubs haven't won a pennant since 1945 or a World Series since Teddy Roosevelt was president; no doubt such lengthy frustration makes a man disgruntled and causes him to lose his judgment.

How else can we explain Will's failure to appreciate the lost grandeur of baseball in the fifties? For the last time the national game held its place as part of nature, timeless and regular as Newton's universe. In the beginning God created sixteen Major League Baseball teams, eight in the National League and eight in the American. Baseball was played on natural grass and mostly in the daytime. Each team played every other team in its league twenty-two times a season, eleven games at home and eleven away; the seventy-seven games at home and seventy-seven away made for a perfectly symmetrical season. The Yankees ruled this world as the Olympian gods ruled theirs. The mighty Dodgers and Giants challenged their supremacy as the Titans and Giants challenged the Olympians, and to no more avail. The Yankees ruled with steadiness, serenity and justice, and only the unworthy gnashed their teeth in envy and prayed for chaos to shatter the unwelcome order.

Then, at last, the forces of disorder held sway. The Yankees, a pale copy of the great teams, won their last pennant of the era in 1964. Then came Götterdämmerung: burning cities at home, frustrating and divisive wars abroad, one president forced not to seek reelection and another to resign his office, debasement of the schools and universities, the rise of a drug culture, the collapse of sexual decorum and restraint.

If, in a future age, Western civilization should come to an end, some perceptive scholar will point with certainty to the era that marked the beginning of its decline. The first clear sign came in 1953, when the Boston Braves moved to Milwaukee; the next year the St. Louis Browns became the Baltimore Orioles. Beginning in 1961 new teams were added, and in 1969 each league was divided into two divisions. The Dark Ages had begun. It is not clear that we shall ever see a Renaissance. It boggles the mind that a serious thinker who passes for a conservative could applaud such a decline.

What must lie behind Will's assessment is his passionate delusion that intelligence, not power, controls the modern degenerate game. Certainly, the men he admires most in the game today all rely on intelligence and on the new informational tools to enhance their success.

The heart of Will's book is a study of four such men: the manager Tony La Russa of Oakland, the pitcher Orel Hershiser of Los Angeles, the batter Tony Gwynn of San Diego and the shortstop Cal Ripken of Baltimore. The choices are by no means obvious. It is true that managers like Casey Stengel, John McGraw and Leo Durocher are no longer around, but it is most unlikely that Will would have chosen them if they were. No more did he choose the Cardinals' Whitey Herzog, the Dodgers' Tom Lasorda, or the Tigers' Sparky Anderson, highly successful managers who resemble those past greats in their blue-collar, extroverted, nonintellectual styles. Instead he chose La Russa, a fine manager who is greatly respected and has had remarkable success with two different teams, and who perfectly fits Will's model of the intellectual in baseball. He is the fifth manager in major league history to hold a law degree and, as Will points out, the other four are in the Hall of Fame.

La Russa's Athletics have won the last three American League championships chiefly because they have the best hitters and pitchers in the league, but La Russa plays and talks a brainy game. It is the game that Will loves, in which runners aggressively take extra bases, and managers engage in intellectual warfare by stealing the enemy's signs and making complicated calculations. Will recounts that La Russa once precisely timed an opposing pitcher's natural delivery to the plate at 1.6 seconds, one-fifth of a second more than a good runner needs to steal second base. La Russa inserted a speedy pinch runner on first to take advantage of the opportunity. The pitcher adjusted to the danger by hurrying some of his deliveries, at the paradoxical cost of losing speed on those pitches. La Russa carefully decided when the next delivery would be slow and signaled the runner to steal. He guessed wrong, but the runner was still safe, although according to the calculation he should have been out. Now Oakland had an advantage, for the runner could score from second on a mere single. On the other hand, the pitcher no longer needed to worry about a stolen base, so he pitched naturally at his highest efficiency. "The tricky stuff was over. Now it was the pitcher against the hitter. The pitcher won. Henderson hit a fly ball caught by the left fielder. Texas won."

However technically sophisticated and intelligent La Russa's strategy might have been, it was confounded by the performance of the pitcher and the batter, which was not intellectual but physical. Besides, it is not even clear that La Russa's strategy was smart. It was based on anticipating the pitching pattern, which he got wrong, only to be saved by the sheer speed of the runner. Was he wise to order a steal at all, and thus to take the pressure off the pitcher? Might La Russa not have done better to keep the runner on first, and to compel a fat pitch that the batter could have demolished? It is not possible to know, as is true of all such decisions. The dictates inside baseball are like maxims; different ones prescribe mutually exclusive courses of action. "A stitch in time saves nine," but "haste makes waste." In the same way, it is good for a pitcher to throw over to first to keep the runner close, but it is bad to do so too often, for that wears him out and distracts his attention from the batter. How often is too often? It depends. Clever managers always tell you about their shrewd moves that worked out, and blame the players' faulty execution for their failures. But by far the most important element in the contest is not intelligence but the natural ability of the players—a point that Will does not make.

Will's preferred game is as old as the hills; it dominated baseball in the era of the dead ball, when power hitting was rare. In recent years it has been most closely associated with Gene Mauch, who managed four different teams over twenty-six years, winning much admiration but no league championships, chiefly because he lacked hitters like Oakland's Rickey Henderson, Carney Lansford, Mark McGwire and Jose Canseco, and pitchers like Dave Stewart, Bob Welch and Dennis Eckersley. It is a game meant to compensate for lack of talent, but even so, natural ability, speed, strength and skill are more important to its success than anything else. In the words of Whitey Herzog, whose speedy, light-hitting Cardinals won three pennants playing that game: "When I managed Kansas City I wasn't too smart because I didn't have a closer. I got smarter in St. Louis because I've had Bruce Sutter, Todd Worrell and Ken Dayley." Today only Dayley is left, and by the last week of the season he had only four wins and two saves. It is no accident, as the Stalinists used to say, that the Cardinals finished last this year and that Herzog is no longer managing.

Will's favorite pitcher, Orel Hershiser, has achieved wonderful things, including breaking the record for consecutive scoreless innings and taking his team to the World Championship in 1988. He is a worthy subject of attention for the student of baseball, but by no means the most obvious. As Will points out, no one in baseball history has had a more sensational first five years than the Mets' Dwight Gooden. He has great speed, an outstanding curve and remarkable control. He is a great strikeout artist and has one of the best winning percentages ever, much better than Hershiser's. Gooden has the best chance of breaking an assortment of pitching records before he is through, yet Will is more interested in Hershiser. The reason he gives is that Hershiser has done something very rare: He is "pitching with steady success in his thirties." That is, indeed, a fine achievement, but the Texas Rangers' Nolan Ryan is still pitching with astonishing success at the age of forty-two! (Hershiser, who turned thirty-two in September, had no success whatever this year, because of a sore arm.) Ryan has struck out more batters and thrown more no-hitters than any pitcher who ever played in the major leagues, won his 300th victory this past season and led the league in strikeouts. Yet Will chose Hershiser, and his real reason is clear. Gooden, Ryan and Boston's Roger Clemens are hard throwers, "naturals," whose success plainly comes from their extraordinary physical abilities. None is very talkative about his skills, which is why Will is less interested in them than in the articulate Dodger, whose success "is more an achievement of mind than muscle."

The story is the same with Baltimore's Cal Ripken. He is a very good hitter; after his first six years in the majors he had a batting average of .283 and 160 home runs, easily the best among active shortstops, with no serious competition. (Some perspective on the pitiful decline of hitting in today's game is provided by the fact that in 1941 seven of the sixteen major league shortstops had a combined batting average of .299, and this was no fluke. Their combined career average, covering 110 years of play, was .297.) He is also the modern iron man of baseball, having played in more consecutive games than anyone except Lou Gehrig. By dint of hard work and ceaseless study he has learned to position himself so as to compensate for his lack of extraordinary speed and agility. He is a fine fielder, but he happens to be a contemporary of Ozzie Smith, whom Will rightly calls "the most elegant shortstop of his era, and perhaps the finest fielder ever." Why, then, is Ripken his chosen subject? Again because Smith is a "natural," blessed with the skills and talents that make him superb. Ripken, on the other hand, is the intellectual's shortstop, relying on thought and knowledge for success. He was voted the "smartest defensive player" by his peers and says of himself, "I'm not blessed with the kind of range a lot of shortstops have. The way I have success, I guess, is by thinking."

Perhaps the strangest of Will's choices, however, is his batter, Tony Gwynn. In general, Will seems to prefer defense to offense, citing with approval the sportswriter Tom Boswell's observation that defense is "the cognoscenti corner of baseball. . . ." If he must have offense, Will prefers running to hitting. If he must have hitting, he prefers thought and finesse to power. Thus it is Gwynn's cerebral approach to batting that explains Will's selection. No student of the art of hitting is more dedicated than Gwynn, whose quest to perfect his style is such that he is distressed at hitting a home run with an imperfect swing, and pleased by a hard-hit out when the ball went where he intended it. He is the first National Leaguer to win three consecutive batting titles since the great Stan Musial won his third straight in 1952, and his .370 average in 1988 is the highest since Musial's .376 in 1948.

But Gwynn, unlike Musial, is a singles hitter. Compared with the outstanding hitters in the game he lacks power, as revealed in home run totals and slugging average, and the dominant hitter's chief contribution, runs batted in. To be sure, there are few Musials in the game today, but there are at least two batters who clearly have a better claim to greatness than Gwynn: the veteran George Brett of the Kansas City Royals and the Yankees' Don Mattingly, Gwynn's baseball contemporary. The statistics in the following table make Gwynn's inferiority clear:

Table:

Career Batting Statistics (through the 1989 season)*

	GWYNN	BRETT	MATTINGLY	MUSIAL
Batting average	.332	.310	.323	.331
Slugging average	.443	.501	.520	.559
Runs batted in**	59	82	102	93
Home runs**	6	17	23	23

**average per full season

*Sources: *The Sporting News Official Baseball Register* (1990 edition), Barry Siegel, ed. (*The Sporting News*, 1990); *The Baseball Encyclopedia* (7th edition), Joseph L. Reichler, ed. (Macmillan Publishing, 1988).

Will's choice of Gwynn instead of Brett or Mattingly crystallizes the shortcomings of his approach to the game. Bemoaning Gwynn's failure to win recognition in spite of his high average, Will complains, "What has all this earned Gwynn? He is called 'the West Coast Wade Boggs.' That is because Gwynn practices his craft at the wrong end of the continent." No, that is because both Gwynn and the Red Sox's high-average hitter have failed to provide the kind of heroic leadership by performance that carries a team to victories and championships, the combination of power and timeliness that drives in runs and inspires teammates.

This year, in an extraordinary departure from the tight-lipped protectiveness usual in the game, Gwynn's teammates have expressed their disappointment. One of the Padres complained that Gwynn "cares only about his hits. . . . He doesn't care about this team. . . . " Another objected to Gwynn's decision to bunt with two men on and nobody out:

If you sacrifice, you can protect your average, but what that does is put the pressure on the other guy. Tony has a chance to be a game-breaking player. We expect him to take his chance and hit. If you sacrifice, the pressure goes to the next guy, and the next guy and the next guy, and they think now they have to get a hit. And when you have to do that, your chances of doing it are going down the toilet, and so are your chances of winning.

A third said:

You like to see a No. 3 hitter with 100 RBI. Tony has the potential to do that. He can drive the ball. He's the type of player who can lead a team to a championship, and he knows that. If I was hitting .350 and there were runners on first or second and they see me bunt and they say to me why don't you hit away, it makes a lot of sense.

Gwynn defends himself as follows:

This is a game based on numbers. It's not based on character or heart or work ethic. It's the numbers. At contract time people say, "Did you hit .300?" The people want to see numbers on the board. I'm a high-average hitter. Some hit for power. Some move a runner over. Some hit for average. I try to do what I am capable of doing, whether people like it or not.

That is not the voice of Roy Hobbs, Malamud's fictional "natural," who literally knocked the cover off the ball in his first at bat in the majors, and whose goal was to be "the best there ever was in the game"; nor is it the voice of the real-life Ted Williams, who said at the age of twenty: "All I want out of life is that when I walk down the street folks will say, 'There goes the greatest hitter that ever lived.'" Gwynn's is the voice of our times, of the antihero who knows his limitations and accepts them, who shuns the burden of leadership, who goes his own way and "does his own thing," who is satisfied with well-rewarded competence and does not seek greatness. And that is what Will likes about Gwynn: "'Stay within yourself is baseball's first commandment.' . . . A player's reach should not exceed his grasp." If Mighty Casey came to bat at a crucial moment today, George Will would want him to punch a grounder through the right side to move the runner to third and leave things up to the next batter.

It would not be fair to suggest that Will has no place for the heroic; it is just that he understands heroism in a peculiarly modern and constricted way. He endorses the novelist John Updike's view that baseball heroism "comes not from flashes of brilliance, but . . . from 'the players who always care,' about themselves and their craft," and adds his own observation that "those who pay the price of excellence in any demanding discipline are heroes."

In his famous essay about Ted Williams' final game Updike spoke of his hero's "hard blue glow of high purpose." For him "Williams is the classic ballplayer of the game on a hot August weekday before a small crowd, when the only thing at stake is the tissue-thin difference between a thing done well and a thing done ill." Such heroism is aesthetic more than it is moral. The game in question was meaningless, for the Red Sox were out of the pennant race. The "high purpose" was entirely personal and made no contribution to a practical or elevated goal. Williams wanted to end his career with a home run. He did so and sat out the team's last few games on the road. In his nineteen brilliant years with the Red Sox they won one pennant and no World Series. In the ten key games of his career—seven in the Series and the other three in which a Red Sox victory would have brought a league championship—Williams hit .232 and made no important contribution. Like Tony Gwynn, but with infinitely greater power and talent, he was a keen student of the game, a tireless perfectionist who refused to swing at a pitch out of the strike zone or to change his style to meet particular situations. What he did he did beautifully and with meticulous care. His last game was a fitting end to the career of a great hitter and stylist—but not of a hero.

Will's concept is less aesthetic but more democratically modern: Everyone is a potential hero, provided that he cares for his craft and works hard to perfect it. That definition flatters us ordinary people, but it also badly diminishes the status of the meritorious, establishing a kind of affirmative-action heroism. It is not what people have sought for millennia in their heroes, who instead are expected to perform great and wondrous deeds, so marvelous that they verge on the magical. Heroes must far outdo ordinary mortals, to the point where their actions give rise to song, story and legend. Heroes do not, however, perform their deeds for themselves alone; instead their deeds are vital to those who rely on them. Achilles is heroic because even other heroes cannot match his speed and strength, without which the Greeks cannot take Troy; Odysseus is heroic because he surpasses all others in cleverness, without which his men will die and never reach home.

Babe Ruth was a true baseball hero, because his achievements dwarfed all others'. When he hit 59 home runs in 1921, the next best slugger had 24; when he hit his 700th homer, only two others had over 300. Even more important, throughout his career his hitting brought victory and championships to his team. Legends sprang up of Ruth's vast appetite for food and drink and women, of his visits to dying children and the fulfillment of his promises to hit home runs for them, of his pointing to the place in the stands where he would drive the next pitch for a home run (and then hitting it there). Will remarks that "[i]t is inconceivable that a protean figure like Babe Ruth could burst upon baseball today," and he is glad of it. He scolds Ruth for his bad habits (the faults of a hero can be as gigantic as his virtues) and concludes that such great superiority in performance could not exist today— not because of the general mediocrity of today's game, but because today's players "are generally bigger and stronger and faster, and they know more about a game that rewards *knowing* [emphasis in the original]."

But the more important point is that none of today's players is likely to match the achievements or epic status of such real heroes as Ruth or Joe DiMaggio. Will is impressed by DiMaggio's commitment to excellence and his knowledge of the game. The one specific achievement that he singles out for praise, however, is that DiMaggio was never thrown out going from first to third! That is what he finds noteworthy about a man who was one of the great batters and fielders of all time, who led his team to ten pennants and to victories in nine World Series in his thirteen years as a player, and who holds what is generally agreed to be the most remarkable and unapproachable base- ball record of all time—a hitting streak of 56 consecutive games.

That streak is the subject of Michael Seidel's recent book, which displays a better understanding of baseball heroism: "The individual effort required for a personal hitting streak is comparable to what heroic legend calls the *aristeia,* whereby great energies are gathered for a day, dispensed and then regenerated for yet another day, in an epic wonder of consistency." DiMaggio's exploits, moreover, had meaning not for himself alone, but carried and inspired his companions, as the deeds of epic heroes do. During his great streak Johnny Sturm, Frank Crosetti and Phil Rizzuto, none of them normally great hitters, each enjoyed a lesser streak of his own. At the beginning of DiMaggio's streak the Yankees were in a terrible slump, five and one-half games out of first place. At its end they had destroyed the will of the opposition and were safely in first place, on their way to clinching the pennant on September 4 (the ear- liest date in history) and finishing twenty games ahead of the next best team. That summer a song swept the nation:

> *From coast to coast, that's all you hear*
> *Of Joe the one-man show*
> *He's glorified the horsehide sphere,*

Joltin' Joe DiMaggio.
Joe . . . Joe . . . DiMaggio . . .
We want you on our side.
He'll live in baseball's Hall of Fame
He got there blow-by-blow
Our kids will tell their kids his name,
Joltin' Joe DiMaggio.

So did the raging Achilles inspire his fellow Achaeans against the Trojans, and, so, at somewhat greater length, did Homer sing of his deeds.

But there is more still to true heroism: the qualities of courage, suffering and sacrifice. These DiMaggio displayed most strikingly in 1949. Before the season he had a bone spur removed from his heel (as with Achilles, a vulnerable spot). The pain was great enough to keep him out of the lineup until the end of June, when the Yankees went to Boston for a three-game series against the team that they had to beat. DiMaggio blasted four home runs in three games, batting in nine runs as New York swept the series. The importance of that manifestation of *aristeia* was very clear at the end of the season, when the Red Sox came into Yankee Stadium for the two final games. Had they won even one of the three played in June, the championship would have been theirs

Joltin' Joe DiMaggio of the Yankees.

already; instead the Red Sox had to win one of the remaining two. DiMaggio had missed the last couple of weeks, felled by a case of viral pneumonia. Once again, the ailing warrior returned to the field of battle. Weak as he was, he managed two hits and led his mates to victory. The next day, the staggering DiMaggio managed to run out a triple and to last until the ninth inning (when weakness and leg cramps finally forced him from the field). The inspired Yankees won the game and the championship.

That is the sort of thing Ernest Hemingway had in mind when he told of the old fisherman in *The Old Man and the Sea,* who struggled in a life-and-death battle with the greatest fish he had ever seen, despite a body cramped with pain and a wounded hand: "I think the great Joe DiMaggio would be proud of me today. I had no bone spurs. But the hands and the back hurt truly." Nor was this the end. In the sad, confused 1960s, when heroism seemed only myth, Simon and Garfunkel caught America's longing for a true hero: "Where have you gone, Joe DiMaggio? A nation turns its lonely eyes to you."

No one ever thought that DiMaggio's greatness came chiefly from intelligence, care and hard work. Millions of people have those admirable qualities without significant result. Heroes arise by means of natural talents that are beyond the rest of us; the secret of their success is mysterious and charismatic. As Toots Shor put it:

Raging Achilles of the Achaeans.

> There never was a guy like DiMaggio in baseball. The way people admired him, the way they admire him now. Everybody wanted to meet Joe, to touch him, to be around him—the big guys too. I'm not just talking about fans coming into the joint. Joe was a hero, a real legitimate hero. I don't know what it takes to be a hero like Joe. You can't manufacture a hero like that. It just has to be there, the way he plays, the way he works, the way he is.

George Will set out to write an antiromantic book about baseball, and he succeeded. In so doing, however, he has missed what baseball is all about. Baseball without romance and heroism is like *Hamlet* without poetry or the Prince of Denmark—just words. We care about baseball not because we enjoy watching working men try hard to improve their craft, or because we seek models for aesthetic appreciation, but because we keep hoping that some hero or team of heroes will come along and do something wonderful and magical, something never done before, something neither we nor any other player could do. Will concludes his book with the words of Malamud in *The Natural:* "When we are without heroes we 'don't know how far we can go,'" but he has curtailed the quotation. The original reads: "Without heroes we're all plain people and don't know how far we can go." His heroes are just like the rest of us, who concentrate their intelligence, work hard and apply themselves to reach a level that is somehow within the reach of anyone with intelligence and discipline. In hard times, however, and all times are in some way hard, we need greater and more potent heroes—to tell us not what all of us can do but what only the best of us can do. Their doing so inspires the rest of us to do the best we can. What we need are heroes like Malamud's Roy Hobbs: "He belonged [the sportswriters wrote] with the other immortals, a giant in performance. . . . He was a throwback to a time of true heroes, not of the brittle, razzle dazzle boys that had sprung up around the jack rabbit ball— a natural not seen in a dog's age, and weren't they the lucky ones he had appeared here and now to work his wonders before them."

Donald Kagan is the Hillhouse Professor of History and Classics at Yale University, and the author of a four-volume history of the Peloponnesian War.

The Romantic Fallacy
in Baseball—A Reply
to Donald Kagan

By George F. Will (*The Public Interest,* Fall 1990)

I AM FORTY-NINE. *The Public Interest* is twenty-five. We who have sat, as it were, at this journal's feet for virtually all of our adult lives have taken to heart its essential wisdom, which is: There are limits. To everything. There certainly are limits to what an author can do to protect his subject from a reader determined to get it wrong.

One reason I wrote *Men at Work* was to rescue baseball from the fell clutches of a certain kind of person who writes about it. I would call that person an intellectual, but let there be no name-calling. That person loves baseball, in his fashion, but does not really think that baseball is enough. Enough, that is, to hold his attention, deserve his admiration and satisfy his desire for entertainment that is elegant, beautiful and inspiring. Sooner or later such a person gets down to his real business, which is loading the game with the freight of theory, until what is a nice sport staggers under the weight of significance. Make that Significance. And then, quicker than you can say "Balk!" there is a lot of clotted talk about the "potentially tragic" and "dramatically heroic" and "Homeric" and "poetic" facets of the game that, lo and behold, is played with the moral equivalent of cavemen's axes. Spare me. Spare it.

I distressed Professor Kagan early, before he got past the dust jacket. He says, "The very name of [Will's] book is ominous." What he finds off-putting is the subtitle: "The Craft of Baseball." Kagan says: Yuck! Will thinks that baseball is just like all other work. I reply (as we do in Washington): Yes and no.

By craft I mean discipline, a set of physical and mental skills subject to constant refinement on the basis of cumulative knowledge. Thus my thesis, which Kagan quotes: "Games are won by a combination of informed aggression and prudence based on information." Kagan scoffs, calling that a "bizarre prejudice" to be explained with reference to my physique and psyche: "This is the fantasy of a smart, skinny kid who desperately wants to believe that brains count more than the speed, power and reckless courage of the big guys."

Hey, Kagan, don't believe me, believe Tony La Russa—the guy over there in the corner of the dugout, the guy with the World Series ring. He's the one who says that baseball "instincts" are actually the result of "an accumulation of baseball information. They are uses of that information as the basis of decision making as game situations develop."

Kagan subscribes to the theory that there is a shortage of great players these days. Well now. The greatest third baseman ever, Mike Schmidt, retired less than two years ago. The greatest leadoff hitter in history, who also is the greatest base stealer, is thirty-one years old—Rickey Henderson. Ryne Sandberg, one of the three best second basemen ever (with Rogers Hornsby and Joe Morgan), just became the third player in history to hit forty home runs while stealing at least twenty-five bases. (The others were Henry Aaron in 1963 and Jose Canseco in 1988.) Roger Clemens (no one ever struck out more men in a game—twenty—than he did on April 29, 1986) isn't chopped liver.* Kagan himself notes that "no one in baseball history has had a more sensational first five years than the Mets' Dwight Gooden." There probably never has been a better late-inning short reliever than Dennis Eckersley, but the Orioles' Gregg Olson may be better, someday. (Olson's is a new kind of baseball career. He stepped off the Auburn University campus and into the Orioles' bullpen. Time was when relief pitchers were worn-out starters. Today the game is too demanding for such recycling of tuckered-out arms.)

In trying to demonstrate what he considers baseball's decline, Kagan scores a few easy hits against some large fish in baseball's small barrel: against domed stadiums, raucous scoreboards, artificial turf. (By the way, in Kagan's Golden Age, before baseball had night games, there were sixteen parks with real grass. There still are.) The trend in baseball is against such stadiums, scoreboards and turf. It is not out of the question that the designated hitter will be gone before this century is.

Professor Kagan's credentials as a critic become suspect when he says that the game is "much more boring" than it was when he and the world (and I) were young, in the 1950s. He cites the fact, as though it is sufficient proof of boringness, that games are longer. No one ever wished that *Paradise Lost* were

*Clemens did it again on September 18, 1996, against the Detroit Tigers.

longer, but fans often wish that baseball games were. And certainly length is not necessarily boring, or otherwise bad, in baseball games.

There are many reasons why games are longer than they used to be. More pitches are thrown, in part because the umpires, lobbied by the batters, have shrunk the strike zone; so there is too much nibbling at its edges, and too many hitters going deep into the count, looking for walks. Also, in the dead-ball era—and even after the coming of the lively ball, before power was distributed, in the form of large hitters, throughout lineups—pitchers were more often able simply to put the ball over the plate and let the fielders do their work. Christy Mathewson once said that a pitcher had to be strong enough to throw as many as 100 pitches occasionally. Today 130 is about normal for nine innings.

Also, today's games are longer because of the increased recourse to relief pitching, which (along with new pitches like the slider and split-finger fastball) makes hitting harder and today's fine hitters especially admirable. Games also are lengthened—not slowed, but lengthened—by the increased emphasis on base running, which results in repeated throws over to first base and other disruptions of the pitcher's concentration.

But if base running is boring to Kagan, perhaps he should pick another sport. Serious fans savor base stealing because it is the baseball achievement in which luck matters least. It is almost entirely a matter of the base runner's—if you will pardon the expression—craftsmanship.

Kagan says that running is "the modern substitute . . . for hitting." But today, as in the 1950s for which Kagan pines, the major league batting average is around .260. And there always have been many more (today in excess of three times more) singles and walks than extra-base hits. The running game is not a substitute for hitting, it is a substitute for standing around and waiting for someone to hit the ball hard enough to wake up the Kagans who are dozing in the stands, uninterested in anything more subtle than a three-run home run.

It is, to say no more, quaint for Kagan to say that baseball's decline, "aesthetically," is apparent in the fact of night baseball. But I will say more, beginning with this: Only an intellectual could believe that.

The wickedness of night baseball is apt to be an article of faith for someone—say, a college professor—who has a flexible workweek and a lot of afternoons free. Factory workers appreciate night games. Furthermore, if baseball's decline began with lights, the era of decline is a lot longer than the predecline. Night games came to the major leagues fifty-five years ago, just thirty-five years into the modern era. It will not be many years before most games in the modern era will have been night games. Kagan, the author of a *conservative* critique, must come to grips with the familiar conservative dilemma, that of deciding when a mere innovation (obnoxious) has been around long enough to become a tradition (venerated).

In his rather sweet meander down memory lane, drenched with sentimentality about the 1950s, Kagan actually celebrates the fact that the Yankees ruled like "Olympian gods," challenged primarily by "the mighty Dodgers and Giants." Yes, indeed. In 1951 all three New York teams finished first. (The Giants and Dodgers tied.) But if you did not live in New York—bulletin: Many fans didn't—that wasn't so swell. Instead of the Olympian reign of New Yorkers, many fans preferred the 1978–87 period when, for the first time in history, ten different teams won the World Series in ten years.

In the 1950s, says Kagan, baseball "held its place as part of nature, timeless and regular as Newton's universe." Oh? As Newton's universe may have seemed but never was.

We know a lot more about the universe than Newton did, thanks to better instruments of observation and measurement. Kagan may think that those instruments take the romance out of the heavens. Be that as it may, we know that the universe involves a lot more wobbling and banging around than used to be apparent. Baseball in the 1950s also was a lot less settled and tidy than it seemed from afar. In just five years of that supposed Golden Age, 25 percent of the teams changed cities. Baseball was not part of nature. It was—there you go again, Will, stomping on romance—a social institution. For example, it became fully integrated two years later than Central High School in Little Rock. (In 1959, when the Red Sox finally discovered that blacks could play the game. By then there had been eight MVP awards to blacks.)

Kagan finds fault with my choices of a manager, pitcher, hitter and fielder on which to focus. But Kagan spikes himself several times. Tony La Russa, he thinks, does not have a sufficiently "blue-collar, extroverted, nonintellectual style." Yes, but what he does have is a team that wins, a lot. So what, says Kagan: La Russa has the best physical material with which to work. That is probably true, but his players are not all that much better than those of teams that do not get the most from their material. Also, Kagan misunderstands the particular play that he analyzes. La Russa did indeed guess wrong about a particular pitch. So Kagan says that La Russa was "saved by the sheer speed of the runner." Indeed. That runner was a pinch runner, put in the game by La Russa *for another pinch runner*. His speed was part of La Russa's calculation.

Kagan thinks it a failing—a moral failing, really; a preference for the mundane over the heroic—that I chose to study Orel Hershiser rather than Dwight Gooden. Kagan prefers Gooden because he is more of a power pitcher, "a great strike-out artist." That he is. (Although in the season I covered Hershiser, he had more strikeouts than Gooden.) But what is so special about strikeouts as opposed to other ways of getting people out? Here we are coming close to the core of Kagan's complaint. Strikeouts are, he thinks, more heroic.

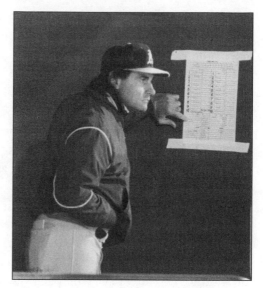

An artist and his canvas: Tony La Russa and the Oakland A's lineup card.

Shortstop Cal Ripken also seems to strike Kagan as somehow, well, banal. Kagan thinks that I chose Ripken because he is "the intellectual's shortstop." I did indeed pick him for the same reason the players picked him as the smartest at his position. He illustrates my thesis about the importance of mind in this physical game. In 1990 Ripken set three remarkable records. He made only three errors. The previous record, set in 1989, was six, set by the Blue Jays' Tony Fernandez, who played on artificial turf and played a lot fewer innings than Ripken played in 1990. Also, Ripken had 431 consecutive errorless chances in one season (the previous record for one season was 331), and his fielding percentage was .996 (the previous record for a shortstop was .992). Are great athletic achievements tainted, are they drained of heroism, if they are produced, in part, by intelligence?

Kagan wrongly emphasizes home runs and strikeouts because he does not appreciate the primacy of winning in the team sport of baseball. The baseball people whom I have been around have icy contempt for players whose goal is not simply to win. When I asked Tony Gwynn what his highest goal was—hitting .400, piling up batting titles, whatever—he looked at me as though I was dim-witted and answered with one word: "Winning."

Perhaps Kagan is too much of a liberal individualist to understand the importance of winning as a team. In any event, he finds Tony Gwynn the "strangest" of my choices of subjects. But Gwynn's ethic of winning explains why Gwynn is not pleased by hitting a home run on a pitch he should not have swung at and with a swing that is not his best. Gwynn has a feeling for the texture of this sport of the long season: Over a span of 162 games he can contribute most to winning by doing what he does best, consistently.

Kagan finds it antiheroic that Gwynn "knows his limitations and accepts them." And here we arrive at the heart of the matter. Listen up, readers of *The Public Interest.* Are we or are we not in favor of facing facts? Here is a fundamental one: There are limits. To everything and everyone. And ignoring them is not smart, let alone heroic.

Kagan, so impatient with Gwynn, prefers Mighty Casey. "If Mighty Casey came to bat at a crucial moment today, George Will would want him to punch a grounder through the right side to move the runner to third and leave things up to the next batter." Well, speaking for George Will, let me say: That depends on who the next batter is, who the pitcher is, the game situation, who is hot and who is not that day or week or month—it depends on a lot of things. These are the sorts of things that Tony La Russa knows; a lot of other people—mostly people who win less often—do not know them. A La Russa will *manage* even a Mighty Casey. And such a manager will have no trouble managing a Tony Gwynn, because he and Gwynn have exactly the same (team) ambition: winning.

If Mighty Casey, instead of swinging for the fences and striking out, had hit a scratch single, he would have earned no praise from Kagan. But there might have been joy in Mudville.

I share Kagan's admiration for Joe DiMaggio, with whom I am privileged to sit on the Baltimore Orioles' board of directors. I share Kagan's awe for the 56-game hitting streak. However, it is not unromantic for me to cite as proof of DiMaggio's genius something other than the streak. I would not admire DiMaggio one whit less if a brilliant defensive play had stopped the streak in the middle by turning a hit into an out. (Or, to be blunt, if a less compliant official scorer had stopped the streak by turning a hit into an error.)

Baseball people will tell you that what made DiMaggio into DiMaggio was judgment of the sort that enabled him to pass through an entire career without ever getting thrown out going from first to third. Other players have been better at the ostensibly "heroic" things—hitting, hitting with power—that Kagan fancies. But no one was ever a more consummate professional—the encomium that baseball people prefer. It is worth pondering that when baseball people want to call someone a hero they do it by semantic indirection, using the word "professional."

"Will's concept [of heroism]," says Kagan, "is less aesthetic but more demo-cratically modern: Everyone is a potential hero, provided that he cares for his craft and works hard to perfect it." (I have been called many things, but rarely, if ever, "democratic" or "modern." This mudslinging must cease.) Not everyone is a greatly gifted athlete. Every major league player is. But not every major league player has the (here I take custody of the word) heroic will-fulness to pull himself above the common major league herd of the merely gifted.

Kagan is a classicist, used to the company of gods. Perhaps for that reason it is beyond my poor powers to get him to share my enthusiasm for the "everydayness heroism" that is elicited—but not from everybody—by the everyday game. Gwynn, unlike Kagan's hero Roy Hobbs, does not perform deeds that are "magical." Gwynn also is unlike Hobbs in another way, one that should seize the attention and kindle the empathy of any author of a "conservative critique": Hobbs is fictional; Gwynn is real.

CHICAGO BASEBALL: "NEVER A LOVELY SO REAL"

1991

CHICAGO HAS A CHIP on at least one of its broad shoulders. The chip was there long before a smarty-pants reporter for *The New Yorker*, A. J. Liebling, firmly affixed to Chicago the label "Second City." And the chip was charred, because the city's foremost formative experience was a fire. Indeed, the wrong American city is named Phoenix. Chicago really did rise from its own ashes. Trouble is, Chicago already had a name, derived from the Indian word for wild onion (*checagou*).

A city with a name like that should be more tangy than glamorous. Chicago is. So has been Chicago baseball.

A major league franchise is a flower, a hardy perennial, that springs from particular social soil. It is shaped by, and shapes, its city. Chicago's two franchises are like that, but with this difference: Each has come to represent a different Chicago as the city has evolved during this century. But we are getting ahead of the story, which began, appropriately, with a calamity.

On October 8, 1871, Mrs. O'Leary, whether drunk or merely negligent we shall never know, left her lantern in the barn while milking the cow. The cow kicked it over, thereby starting the fire that consumed much of Chicago, which was mostly made of wood, right down to its sidewalks. Until then the city had been emblematic of the restless energies of a nation recuperating from civil war and filling its frontier reaches with production. From grain to cattle to iron ore, Promethean Chicago was the great processor of raw materials. Then thirty-six hours of flames reduced much of the city to the condition Richmond and Atlanta had been in six years earlier. Chicago suddenly became emblematic of another facet of the American dream, the fresh start.

Chicago's trauma confronted America with a sobering fact: Progress can come to a screeching halt. Even mankind's most sophisticated artifacts, cities, can be quickly brought low. But the fire was invigorating. Ross Miller, in *American Apocalypse: The Great Fire and the Myth of Chicago,* writes that Chicago was suddenly transformed into an environment of productive disorder, instantly hospitable to innovations of all sorts. It was a blank slate to be written on by strong hands. A popular novel about the fire, published in 1872, was titled *Barriers Burned Away.* The fire loosed a euphoric sense of expanded possibilities for bold strivers.

Onto that level playing field stepped some pioneers of what already was well on its way to becoming the national pastime. The pioneers included a young pitcher and budding entrepreneur whose name was to adorn one of the nation's most famous trademarks: A. G. Spalding. So important was Spalding to the development of professional baseball in Chicago, it is almost fair (a Chicago-style approach to fairness) to say that Chicago was, in baseball terms, a suburb of Rockford, Illinois, where Spalding starred for the Forest Cities team before heading for the big city. He came to Chicago via Boston, at a time when Chicago did not just have rough edges, it was almost all rough edges. In the late nineteenth century it was growing at a pell-mell pace and was not a place for the squeamish. In the 1890s there were 1,375 miles of railroad tracks in the city traversing streets at grade level in about 2,000 places. One result was constant carnage.

By 1893, when Chicago threw a grand party called the Columbian Exposition, the city had a population of one million, up from 300 when the city had incorporated sixty years earlier. Railroading was king and Chicago was the greatest hub from which people and goods radiated, from farms to cities and back. Giving off a blue glow of energy, Chicago embodied modern America's dilemma, the tension between restless individualism and the yearning for the settledness of community. Chicago was rapidly turning into a city of many communities, and they did not feel real neighborly toward one another. White ethnics of European extraction preserved many of the mutual hostilities that had made Europe a place from which to flee to places like Chicago. But Chicago's basic division, like the nation's, was between north and south. The problem was not ethnicity but race.

It is said that baseball is Greek because it is based on rivalries of city-states. But Chicago baseball has a different dimension because it mirrors a city divided between its North and South Sides. Chicago, wrote a local novelist, Nelson Algren, "has grown great on bone-deep grudges." One grudge is directed outward, against New York, but most are intramural. The grudge between Cub and Sox fans is durable and sometimes fierce because the location of the teams has guaranteed that the loyalties of the fans will reveal fault lines in the city's social soil.

A good guide to Chicago, even now, was written sixty years ago by novelist James T. Farrell. His Studs Lonigan trilogy is suffused with the tensions between the city's unmelted and unreconciled ethnic blocs, their strong sense of territoriality, street by street, and their border skirmishes. The world's third-largest Polish community—larger than all Poland's cities other than Warsaw and Krac\'ow—is in Chicago. Chicago's black population is larger than the population of all but two black African cities. Where was Lorraine Hansberry's play *Raisin in the Sun* set? The same place where Richard Wright's *Native Son* lived—Chicago's South Side, America's largest concentration of black Americans and, in a sense, the capital of Black America.

Long ago—well, not *that* long: in the 1940s and 1950s—the Illinois Central railroad, "The Main Line of Mid-America," was for hundreds of thousands of southern blacks the steel highway to the promise of a better life in Chicago. Before such trains as The Louisiane, The Seminole and The City of New Orleans got the disappearing-railroad blues, they deposited the trunks of hundreds of thousands of southern blacks in the cavernous lobby of Chicago's Twelfth Street Station, on Michigan Avenue, hard by the lake. There the postwar pilgrims collected their worldly goods and began the final leg of their journey north by turning south into White Sox territory. There many turned into White Sox fans.

Zeke Bonura, 1930s White Sox first baseman. "He was no intellectual giant, but he understood better than anybody the rule that says you can't be charged with an error if you don't touch the ball. And so he assiduously avoided touching anything that looked difficult." (Edward Bennett Williams)

But not nearly as many became White Sox patrons, buying tickets. No one knows for sure all the reasons why blacks are underrepresented in baseball crowds. Everyone sensible in baseball knows this is a moral as well as financial failure on the part of baseball. The primary reason, probably, is that blacks were for so long banned from the field and unwelcome in the stands. Baseball, by its very prominence in American life, became an especially galling instance of the caste system when that system was still strong.

Professional football and professional basketball are essentially post–World War II phenomena. True, the National Football League was functioning in the 1920s and 1930s, but the burgeoning of the sport coincided with the growth of the civil rights impulse in society. Back when blacks did not play pro football, few blacks went to games, but few whites went either. The explosive growth of professional basketball did not just coincide with the arrival of black players, it was caused by it. Neither the NFL nor the NBA has what baseball has, a long-remembered record of inhospitable treatment of blacks. Such treatment is in the past, but memory is in the present.

If the White Sox cannot break the invisible but durable barriers between blacks and the bleachers, no franchise can. If the White Sox can, they can supplant the Cubs as the city's emblematic team. Chicago's Near North lakefront, with Michigan Avenue's "Magnificent Mile" and the Gold Coast apartments, is one of the world's most striking cityscapes. But just as representative of modern Chicago are the thirteen-story buildings of the Robert Taylor housing project on the South Side, near Comiskey Park. There are few meaner streets in America than those around "the projects," even if one of baseball's first $3 million players, the Twins' Kirby Puckett, came from those streets.

For decades Comiskey was not far from, and frequently downwind of, the stockyards, back when Chicago really was the hog butcher and wheat stacker. The Sox were, depending on whom you talked to, agreeably down-to-earth or just déclassé. In any case, the Sox came, for a while, into the playful hands of Bill Veeck, baseball's master promoter. Those playful hands also were politically active. Veeck was second only to Branch Rickey as a baseball integrationist, and not second by much. In 1947, the season Jackie Robinson integrated baseball, Veeck, then the owner of the Cleveland Indians, made Larry Doby the first black in the American League. In 1948 he brought Satchel Paige (and his rocking chair) to Cleveland. During Veeck's subsequent White Sox years the Comiskey Park experience, exploding scoreboard and all, was not for the staid. The Wrigley Field experience was, for a long time, too staid.

While pyrotechnics were lighting the night sky over the South Side, on the North Side the Cubs did not even welcome the incandescent lightbulb until 1988, fifty-three years after night baseball first came to the big leagues. Somewhere along the line, Cub fans became a tad precious. They acted as if losing were cute, and they nattered on at nauseating length about the sin of playing baseball after the sun had set. They seemed to think that the Cubs were morally (certainly not competitively) a cut above the other twenty-five clubs. The Cubs were slow to admit what everyone on the South Side knows: A lot of people have to work while the sun shines.

Work is something Chicago understands. In Chicago, wrote Theodore Dreiser in *The Titan* (1914), the world was young and life was doing something new: "Here happy men, raw from the shops and fields, idylls and romances in their minds, builded them an empire, crying glory in the mud."

Chicago's go-getters (Aaron Montgomery Ward, Misters Sears and Roebuck, Hugh Hefner of *Playboy,* Ray Kroc of McDonald's) have had a genius for inventing and marketing basic commodities and catering democratically to mass appetites. Chicago novelist Saul Bellow, winner of the Nobel Prize, has one of his characters, Augie March, say with nice concision that Chicago is "not mitigated." The city, where even the lovers' feast of St. Valentine is associated with machine guns, produced America's first saint, Mother Cabrini. But Chicago got sanctity out of its system early. Surely only in Chicago would a division-winning team (the 1983 White Sox) adopt the slogan "Winning Ugly." The Chicago tone—unminced words about elemental things—was struck in a 1986 headline about the reaction of the Cubs general manager, Dallas Green, to his team's play: CUBS NAUSEATE GREEN.

Chicago baseball has had its share of bad moments, even when a Chicago team has been enjoying the splendor of participation in a World Series. In the 1932 Series, where did Babe Ruth's "called shot" land? In Wrigley's bleachers. That is the most famous thing that ever happened in Wrigley. The most famous thing that ever happened in Comiskey Park is the most infamous thing that ever happened in baseball, the fixing of the 1919 Series.

Even Chicago's baseball glory seems often to come alloyed with mortification. The 1906 White Sox won the pennant but earned the name "hitless wonders," compiling the lowest batting average (.230) of any pennant winner. But the "hitless wonders" were powerful enough to beat the National League's entry in the World Series. What team was that? The Cubs. Four years later the White Sox set season records for the lowest club batting average (.211) and slugging percentage (.261). Such achievements are something of a South Side

"Old Aches and Pains": Luke Appling.

tradition. Twice, in 1918 and 1947, the Sox lost eighteen-inning games without scoring a run.

It is arguable that the best player in the history of each Chicago franchise was a shortstop. Luke Appling, who played twenty years with the White Sox, was known as "Old Aches and Pains" because of his constant complaining about his ailments. He retired in 1950, never having made it to a World Series. Three years later a string bean of a shortstop played his first game across town. Ernie Banks was to play nineteen seasons with the Cubs. He never made it to a

World Series. (Ted Lyons, a pitcher, holds the record for most seasons—twenty-one—with a club without playing in a World Series. His club? The White Sox.) On October 12, 1929, the Cubs played the Athletics in Philadelphia and helped to produce one of the—for Chicagoans—most dismal game lines in Series history:

Chicago	0	0	0	2	0	5	1	0	0	8
Philadelphia	0	0	0	0	0	0	10	0	X	10

On June 18, 1911, the Sox roared to a 7–0 lead in the first inning against the Tigers, led 13–1 in the middle of the fifth—and lost, 16–15. What team once gave up 13 runs after two were out in the second inning? The 1956 White Sox.

The Cubs once scored a record 5 runs in the bottom of the eleventh inning, and lost. (The Mets had scored 6 in the top of the inning.) The Cubs once scored a record 22 runs in a losing effort. A Cub (a good one, too: Glenn Beckert) holds the major league record for most runners stranded in a nine-inning game (12).

In 1962 the National League expanded from eight to ten teams. It was the first season in which a team could finish ninth. The Cubs did, 42½ games out of first and six games behind an expansion team, the Houston Colt .45s. For-

tunately for the Cubs, who lost 103 games, the Mets lost 120. But in 1966 a team finally finished below the Mets. Don't ask which team.

Several generations of Cub fans have come and gone knowing that the last time the Cubs won a pennant, in 1945, the nation's best athletes were at war. In the postwar period, 1946 through 1990, the Cubs were 526 games below .500. That means they could have gone undefeated through 1991, 1992 and 1993 and still have been 40 games below the flat mediocrity of .500.

White Sox owner Charles Comiskey.

But if you can't enjoy the game unless you are pretty sure your team is going to win, baseball is not the game for you. Remember, the best team in baseball in any year is going to be beaten about sixty times. And judging by the most recent ninety years of Chicago baseball, Chicago fans should start a 162-game season expecting their team to lose seventy-nine, maybe eighty times. Which is to say, Chicago baseball is generally a struggle to keep one's chin above the choppy water. But taken on those terms, it is a successful struggle.

A very Chicago way of talking, that: "taken on those terms . . ." Chicago, an upstart that had to start up a second time with soot in its hair, has learned to take life on life's terms. A lot of life, like a lot of Chicago, is not pretty. Giving Chicago two baseball teams is, perhaps, life's way of making amends.

Baseball is a pretty sight and a nice experience, win or lose, particularly if it is watched in a nice park. Chicago has not had the best teams, but it has had the best baseball architecture. Just as there have been Chicago styles of sky-scrapers, jazz, blues and pizza, there have been Chicago styles of baseball. Two of them, of course. They are, at least in part, products of two quite different ballparks.

The original Comiskey Park was one of those rarities, a stadium that seemed made for pitchers. That is not surprising. A pitcher, Ed Walsh, had a hand in making it. He and an architect surveyed major league parks for the best features and, by golly, wonder of wonders, the House Walsh Helped Build wound up with a capacious outfield that swallowed long flies. From time to time the Sox management fiddled with the fences, moving them in and out, and once even moving out the infield, but Comiskey remained congenial to pitchers. Thus the all-time Sox career home run record, through 1990, was just 192. It was held by Carlton Fisk, who did not even put on a White Sox uniform until he was thirty-two years old.

All baseball fans owe a vote of thanks to Walsh and Comiskey Park. Perhaps because the park encouraged the virtues of the past, the Sox in the 1950s helped lead baseball back to the future. The Sox showed the way out of the sterile station-to-station baseball of the 1940s and 1950s, the unimaginative, risk-averse baseball of standing around waiting for some slugger who swings from his heels to belt the ball into the seats. The "Go-Go" Sox of the 1950s were powered, if that is the right word, by steals and hit-and-run plays.

The transformation of baseball into the more varied brand we enjoy in the 1990s may have begun in 1950 with the arrival at Comiskey of shortstop Chico Carrasquel from Venezuela. He was the first of many Latin shortstops who would bring speed and sparkle to North American diamonds. He was succeeded as the Sox shortstop by another Venezuelan, a future Hall of Famer, Luis Aparicio. In 1959 Aparicio and second baseman Nellie Fox proved that two small middle infielders could be the heart of a pennant-winning attack, if "attack" is not too strong a term for the spray-hitting they did. And think of the hitting they prevented. They had one of the best up-the-middle trios in the American League: Aparicio, Fox and center fielder Jim Landis, each of whom led his position in putouts in 1959. Soon the Cardinals of Lou Brock and the Dodgers of Maury Wills, Tommy Davis and Willie Davis were playing the new-old baseball that was born again on Chicago's South Side.

Wrigley Field, cozy and well-swept, is a hitter's park (although the wind can blow in, too). Unfortunately for the Cubs, baseball is not just, or even primarily, a hitter's game. The Cubs have a melancholy tradition of long-ball-hitting teams that fall short, often far short. For example, in 1971 the Cubs had three players with 300 or more career home runs (Hall of Famers Ernie Banks and Billy Williams, and should-be-a-Hall-of-Famer Ron Santo), and still they finished third, with an 83–79 record. In 1987 the Cubs clubbed 209 home runs, more than any other National League team in three decades. Alas, they still were outscored by 81 runs by opponents, who got 229 more base runners than the Cubs got.

Comiskey Park and Wrigley Field were two of the fourteen concrete-and-steel parks built between 1909 and 1923. Wrigley, Fenway Park and Tiger Stadium are the only ones still in use, and the vandals are menacing Tiger Stadium. The superiority of the old parks is not a mystery or a matter of mere nostalgia. Rather, it is a marriage of form and function. The point of going to a baseball game is to see the game. Baseball is the most observable of team games—everyone is nicely spread out on an eye-pleasing green stage. And the rhythm of the game and the general absence of hysteria make for an intimacy between game and spectator, when the park permits it.

Older parks do. They were built before the idea of a "multipurpose" facility was hatched. Football was played for years in Comiskey and Wrigley, but neither was built with football—or rock concerts or tractor pulls—in mind. And no one had thought of "skyboxes" because no one thought it would be neat to watch baseball from high in the sky.

The point of going to a game is the pretty game itself. The thrill of victory is nice, but not necessary, for which Chicagoans give thanks. Here is the list, through 1990, of the professional sports franchises that have gone the longest since winning a championship:

Cleveland Indians	42 years
Phoenix/Arizona Cardinals	43 years
New York Rangers	50 years*
Boston Red Sox	72 years
Chicago White Sox	73 years
Chicago Cubs	82 years

The Cubs' combined winning percentage from 1901 through 1990 was .509, the White Sox's was .502. Among cities with at least two teams, Chicago is second (of course) to New York, which has a ninety-year Yankees-Giants-Dodgers-Mets winning percentage of .536. But Chicago has done better than St. Louis (.482 with the Cardinals and the Browns) and a lot better than long-suffering Philadelphia (.464 with the Phillies and the Athletics). From 1901 through 1990, the Cubs and White Sox combined had played 27,773 games and had won 301 more than they had lost.

That may not be much of a basis for bragging, but, say Chicagoans, a lot of people have less. Chicagoans inhabit a city planted not all that long ago, in the teeth of prairie winds, and they know that you get only what you wrest from the whirl of things. A city known for raw weather, rough politics, tough characters and baseball just an inch above the .500 waterline has had no trouble supporting two teams with a remarkably high ratio of fan loyalty to team artistry.

Chicago is still the divided city where America is most visibly working out its dangerous but exhilarating destiny, bringing unity from diversity. For black and white Chicagoans, living many miles and vaster social distances apart, there is, in baseball, a common vocabulary, and a shared affection. There are seeds of community feeling in baseball, with its own tidy universe of regulated striving and objective results and second chances every tomorrow.

Bear in mind the big, agreeable numbers that tell the city's won-lost record from 1901 through 1990: 14,037–13,736. It is *the city's* record, its collective baseball experience from both sides of town.

It is the summers of baseball in the Second City, the capital of mid-America, a tale of ups and downs averaging out to middlingness. What Nelson Algren said of Chicago, all Chicagoans can say of their baseball, whichever team is theirs: "Like loving a woman with a broken nose. You may well find lovelier lovelies, but never a lovely so real."

---

*The New York Rangers broke their streak by winning the Stanley Cup in 1994.

BASEBALL ALONG
THE BACKROADS

March 31, 1991

WAUCHULA, FLORIDA—When the hubbub of life over in Avon Park sets your nerves jangling, you can drive down the undulating road to this hamlet set in the center of Hardee County, in the center of the peninsula, midway between most places. Here, far from Florida's beachfront condominiums and flashy tourist attractions, the Hardee Wildcats are hosting the St. Alban's Bulldogs, who are down from Washington, rounding into shape for the high-school baseball season.

The night is cool but the coffee at the concession stand is hot and strong and a smattering of high-school girls wearing shorts and tans and orange satin Hardee jackets glow beneath the lights. After a rocky start, this trip has righted itself.

Picture this. Since September about three dozen teenage boys—a critical mass of critical masses—have put up with school and winter so they could get down here for the pleasure of eating badly and playing ball. And it has rained. They are living on doughnuts, pizza and, 'round about midnight, nachos from the Circle K store out on the highway that is sown so thick with fast-food joints that just a drive down it elevates your cholesterol level. Furthermore, something in (or perhaps not yet in) these young men causes them to express emancipation from parents by dropping Doritos into the retentive shag of a Days Inn motel carpet.

There are serious sides—well, slivers—to the trip. For example, the short-stop was sent south packing a stack of 3 x 5 cards containing SAT vocabulary words. One afternoon found him standing at a pay phone along U.S. Route 27, getting a long-distance vocabulary quiz, administered by his father, as the 18-wheelers whined by hauling oranges north.

The other night the Bulldogs were rolling, 9–1, over Avon Park's Red Dev-

181

ils. (An adequate name, but not up there with Toledo's Mud Hens or the old drug company semipro team, the Paregorics.) Then the wheels fell off. A relief pitcher found the plate moving around on him and a Red Devil homered over the best outfield fence sign in America: "Beef and Baseball." (That's the full text. That's enough. It is put there by a local ranch that understands the two basic food groups.)

Anyway, there were eight Red Devil runs, then extra innings, before the Bulldogs won. It was a victory doubly sweet because it came on hallowed ground: Tom "Flash" Gordon of the Kansas City Royals began his ascent to glory from Avon Park's pitcher's mound.

The Bulldogs win again the next night in Wauchula. After the game the Wildcats grab rakes and restore the infield's smoothness, getting the everyday sport ready for tomorrow. The Bulldogs sprawl on the wet grass for a critique from their coach. He is wise beyond his years (twenty-six of them) and bilingual, fluent in English and a dialect, baseball.

"We had too many backward Ks tonight." (K is the scoring symbol for a strikeout; a backward K indicates a called third strike.) "That is a quick way to

"Mastering the satisfying pressures of this pretty game" in Avon Park, Florida.

the pine." (To get benched.) The reliever who got lit up by Avon Park did well tonight and is praised for "getting back on the horse." Now it's nacho time.

"In our sun-down perambulations, of late," wrote Walt Whitman in 1846, "through the outer parts of Brooklyn, we have observed several parties of youngsters playing 'base,' a certain game of ball. We wish such sights were more common among us." Whitman didn't have long to wait.

Lincoln interceded for boys whose ball game had been shooed off the White House lawn. The Civil War, which moved millions of young men hither and yon, acquainting them with the variety of American experiences, simultaneously spread baseball like honey across bread. It has been everywhere ever since: When Geronimo escaped from a reservation near Fort Apache, soldiers had to stop a baseball game to saddle up.

Every spring baseball brings American boys to places they otherwise would never visit, or even hear of. Some of the city boys from Washington were hauled off to see London, Paris and Florence years before they were allowed to see Kissimmee, Okeechobee and Frostproof—the music of American names!—but I will wager they learned more of lasting value along Florida's backroads than ever they did being marched through Florence's Uffizi gallery. I know they had more fun.

For many fans this spring, the flavor of the dawning baseball season is being soured by the well-publicized tantrums of a few players at the pinnacle of baseball's steep pyramid. They are childish men who wonder aloud whether they can be "motivated" by a mere $2 million or so. But down at the pyramid's broad base, where baseball is perennially renewed, boys still play for the sheer exhilaration of mastering the satisfying pressures of this pretty game that they play in front of small, quiet crowds, mostly family and friends, after a scratchy recording of the national anthem and before late-night pizza back on the highway.

"I CAN'T STAND IT,
I'M SO GOOD"

April 7, 1991

Boston's Red Sox are the wrong team for that neighborhood. The Sox are prone to melodramatic falling-short, and New England is planted thick with writers ready to wax metaphysical about such things. (Ernest L. Thayer, the author of "Casey at the Bat," the poem about baseball and community woe, was a Massachusetts man, naturally.) The Red Sox were winners of five of the first fifteen World Series but have not won one since 1918. They have been in four Series since then but lost them all—all in the seventh games. There have been two one-game playoffs in American League history. The Red Sox lost both.

Nineteen eighteen was a while ago; Czar Nicholas II died that year. But Teddy Samuel Williams (that is what the birth certificate says; his father admired the Rough Rider) was born in 1918 in San Diego. Twenty-one years later, thin as a rail and full of purpose, he arrived at the Hub, an adolescent Ahab in baggy flannels pursuing the white whale of perfection.

A hitter's perfection consists in failing only 60 percent of the time. Williams did that in 1941, batting .406. Now two books arrive to celebrate him and the fiftieth anniversary of what actually may have been only his second-best season.

When Williams arrived in Boston he announced, with the openness of a Westerner and the innocence of an adolescent, "All I want out of life is that when I walk down the street folks will say, 'There goes the greatest hitter who ever lived.'" Michael Seidel's rounded biography, *Ted Williams: A Baseball Life,* and Dick Johnson and Glenn Stout's *Ted Williams: A Portrait in Words and Pictures,* an alternately lively and reverential mixture of narrative, photographs and short essays by assorted Williams fans, explain why many people now say what Williams wanted them to say. Mr. Johnson and Mr. Stout

The final appearance at the plate,
and the 521st home run of Ted Williams' career,
September 28, 1960.

include scrumptious tables of statistics. (Want to know Williams' career batting average against the St. Louis Browns? It was .393.) Both books suggest, delicately, why, in spite of his virtuosity at the plate, he does not belong on any all-time All-Star team.

Overflowing with childlike ebullience, Williams would exclaim in the batting cage, "I can't stand it, I'm so good." He was—at bat. But as baseball people never tire of saying, and Williams quickly tired of hearing, the greatest players do five things well—run, throw, field, hit and hit with power. Even when Williams was paying attention, he was an indifferent outfielder in baseball's smallest left field. He had a mediocre arm and was slow afoot. The best person playing left field in the 1940s and 1950s was not Williams but Stan Musial.

Still, as a pure hitter Williams was in a class by himself. Readers of these two books can decide whether that speaks well of him.

What makes him so fascinating that books are still written about him is the terrible simplicity of his passion. A baseball career—any athletic career—involves a narrow focus. But Williams' focus was unnecessarily narrow. The authors—Mr. Seidel previously wrote *Streak: Joe DiMaggio and the Summer of '41;* Mr. Johnson is curator of the Sports Museum in Boston and Mr. Stout is a freelance sportswriter—provide ammunition for critics who say Williams may have been baseball's best hitter but he was not a satisfactory member of a baseball team. There is a point, a point Williams passed, when the pursuit of personal excellence becomes, in the context of a team sport, evidence of a character flaw.

If Williams had not lost four and a half years to World War II and the Korean War, his career numbers would probably place him first or second in runs, runs batted in, total bases, extra-base hits and, perhaps, home runs. He had the highest on-base percentage in history, .483. He was as effective as he was elegant.

But critics stress ethics, not aesthetics. Their complaint is that extremism in pursuit of a batting virtue is a vice. The virtue is selectivity—waiting for a good pitch to hit.

Pitcher Bobby Shantz once recalled the unhelpful advice he was given for dealing with Williams: "He won't hit anything bad but don't give him anything good." Williams defined himself by his almost manic discipline. He swung at nothing out of the strike zone, taking a walk rather than a hack, no matter what. Because he walked so often, he never had a 200-hit season. It is arguable that over a long career in the sport of the long season, absolute fastidiousness about the strike zone maximizes not only a batter's personal career totals, but also his ability to help his team. But in some situations such discipline almost certainly sacrifices the team's welfare.

As Luke Salisbury, the author of *The Answer Is Baseball* and one of the nine essayists in *Ted Williams: A Portrait in Words and Pictures,* says, "Hitting is a solitary business. Winning is not. When Williams took that pitch a half-inch outside with the tying run on second, he set himself apart." Apart, that is, from players seeking team rather than personal attainments, like Joe DiMaggio. In *Ted Williams: A Baseball Life,* Dom DiMaggio, comparing his teammate Ted and his brother Joe, says: "Joe would swing at a bad pitch if the situation called for it. Not Ted, who was always the perfectionist." His lonely splendor was not always applauded by teammates.

What has been said about the study of the law—that it sharpens the mind by narrowing it—is often true about intense concentration on any excellence, especially in athletics. That is one reason why so many athletes' biographies are boring beyond endurance. Williams' story is not boring, but it is tedious, for two reasons: his tantrums and his monomania.

Because of the team's role as a regional franchise, and because of Boston's peculiarly carnivorous journalistic culture (one sports columnist cheered when the Boston Braves manager Casey Stengel was hit by a taxi), the Red Sox are baseball's most intensely reported team. Journalistic competition does not always purify. Boston has had some reckless baseball reporters. Williams, so preternaturally controlled at the plate, was thin-skinned and volatile everywhere else. He carried emotional adolescence into middle age, often throwing tantrums and spitting, actually as well as figuratively, at journalists and spectators.

Because athletic careers compress the trajectory of life, from aspiration to apogee to decline, writers about athletes are constantly tempted by facile pathos. Both of these books avoid this. And if you take Williams on his terms, apart from the team game, he was an entrancing spectacle as he approached the age of forty. He came to look, sound and even walk as John Wayne did when playing Rooster Cogburn in *True Grit.* "I may not have been the greatest hitter who ever lived," Williams once said, "but I know I was the greatest old hitter." Yes. In 1957, he had perhaps an even better season than in 1941. He batted .388 when his thirty-nine-year-old legs surely cost him the five hits that would have given him his second .400 season.

After 1949 the weakness of the Red Sox teams encouraged his self-absorption. The franchise's oldest tradition, that of bonehead decisions, started with the sale of Babe Ruth to the Yankees after the 1919 season. In 1945 Jackie Robinson was given a perfunctory tryout with the Red Sox and was rejected. In 1949 a Red Sox scout was sent to see a young player on the Birmingham Black Barons. The scout reported that Willie Mays was not the Red Sox type. The Red Sox were the last team to integrate.

Perhaps Williams was the Red Sox type. He was a glittering star in a gray firmament, spectacular in one dimension but one-dimensional and not, shall we say, a martyr to the ethic of team play. What he called "the most thrilling hit of my life" was not hit for the Red Sox or in a game that counted. It was the ninth-inning three-run home run that won the 1941 All-Star Game. It is altogether appropriate that between seasons and in retirement Williams' patience and passion for precision made him one of the world's greatest sport-fishermen. Fishing is the right pastime for this solitary man, who only seemed happy when isolated in the one-on-one duel with the pitcher.

In his last at bat he hit a home run that moved a spectator, John Updike, to write one of baseball's finest essays. Later, Williams wrote one of baseball's better memoirs, *My Turn at Bat.* Maybe he belonged in wordy New England after all.

When Ted Williams retired in 1960, a sportswriter said that Boston knew how Britain felt when it lost India. Indeed. Britain felt diminished, but also a bit relieved.

THE SEASON OF '41

April 8, 1991

I WAS BORN IN MAY 1941, in the nick of time. I had eleven days to get my bearings before it began—The Streak. It was the greatest event of a baseball season that flared dazzlingly on the eve of darkness.

There were just sixteen teams in ten cities, and St. Louis was baseball's westernmost outpost, but the future—California—was present in San Francisco's Joe DiMaggio and San Diego's Ted Williams. Williams was as volatile as a colt and as one-dimensional as a surgeon. DiMaggio's cool elegance concealed a passion to excel at every aspect of the game.

Williams used a postal scale in the clubhouse to make sure humidity had not increased the weight of his bats. An official of the Louisville Slugger company once challenged Williams to pick the one bat among six that weighed half an ounce more than the other five. He did. He once sent back to the factory a shipment of bats because he sensed that the handles were too thick. They were, by .005 of an inch.

In 1941 Williams was hitting .39955 going into the season-ending doubleheader in Philadelphia's Shibe Park. Daylight savings had ended the night before, so the autumn shadows that made hitting hard would be even worse. If Williams had not played, his average would have been rounded to .400. Instead, he went 6 for 8, including a blazing double that broke a public-address speaker. He finished at .406. Today when a batter hits a sacrifice fly he is not charged with an at bat. In 1941 he was. Williams' manager, Joe Cronin, estimates Williams hit 14 of them, so under today's rules his average would have been .419. Since then, the highest average has been George Brett's .390 in 1980.

Williams' achievement is one of the greatest in baseball history, but not the greatest in 1941. Nothing in baseball quite matches DiMaggio's 56-game hitting streak.

The Yankees were on a tear, so at home they rarely batted in the bottom of the ninth. DiMaggio had to get his hits in eight innings, and in the 38th game he was hitless entering the bottom of the eighth with the Yankees ahead 3–1. He was scheduled to be the fourth batter. The first batter popped out, the second walked and Tommy Henrich was up and worried. He was a power hitter who rarely bunted, but if he hit into a double play the streak probably would end. He returned to the dugout and got manager Joe McCarthy's permission to bunt. Then DiMaggio hit a double.

On July 8 in Detroit the American League won the most exciting All-Star Game when, with two out in the bottom of the ninth and the National League leading 5–4, Williams hit a three-run home run to Briggs Stadium's upper deck. When play resumed after the All-Star break, with DiMaggio's streak at 48 games, he erupted for 17 hits in 31 at bats. As the pressure intensified, DiMaggio's performance became greater. He had four hits in the 50th game, went 4 for 8 in the doubleheader that ran the streak to 53, had two hits in the 55th game and three in the 56th. The streak ended in Cleveland when the Indians' third baseman, Ken Keltner, made two terrific stops of rocketed grounders. Both times his momentum carried him into foul territory, from which he threw DiMaggio out by a blink.

In those 56 games DiMaggio hit .408 with 91 hits, 35 for extra bases, including 15 home runs. He drove in 55 runs and scored 56. The next day he began a 16-game streak. When it ended he had hit safely in 72 of 73 games (not counting his hit in the All-Star Game).

Most records are improved by small increments. Not this one. The consecutive game-hitting record for a Yankee had been 29. The modern major league record had been George Sisler's 41. The all-time major league record had been Willie Keeler's 44. DiMaggio fell short only of two other professional baseball hitting streaks—69 games by Joe Wilhoit for Wichita of the Western League in 1919, and 61 in 1933 by an eighteen-year-old playing for the San Francisco Seals: Joe DiMaggio.

The Yankees clinched the pennant on September 4, earlier than any other team before or since. In the National League the perfectly matched Dodgers and Cardinals (they played twenty-three times, each winning eleven, with

July 16, 1941: Joe DiMaggio singles in the first inning of a game against the Indians . . . the 56th and final game of his record-setting streak.

one tie) scratched and clawed down to the wire. The Dodgers won by two and a half games, even though in late September the Cardinals got 20 hits in twelve games from a young outfielder from Donora, Pennsylvania. Stan Musial had begun producing one of baseball's prettiest numbers: 3,630 hits, 1,815 at home, 1,815 on the road.

Today, Robert Creamer writes in his book on the 1941 season, the Yankees are like Austria, "an unimportant little country" full of monuments to golden days. That is unfair. To Austria. However, in 1941 the Yankees were the Bronx Bombers. For decades the Dodgers had just been the Bums, often aspiring only to mediocrity. In one five-season stretch they finished sixth every time, causing a newspaper to say "overconfidence may yet cost the Dodgers sixth place."

In the 1941 World Series, with the Yankees leading two games to one, the Dodgers were leading the fourth game 4–3 with two outs in the bottom of the ninth and two strikes on Henrich. Dodger pitcher Hugh Casey was one strike from evening the Series, and he got it. Henrich swung and missed. But Dodger catcher Mickey Owen missed it, too. Henrich sprinted to first. The next batter was DiMaggio. The Yankees won the Series 4–1.

During DiMaggio's streak, radio broadcasts had been interrupted to bring bulletins about his progress. But once radio interrupted baseball. On the night of May 27, when the Braves were playing the Giants in the Polo Grounds, both teams left the field for a while at 10:30 and the public-address announcer said, "Ladies and gentlemen, the president of the United States." About 17,000 fans listened to FDR's radio address describing the lowering clouds of danger.

Michael Seidel, author of *Streak: Joe DiMaggio and the Summer of '41*, says DiMaggio was a lot like the taciturn, enduring characters then played in movies by Jimmy Stewart and Gary Cooper (who was soon to play Lou Gehrig). DiMaggio (number 5), was the successor to Lou Gehrig (number 4), who died on June 2, 1941, of the disease that now bears his name. Gehrig was seventeen days shy of his thirty-eighth birthday. He died sixteen years to the day after he became the Yankees' regular first baseman, in game two of a streak of 2,130 games. DiMaggio's similar stance toward life—a steely will, understated style, relentless consistency—was mesmerizing to a nation that knew it would soon need what he epitomized, heroism for the long haul.

THE COLLISION BETWEEN
BART AND PETE

June 27, 1991

Baseball is a game of episodic action. Discrete events stand out. The players are dispersed around a large space. And it is the American sport with the longest season and longest history. These are among the reasons it has such a strong institutional memory. One savors one's memories of episodes, so much so that A. Bartlett Giamatti, the late commissioner, said that baseball is, in a sense, the conversation about it.

The conversation often concerns the most famous this or that. The most famous home run? Perhaps Bobby Thomson's "shot heard 'round the world," the one by which the Giants beat the Dodgers in the 1951 playoff. Or perhaps the one by the Pirates Bill Mazeroski against the Yankees in the seventh game of the 1960 World Series, [until then] the only home run to end a Series.* Or perhaps Babe Ruth's "called shot" against the Cubs in the 1932 Series. The most famous pitching performance? Perhaps Don Larsen's perfect game for the Yankees in the 1956 season, or Orel Hershiser's 59 consecutive scoreless innings at the end of the 1988 season. The most famous defensive play? Probably "The Catch" by Willie Mays, the over-the-shoulder masterpiece in game one of the 1954 Series.

Baseball's most famous collision at home plate is so famous not just because it involved a superstar and occurred in front of a huge national television audience, but also because it occurred in a game that did not matter. It happened during an All-Star Game, baseball's midseason picnic, when work is suspended and the business of baseball becomes pure play for a day. The All-Star gathering is the community of baseball condensed and at ease, a mingling of players who have competed against one another since they were deep

---

*In 1993, Joe Carter's homer gave the Blue Jays a Series victory over the Phillies.

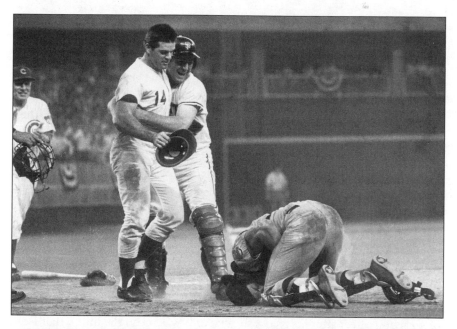

Two separate collisions at home plate for Pete Rose:
With Indians' catcher Ray Fosse during the 1970 All-Star Game,
and in 1989 with Commissioner Bart Giamatti.

in the minor leagues, and of executives, many of whom played against each other long ago.

The 1970 game was played in Cincinnati's new Riverfront Stadium, with the president of the United States present. In the bottom of the twelfth inning, with the score 4–4 and two out, Pete Rose, a product of Cincinnati's sandlots and by then a hero of the Reds, came to the plate. He singled, then advanced to second on another hit. The next batter lined a single on two bounces to the American League's center fielder, who played the ball cleanly and came up throwing, as Rose, the potential winning run, raced around third. The throw was headed for Ray Fosse of the Indians, who at twenty-three was baseball's premier young catcher. He was in the most vulnerable position a player can be in, his eyes on the incoming ball, with a runner barreling toward him. He was prepared to catch the ball and sweep his glove at Rose, who presumably would be trying to hook-slide around Fosse's tag.

But Rose was not sliding. He made of himself a missile, slamming Fosse with his left shoulder. Fosse never touched the ball. And he never had much of a playing career after his recovery, such as it was, from the injury that Rose inflicted.

After Rose's fall (James Reston Jr. says in *Collision at Home Plate* that it is hard to think of any American, other than the president who was at that game, who has fallen farther faster) this was frequently said: Poor Pete was fine between the white lines but just couldn't handle life off the field. That judgment misses the connection. The Rose who swerved across the lines of common sense, and then of legality, was the same headlong charger who hit Fosse. What Rose did in the 1970 All-Star Game was within the rules. It also was unnecessary, disproportionate and slightly crazy.

Baseball is not a game like football, a game of adrenaline rushes and manufactured frenzy. The crucial baseball skills—throwing a ball fast and with movement into a small space over a 17-inch-wide plate; hitting such a ball with a round bat; catching a batted ball and knowing what to do with it—require a combination of force and delicacy, strength and precision. To exercise these skills with the consistency demanded by a 162-game season requires a remarkable equilibrium of temperament, a combination of intense concentration and relaxation. To sustain this equilibrium, baseball has evolved a set of unwritten and rarely even spoken norms, mores, habits and customs. These make up a silent, almost intuitive, code of the kinds of competition that are appropriate, and those that are not. The code governs such matters as when it is appropriate to pitch at, or very close to, a batter; when and how to retaliate for that;

which displays of emotion are acceptable and which constitute "showing up" an umpire or opposing player; what sort of physical contact, in what sorts of game situations (breaking up a double play at second, trying to score when the catcher is blocking the plate), is acceptable.

Rose's slide broke rules no less real for being unwritten. In time, he would shred written rules, of baseball and society.

Soon after the 1970 All-Star Game Rose was lying about what boon companions Fosse and he had become the night before the game. He bragged, "I could never have looked my father in the eye again if I hadn't hit Fosse that day." Rose's father was a blue-collar worker and semipro football player who was not really big enough to play without getting hurt but was tough enough to play hurt. He was, in his way, as representative of Cincinnati as any Taft ever was.

A century and a half ago, when Cincinnati was the most vibrant metropolis west of the Alleghenies, Charles Dickens and Frances Trollope went there in anthropological moods to observe the manners of elemental Americans. It was there, in 1869, that baseball took a large step from pastime to profession, with the founding of the Red Stockings professional team. So Cincinnati has a fair claim to being the birthplace of Major League Baseball as well as of Pete Rose. Cincinnati has a genteel tradition that produced a president whose son Robert became a Hall of Fame senator. (Literally: His visage is on a wall of honor outside the Senate Chamber.) But the city also has a rough side that lingers from the days when it was known as Porkopolis, a hog butcher before Chicago got into that business in a big way.

Six hundred miles northeast of Cincinnati, Angelo Bartlett Giamatti, who was three years older than Rose, grew up in academic gentility. He had, writes Reston, a quiet and graceful upbringing suffused with the decorum and public-spiritedness of a Yankee village. His father had grown up in the Italian tenements of New Haven, where he rode the trolley and a four-year scholarship to a Yale degree. He received a Ph.D. from Harvard and taught Italian literature at Yale before moving to Mount Holyoke, where Bart was born. The Giamatti house was pervaded with the father's love of Dante's books, and Dante's categories—damnation, purgatory, salvation, allegory and symbolism. The young Bart learned from his father that all of those are relevant to real life.

Bart's town was filled with talk about the Red Sox, "the lingua franca of the place." Baseball would one day see the results of the boyhood in which, Reston writes, Bart acquired "an Italian sense of nobility" and a "Latin sense of the expansive gesture." By his middle teens he had twice lived for a year in

Italy, acquiring, he said, an Italian feel for history and the fragility of institutions. This he combined with his American idea of possibility.

Upon his second return from Italy at age sixteen, he entered Andover, which fostered another Mediterranean idea, the Greek ideal of the scholar-athlete. Bart was skinny and clumsy but charming and popular. He was pleased to find, in the Greek elevation of the great athlete to the level of the great artist, a distinguished pedigree for his enthusiasm for sports.

In 1989 Rose was to have another famous collision, his last in baseball. This time he collided with a portly, chain-smoking and utterly unathletic fifty-one-year-old former Yale professor of Renaissance Literature. When the dust settled, Rose was sprawled in it, and Bart Giamatti, the commissioner of baseball, was standing. Rose was out, banished from baseball because he had bet on it.

A few days after that decision was rendered, Giamatti was dead from a heart attack that may have been hastened by the strain of his struggle with Rose. Giamatti's father had suffered a serious coronary attack at age fifty-one. Rose did not kill Giamatti—an unhealthy constitution and habits did. But Giamatti condemned Rose to a kind of death-in-life by severing him from the game that was the source of his vitality.

James Reston Jr. has written a brisk narrative of the two remarkably different lives that intersected so dramatically in the summer of 1989. It is a story suited to a novelist, which Reston is, and to a biographer, which Reston also is. It could become a wonderful play in the hands of a playwright, which Reston is as well. It touches on some of the great themes of literature—love, waste, regret. It concerns two radically different temperaments that came together at one fateful place, a shared love for baseball.

Rose spent five years in high school in Cincinnati, repeating his sophomore year, which he had flunked. Then he went into professional baseball, weighing 155 pounds. He was carrying his father's heavy expectations and, Reston says, wearing "the desperation of his situation on his sleeve." Remember the famous report on Fred Astaire's first screen test? "Can't act. Slightly bald. Can dance a little." The Reds' scouting report on the puny switch-hitting infielder said: "Can't make a double play, can't throw, can't hit left-handed and can't run." At that time the report was correct, but it missed an ingredient—Rose's fanatical concentration of his meager athletic gifts on whatever task was at hand.

An occupational hazard of any demanding craft or profession is the intense concentration that can also become a deformation of character. That hazard is particularly acute in the life of a professional athlete, for two reasons. His attention is focused on his physical self. And many people are poised to make the world smooth and undemanding for him in order to banish all distractions from his small universe of physical exertion.

As Giamatti was to say about baseball players:

> You can't get to the top of your profession without having lived a life where a lot of people are taking care of you. It's an adulated, isolated life, and you're vulnerable. These people who have developed their physical gifts haven't necessarily developed the rest of themselves.

This is one reason why professional sports teams have a lot of louts. And it is one reason why great athletes of fine character deserve special admiration.

Rose made himself a great player by sheer strength of will. That will was, he now suggests, extinguished by a gambling "addiction." But Rose's behavior, as Reston reports it, looks like extreme willfulness.

Rose's willfulness on the field made him much loved in baseball's inner circles, and in the bleachers. His success, Reston writes, was accessible, not exotic. He excelled because he tried harder than anyone else. That is why the public perception of Rose was so positive, at least until the 1970 collision at home plate.

But the force of his severely narrowed will, which made him an All-Star, had—had to have—its dark side. In the process of becoming a star, by dint of extreme concentration he became unusually self-absorbed and blind to the rules of living. Those are rules which, ignored long and thoroughly enough, can take a fearful toll.

With cold calculation Rose cultivated a hot manner, a swagger, to supplement his slight physical gifts. He bought a green convertible. During spring training he bet at Florida dog tracks and jai alai frontons.

As Rose's life became more garish, Giamatti was cultivating his garden at Yale. As a graduate student in the early 1960s, he became interested in the image of the garden in literature, the garden as conducive to spiritual experiences. Games, Giamatti thought, could be an adjunct to such a garden. Games are a space for ordered striving, under rules made not by Nature but by free choices. Hence games are apprenticeships for self-governance. "Order and disorder preoccupied him," Reston writes.

In several of his academic essays, Giamatti focused on the image of the wild horse. The unchecked, riderless horse is in Renaissance poetry a metaphor for "appetite run wild, a people completely leaderless." The rider, by contrast, represents the rationality of man. The combined image of the horse and the rider were the halves of man himself.

Giamatti taught a course on Spenser's *The Faerie Queene*, an allegory of justice and virtue, and wrote a book about it. He identified with Talus, the enforcer of righteous decisions:

> *made of yron mould*
> *Immoveable, resistlesse, without end*
> *who in his hand on yron flale did hould*
> *With which he thresht out false-hood, and*
> *did truth unfould.*

Giamatti's preoccupation, academic and otherwise, was with excellence within rules. Reston says Giamatti's trips to ballparks usually included visits to the spartan (or worse) rooms for the umpires, "the keepers of the rules, the ones who controlled the fire of competition."

Giamatti, a man devoted to order and excellence, could not fathom the forces raging in Rose's life. Reston gives new depth to the term "lowlife" as he recounts Rose's slide into gambling, debts, drugs, incessant adultery and the company of muscle-bound dimwits resembling characters who wandered out of a Damon Runyon short story that had been rewritten by Elmore Leonard. Rose was surrounded by bodybuilders whose narcissism was so great they did not notice his own. His retinue included drug dealers and other hangers-on, who greased his slide into criminality. By 1987 he was losing $30,000 a week to bookies—$34,000 on a single Super Bowl bet. His need for money intensified his avarice. During the game in which he broke Ty Cobb's career record for most hits, he changed his uniform shirt three times—one shirt for himself, one for the Reds' owner and one to sell. Reston says that by March 1989, ten collectors claimed to have the bat with which Rose broke Cobb's record.

The flavor of Rose's runaway life is caught in Reston's description of Rose and a lackey named Janszen driving to a baseball card show in Cleveland.

> As they started out of Cincinnati, Rose made an unscheduled stop at a house, and out came a young woman whom Janszen knew. The threesome proceeded happily to Cleveland and checked into adjacent rooms in a Holiday Inn. A half hour later, there was a bang on the door, and there stood Pete's wife. Long-suffering and often cheated upon, Carol Rose had finally put a sleuth on her husband's tail.
>
> Janszen described what took place next: Pete is frantic. "Paul, would you please take the blame. If I put the girl in your room, we'll lock the middle door. I'll tell my wife you are with the girl." So he lets Carol in, and they are fighting

and arguing, you know. And she thinks there's two girls. He finally throws her out of the room. I said, "Pete, why don't I take this girl to the airport. Just get in there with your wife." . . . Carol was going crazy. . . . "Pete," I said, "just have Carol come in the room, stay with her, and I'll take the blame." "Hell with that," he says. "I didn't drive 200 miles to sleep with my own wife!"

So his wife is in the hallway crying. She finally gets a room. I go down and find out what room she's checked in. I am down in her room. She is crying. I'm upset, trying to explain to her, I am with a girl that I'm not with. And Pete is up in the room, having sex with this girl.

Rose's first wife, Karolyn, was the functional equivalent of a green convertible. She was given, Reston writes, to wearing tight-fitting T-shirts with off-color slogans written on them. Her husband was a moderating influence of sorts, vetoing her request for a CB radio in their Rolls-Royce. Rose took his girlfriends on the team plane and lent them his cars. When his first wife saw her Porsche being driven by a Philadelphia Eagles cheerleader, Mrs. Rose "did a fast U-turn, caught up with her Porsche at a stoplight, jumped out and tapped on the window. When the blond rolled it down, Karolyn punched her in the nose."

When Rose was getting divorced, he was asked if it upset him. "Nothin' bothers me," he said. "If I'm home in bed, I sleep. If I'm at the ballpark, I play baseball. If I'm on the way to the ballpark, I worry about how I'm going to drive. Just whatever is going on, that's what I do." As Reston notes dryly, the day Karolyn filed for divorce, Rose went 5 for 5. He did what he wanted to do. Karolyn knew the score: "He's making so much money now that he thinks he doesn't have to play by the rules."

Major League Baseball's rules are posted in every clubhouse. The most important, because of baseball's history, forbids gambling. The office of baseball commissioner was invented in the aftermath of baseball's worst trauma, the 1919 Black Sox scandal of the fixed World Series. Baseball and gambling were dreadfully entangled in the game's early days. Stories are told of bullets splatting into the grass at the feet of outfielders as they were about to make catches that would have upset the calculations of gamblers. In 1867 *Harper's Weekly* reported:

> So common has betting become at baseball matches that the most respectable clubs in the country indulge in it to a highly culpable degree and so common . . . [are] the tricks by which games have been "sold" for the benefit of gamblers that the most respectable of participants have been suspected of this baseness.

In the bidding by cities for star players, gamblers joined politicians in offering fringe benefits. In 1872 *The New York Times* thundered on behalf of amateurism: "To employ professional players to perspire in public for the benefit of gamblers . . . furnishes to dyspeptic moralists a strong argument against any form of muscular Christianity." In 1908 some Phillies threw a gambler down the long flight of clubhouse steps at the Polo Grounds because he had tried to bribe them to throw a game. By then Major League Baseball was beginning to put gambling behind it. But the worst episode, the Black Sox scandal, was still to come.

By the time Rose's gambling became too lurid to remain private, there was an interesting contradiction between baseball's de jure culture and the nation's civic culture. By the late 1980s, state governments coast to coast were in the business of promoting gambling. But gambling remained baseball's capital crime. And rightly so. Baseball's nightmare is a player or manager in hock to the mob. The severity of that nightmare is one reason why all commissioners have, if they husband it, veto power.

From time to time commissioners have made decisions that have, in effect, seized owners' properties. The first commissioner, Judge Kenesaw Mountain Landis, made some players free agents because he did not like the way certain clubs were hoarding talent. In 1976 Commissioner Bowie Kuhn blocked Charles Finley, then owner of the Oakland Athletics, from selling three players for $3.5 million, at that time an imposing sum. Kuhn did so under the vast grant of power by which commissioners are entitled to act "in the best interests of baseball." Denny McLain, the Tigers pitcher, was suspended for ninety days in 1970 for associating with gamblers. Leo Durocher, the Dodgers manager, was suspended throughout the 1947 season for the same offense.

Some flaws in Reston's report are not entirely his fault. Some significant participants in Major League Baseball's final skirmishes and maneuverings with Rose, including Fay Vincent, who is now commissioner, have chosen not to talk to Reston or anyone else about the details of the case. John Dowd, the Washington attorney who conducted baseball's investigation of Rose, says that Reston never tried to interview him. In piecing together what happened, Reston gets some details wrong, including some points of law, particularly about what was and was not owed to Rose as his due process rights.

For example, Reston is mistaken when he says baseball rode "roughshod" over Rose's constitutional rights by compelling him to copy notations he had made on betting slips. Rose was not required to copy anything. He was required to write certain numerals and letters, but the Supreme Court has held that compelling a person to give handwriting samples does not violate Fifth Amendment protections against self-incrimination. Anyway, baseball's investigation did not constitute a trial or any other facet of the criminal justice system. It was a housekeeping function by the commissioner, who was exercising the broad powers conferred in his charter. Rose, like all others in uniform, had acknowledged the authority of Major League Baseball's governing structure. What Rose got from baseball was justice, not perhaps as exquisitely refined as an Earl Warren would want it for every stage and procedure of the criminal justice system, but fundamental justice nonetheless.

Also, and in a related point, Reston does not do justice to how close the Rose case came to becoming another case of a familiar political pathology. Yet another functioning American institution—the commissioner's office—almost became a victim of judicial overreaching. Today's courts have an unhealthy itch to supervise and fine-tune virtually every equity judgment in American life. Rose's legal strategy was to find a judge willing to insinuate himself into baseball's disciplinary procedures. If Rose had succeeded, the commissioner's office would have been irreparably damaged. Its core function, which is disciplinary, would permanently have been put in question. Another of civil society's intermediary institutions—those that stand between the individual and the state—would have been broken to the saddle of government. A nannylike judiciary would henceforth have made the commissioner's office negligible—another hitherto private institution permeated by state power.

Government action was not involved in Major League Baseball's agreement with Rose, a standard agreement signed by whoever wears the uniform. The full panoply of constitutional due process rights did not apply. The "constitutional" rights involved were the commissioner's. Rose, like everyone else who signs the standard agreement, had acknowledged them.

If Rose's strategy had succeeded, the thin end of the government's large wedge would not have been the constitutional rights of the players. It would have been today's all-purpose word, "fairness." Some judge probably could have been found to rule that it is unfair, and therefore unconstitutional (much recent constitutional law rests on that non sequitur), for the commissioner to be both investigator and adjudicator. Actually, uniting those functions is no novelty in American institutions: The Federal Trade Commission and the Securities and Exchange Commission have similar responsibilities.

In the end, the case was resolved only when rhetoric superseded legalisms. Rose dropped his legal challenge to the commissioner's powers. In exchange,

Major League Baseball issued a statement that did not include a formal finding that Rose had bet on baseball. But at the press conference announcing the agreement, Giamatti stepped up to the microphone like DiMaggio striding to the plate. In response to a question, he said he was convinced by overwhelming evidence that Rose had bet on baseball. He was able to say so because the investigation he had commissioned by John Dowd had made the facts of Rose's betting entirely clear.

The evidence included the testimony of eight eyewitnesses, and Rose's handwriting on betting slips, and telephone records showing that during a ninety-day period, thirty minutes before every game—home or away, night or day—Rose placed calls to people who placed bets.

Giamatti said much more and, as he spoke, the injury to baseball began to heal, and a national sense of ethical standards was strengthened. Baseball had been hurt, but as Reston writes:

> It would emerge stronger, however, for the commissioner's office had come through a difficult test with its absolute powers affirmed and the principle established that no man, no matter how exalted, was above the game itself. For Giamatti, the whole episode had been about two things: living by the rules, and taking responsibility for one's actions. . . .
>
> The country was witnessing a rare sight. The words alone were surprising: *disgrace, banishment, integrity, authenticity, idealism,* and the *purchase* that the national game had on the national soul.

Baseball was integrated before the armed services were; its Black Sox scandal of seventy-two years ago is more indelibly etched on the nation's memory than the Watergate scandal of nineteen years ago. In the Rose crisis, baseball supplied a sight for the nation's sore eyes—eyes made sore by looking for leaders in the years since Watergate. Reston writes:

> Here was a leader [Giamatti] who had been through a difficult and painful and debilitating process, who had agonized and had even been badly mistaken along the way, but who, at the end, spoke plainly and directly from the heart with natural eloquence. . . . He did not get technical or legalistic. There were no pauses or mumbles. Without regret or qualification, he took a simple and clear moral position. . . . To the wider world, this moment of leadership was stunning and uplifting. . . .
>
> The commissioner was talking about baseball, but his message applied to all American institutions; therein lay the power of the moment.

"There was," Reston writes, "something biblical—indeed, Old Testament—about the punishment." Rose, like Adam, was banished from the garden that Giamatti tended. Rose had become, by that point in his downward-spiraling life, a moral monster. This was not because his sins were so scarlet—although they were scarlet—but because of the coarseness of his self-absorption. He injured baseball a bit and affronted many people who had admired him in undiscriminating ways, but mostly he ruined himself.

Giamatti once said, "At the moment where an athlete makes something happen, everyone watching is elevated." In his handling of Rose, Giamatti was an athlete of governance. Nowadays, when thinking well of a public person may be considered a dereliction of journalistic duty, it is rare for a writer to face the discomfiting fact that one of his subjects is a fine person. So a tip of the cap to Reston for his simple affirmation that Giamatti was "a wonderful human being." A sentimental judgment? No, good reporting.

Marvin Miller: Sore Winner

August 18, 1991

*F*ollow *the bouncing ball and sing along: "Arise ye prisoners of starvation. . . ."*

Baseball players have risen. And how. There has been a 2,000 percent increase in salaries in twenty years, and a commensurate increase in the dignity of their status relative to their employers.

Before the players organized a union, the owners were, more often than not, an overbearing lot. The players were among the last Americans to gain the right to negotiate the terms of their employment. But in the twenty-five years since Marvin Miller became head of the players' union, the Major League Baseball

Players Association, the players have gone from chattel to domination, from relative penury to riches beyond the dreams of even 1970s avarice.

The short, eventful history of the MLBPA is quite a story. Miller, who breathed life into the MLBPA and made it mighty as its head between 1966 and 1982, tells the story in *A Whole Different Ball Game: The Sport and Business of Baseball*.

The heart of the story is the overthrow of the reserve clause that bound a player to one club for as long as the club wanted. When in 1976 players won the elemental right to leave one employer and seek another, the owners were unreconciled. Strife—lockouts, collusion, strikes—has been one result. Another is an average salary of almost $900,000. Miller recounts all this, and other fascinating arcana such as the business of bubble-gum cards, with polemical punch. And worse.

There is a problem inherent in the memoir genre, a tension that often results in the triumph of ego over editing. It should be instructive to read the reflections of people who have achieved big things. But the confidence, single-mindedness and moral certitude that serves such people in the realm of action often disfigures their reflections. As Miller tells it, his adversaries, the owners, were mostly wicked, boorish, corrupt and stupid, and his allies, the players, were often inconstant and uncomprehending. So blinkered is he by his egomania, he does not understand that if the owners were as dim-witted as he says, then his triumph over them was not as much of an achievement as he supposes.

His book is unrelievedly unpleasant. It is arrogant in tone, ad hominem in argument, ungenerous toward vanquished foes and mean-spirited toward former allies. This is particularly disappointing because it tarnishes a story that should sparkle. Miller played a large, indeed decisive role in a just cause, winning an unbroken skein of victories that made the national pastime, and hence the nation, better.

In fact, an even better case can be made for the union's work than Miller, in this lazy, score-settling book, bothers to make. The redistribution of baseball's burgeoning revenues has been good for the game. Baseball is played better because better athletes are drawn to it by the money, and are motivated to train and improve year-round because long careers are so lucrative.

The owners were wrong about many things, but particularly in their warnings that the end of the reserve clause would bring the end of competitive balance. The worry was that a few rich teams in their biggest cities would corner the market on talent and monopolize the World Series. Actually, free agency has coincided with splendid turmoil in the standings. Consider:

From 1949 through 1953, the Yankees won five consecutive pennants. If the Dodgers had won two particular games—against the Phillies in the last game of the 1950 season, and the 1951 playoff game that Bobby Thomson's home run won for the Giants—the Dodgers, too, could have won five pennants from 1949 through 1953. And five Series would have been played entirely in two parks. But since the 1977–78 Yankees—since, that is, free agency began to work—only one team has won two consecutive Series: The Toronto Blue Jays won two in a row starting in 1992.

Miller rightly gives short shrift to woolly-headed rubbish about how lovely baseball was "before money mattered." When was that? Miller is properly impatient with people who blame players for society's priorities. (No teacher is paid poorly because players are paid well.)

America's pastime is one place where Marx's labor theory of value makes much sense. The players are the central, indispensable ingredients in the creation of considerable wealth. This year fans will buy about 56 million tickets to major league games (perhaps 4 million in Toronto). Not one fan will pay, or tune in to the broadcasts now earning baseball more than half a billion a year, to see an owner.

Miller is justly proud of his success in redistributing baseball's revenues, but he is not alone responsible for the dazzling growth of those revenues. For many reasons—the growth of leisure spending in an increasingly affluent society; better marketing of the game; a better game to market; and, yes, the excitement of competitive balance enhanced by free agency—baseball is much more popular than it used to be.

In 1933 the St. Louis Browns drew 88,113—for the year. They drew 1,184,076 for the entire decade of the 1930s, about half what that transplanted franchise (it moved in 1954) will draw in Baltimore this year. Forty years ago this fall there occurred perhaps the most famous game in baseball history, that playoff game in which Bobby Thomson's ninth-inning home run capped the Giants' come-from-behind (from thirteen and a half games behind on August 11) pennant rush to beat the Dodgers. The game was played in the Polo Grounds, and about 20,000 of the 55,000 seats were empty.

If one is to judge from these pages, Miller's thinking about baseball's collective health as an industry is primitive. When he goes beyond reiteration of the fact that revenues are rolling in, he simply assumes that the union exists to get as much of the money as possible for the players, right now, and that baseball will prosper because it has been prospering.

But both CBS and ESPN have baseball contracts spewing red ink. The

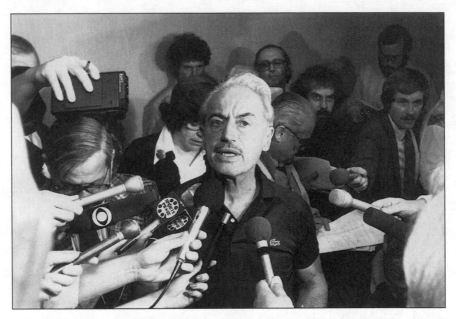

Marvin Miller: *Ecce Homo Economicus.*

next national television contracts may necessitate wrenching readjustments on the part of teams that have unwisely anticipated, and improvidently spent (on long-term contracts), profits that may not happen.

Miller is of the species *homo economicus.* He is not inclined to think about the nimbus of consequential intangibles surrounding baseball, particularly its role as a quasi-public utility serving the emotional lives of communities. A cautionary fact: In 1958, the year the Dodgers and Giants went west, leaving the Yankees alone in New York, the Yankees' attendance declined. Miller is comfortable thinking about economic matters, things that can be quantified and fought over, but not about the precious, perhaps perishable hold baseball has on its public.

Miller, the single-minded salary-maximizer, probably would welcome the migration of some franchises (the Mariners, Giants, Indians, Pirates) to greener pastures. But, then, Miller, the trade unionist, is not used to thinking about the future of baseball as an industry, any more than the steelworkers' union, from which Miller came to baseball, thought much about the future of the steel industry. It should have.

Today, the Red Sox payroll is larger than the Mariners' gross; the Athletics payroll is larger than the Twins' gross. The Yankees rake in more local broadcasting revenues (about $57 million) than do the Brewers, Twins, Mariners, Royals, Pirates, Rangers and Giants combined. There is some level at which such disparities will produce competitive imbalances incompatible with baseball's health. The fact that owners have frequently been wrong and sometimes cynical in forecasting hard times does not mean they can never be right.

In 1966 the salaries of all major league players totaled $9.5 million, about what Roger Clemens and Tony Gwynn together make in 1991. Last year, when players won their arbitration cases, their average increase was 141 percent. When the clubs beat the players, the players' average increase was still a thumping 110 percent. In 1990 the Brewers' Robin Yount became the first player paid $3 million for one season. In 1991 there are thirty-two $3 million men. Such exponential growth never goes on for long.

This year, baseball is soggy with nostalgia for 1941, a glittering season—DiMaggio's 56-game hitting streak, Williams' .406 average—in baseball's supposed Golden Age. That, say sentimentalists, was baseball before The Fall, before players were contaminated with rights, and before they were tainted by salaries reflecting the market value of their talents.

In a 1941 game, the Yankees twenty-four-year-old shortstop, Phil Rizzuto (5 feet 6, 150 pounds), won a crucial game with one of his rare home runs. As he rounded the bases he was mobbed by fans, one of whom snatched his cap. Rizzuto was tempted to chase the fan to retrieve the cap. "In those days," Rizzuto recalls, "we had to buy our own shoes, our own sweatshirts, our own caps."

In 1941 the average major league salary was less than $10,000. DiMaggio was paid $35,000. DiMaggio's manager was paid as much. The baseball commissioner was paid $60,000. As Robert Creamer, the baseball historian, says, "The players were low men on the baseball totem pole." They are no longer, thanks in large measure to Miller, who should lighten up and enjoy his laurels more graciously.

Recently, General John R. Galvin, NATO commander, was in Washington giving General Colin Powell a grim assessment of the continuing Soviet threat and U.S. procurement needs. Powell interrupted: "Jack, smile. We won." Smile, Marvin.

LOCAL OWNERSHIP
AND OTHER TRADITIONS

February 6, 1992

Get this: Baseball owners, who have put designated hitters into baseball and baseball indoors on plastic grass with costumed and cavorting "mascots" and volcanic scoreboards spewing fireworks and rock 'n' roll trivia quizzes, and who for financial reasons are flirting with the idea of "wild card" teams in another layer of postseason playoffs—these people are worried that Japanese participation in the ownership of Seattle's Mariners might imperil baseball's traditions.

The somewhat visceral opposition of some (not all) major league owners has brought down upon baseball an acid rain of charges of xenophobia and racism. Granted, there are legitimate, complex considerations about how cultural institutions should preserve their valuable and complex relationships with their publics. But are legitimate considerations the ones at issue here?

Each baseball franchise is a native flower that flourishes, if it flourishes, in the native soil of its particular community. Each major league community has evolved, through the everydayness of the sport of the long season, its distinctive, organic relationship with its team. So baseball rightly values strong local components in ownership. But no community has suffered more than Seattle from the lack of such ownership. That is why reflexive rejection of Seattle's potential new ownership would be puzzling. Consider some history.

The Mariners were created because after just one season, 1969, Seattle's first major league team, the Pilots, left to become the Milwaukee Brewers. Seattle sued Major League Baseball. When a whopping judgment against baseball seemed likely, baseball agreed to award Seattle a franchise as part of the expansion that first brought foreign ownership into the game, in Toronto.

Seattle has had three ownerships. Two were from California. The current owner is from Indianapolis. Baseball's "local ownership" preference is just that—

Rookie owner: Minoru Arakawa of the Seattle Mariners.

a preference, not an enforced principle. The Houston Astros' owner lives in New Jersey; the principal owner of the San Diego Padres lives in Los Angeles; the owner of the Orioles has put down roots in Baltimore but lives primarily in New York; no one knows who, if anyone, is in charge of the Yankees, but The Boss used to be George Steinbrenner, a Clevelander, who seems to live in Tampa.

The Mariners' current owner does not believe baseball can be a paying proposition in Seattle. Certainly he, a broadcasting investor deeply in debt, cannot make it pay, and he is eager to get to a greener pasture. But before he can skedaddle to Tampa-St. Petersburg he must offer the team for sale, for 120 days, at a price set by an independent appraiser. The price is $100 million.

Perhaps the hope and expectation was that no Seattle group would come up with that sum, thus enabling the American League to seize a share of the Florida market. (The National League's Miami franchise begins play in 1993.) But a Seattle group has come up with $125 million to purchase and reorganize the club.

Here's the rub: Sixty percent comes from Hiroshi Yamauchi, president of Nintendo of Japan. He is not an aggressive investor. His participation, which he calls an expression of gratitude to the region, was solicited by Washington's

Republican Senator Slade Gorton through Yamauchi's son-in-law Minoru Arakawa.

Arakawa, a Japanese citizen, has an advanced degree from M.I.T. and has lived in Seattle for twelve years, supervising Nintendo of America's 1,400 employees. He would have an irrevocable proxy from Yamauchi, who would have no direct involvement in Mariners operations. Other investors are senior officials of such local corporations as Microsoft, Boeing, McCaw Cellular and Puget Sound Power & Light.

All major decisions would require a supermajority of the board—that is, a majority of the minority shareholders. If the Mariners were to be put up for sale for successive 120-day periods, members of that group would have first right of refusal; then it could be sold only to people from the Pacific Northwest; then only to people committed to keeping the club in Seattle.

Baseball cannot have it both ways, restricting potential buyers but assuming franchise values will increase. It recently put a $95 million price on two expansion franchises, thereby raising the floor under the value of existing franchises. But if franchises are to command rising prices, the pool of potential owners will not be large. It will be particularly small if the only eligible buyers are U.S. and Canadian residents of the cities with franchises. Relaxing the local ownership requirement may be necessary to maintain the growth in values or even maintain the values of franchises.

This is not a propitious moment, politically, for anyone Japanese to try to become even a passive owner of even just 60 percent of one-twenty-eighth of Major League Baseball. (There are twenty-eight franchises, counting the infants in Miami and Denver.) But if baseball summarily rejects Seattle's plan, it will need better reasons than so far adduced, or racism will be assumed. And baseball will again be dragged into the second national pastime: litigation.

LOVE AT CAMDEN YARDS

April 5, 1992

Baltimore—Recreation, as Bart Giamatti liked to say, is re-creation, an attempt to renew ourselves according to some standard, to make a vision palpable. Thus, paradoxically, recreation implies both leisure and what Giamatti called "a rage to get it right." The people responsible for the Orioles' new ballpark did.

It was an architect who said God is in the details. Could have been a baseball person. "Baseball people," Giamatti said, "have the keenest eyes for details I have ever known"—this from a professor of poetry. Hear baseball people dissect a batter's swing, or catalog minute variations in a pitcher's release point, or deplore the way a shortstop by leaning betrays the kind of pitch that is coming. It is, therefore, splendidly right that Oriole Park at Camden Yards sets a new standard for detailed excellence.

Three related reasons why the park is receiving standing ovations from critics are its urban setting, its asymmetry and its intimacy. All these suit it to the ceremony of sport and especially to baseball.

The park speaks well of Maryland's Governor William Donald Schaefer, who again has provided proof that government can do things right. One of the primary shapers of the park is Orioles owner Eli Jacobs, a carrier of the torch of baseball traditionalism. His tastes were shaped by quirky parks shoehorned into city neighborhoods—Brooklyn's Ebbets Field and Boston's Fenway Park. Another shaper is Orioles president Larry Lucchino, a baseball purist who hired a kindred spirit, Janet Marie Smith, thirty-four.

Like Will Clark, Smith is one of Mississippi State University's great gifts to the national game. This willowy dynamo is an urban design specialist (she worked on development of New York's Battery Park City and Los Angeles' Pershing Square) who knit the new park into the fabric of this old city.

Baseball is, as Giamatti said, "strenuously nostalgic," but not for a pastoral

211

past. Baseball's codification occurred not in Farmer Phinney's pasture near Cooperstown but in a Manhattan meadow where in 1845 Alexander Cartwright—baseball's James Madison: its greatest constitutionalist—laid out a diamond with the bases 90 feet apart. Western philosophy is a series of footnotes to Plato, and baseball's evolution has been but footnotes to Cartwright.

Baltimore baseball history will henceforth be made where much history has happened. General Rochambeau's French forces camped at Camden Yards en route to Yorktown in 1783. At 3 A.M. February 23, 1861, President-elect Lincoln passed through Camden railroad station, which is just beyond center field, on his stealthy journey to Washington. Lincoln passed through Camden Yards in November 1863 traveling to Gettysburg, and in April 1865 going home to Springfield.

The center-field bleachers are near where the first Civil War fatalities occurred. Southern sympathizers fought with Massachusetts infantry that was passing through Camden station en route to Washington after the attack on Fort Sumter (where both sides together fired 4,000 shells and killed no one).

Oriole Park is not the first built on sacred soil. Second base at Cincinnati's Riverfront Stadium is on the site of the birthplace of Roy Rogers. The Ori-

The old Baltimore & Ohio warehouse, partially concealed
by a baseball park: Camden Yards.

oles' new center field was once the site of a saloon where George Herman Ruth Sr. sold nickel beer and dime soup. The barkeep's son had "warehouse power." That new baseball term describes batters who can hit the old brick B&O warehouse 460 feet from Camden Yards' home plate, down the right-field line.

The foul lines in Oriole Park are different lengths; the outfield wall is 25 feet high in one stretch, 7 feet elsewhere. Good. Baseball has blithe disregard not only for the dictates of clocks but also for numerical or spatial symmetries. Even baseball's numbers are odd—three strikes and you're out, five ball-and-strike calls make a full count, nine players to a side, nine innings to a game, get twenty-seven outs and you can go home—unless there is then the impermissible symmetry of a tie.

Bradd Shore, an anthropologist, notes baseball's social asymmetry: One team never confronts the other. Nine defenders confront one batter and at most three base runners at a time. So Oriole Park, with eight angles in its out-field wall, is a suitable frame for an asymmetrical game.

It is the most observable game—players are dispersed on green—and should be seen up close. We make buildings, then they make us, and Oriole Park will make baseball fans by making the game's elegance and nuances as observable as they now are only in Wrigley Field, Tiger Stadium and Fenway Park, the parks built before the world went mad (World War I).

Oriole Park's 48,000 seats are enough. Last year the Cleveland Indians, playing in a stadium that seats 80,000, played at home in front of 5,055,743 empty seats.

Giamatti, who rose from Yale's presidency to the splendor of baseball commissioner, said that we associate leisure with happiness, and leisure at a sporting event with a shared absence of care. Giamatti hinted ballparks can be intimations, or echoes or remnants, of paradise.

A ballpark can be an active ingredient in transforming a crowd—a mere aggregation—into a community. A sporting event can be a moment of harmony, and a ballpark can be a setting for surcease from the competitive strivings of urban life. In an age when religious ceremonies are decreasingly central to most lives, and in a republic in which civic rituals are purposely few and spare, sport can satisfy a yearning for ceremony. Baltimore's jewel of a ballpark is worthy of such yearnings.

It already has been the scene of one small ceremony. Late one afternoon last August, before the sod was down, at the place where home plate now is, I proposed marriage to the Oriole fan who now is Mrs. Will. Hey, call me romantic, but I wanted Mari to know that in my heart she ranks right up there with baseball.

THE LURID MONOTONY OF BILLY MARTIN

April 5, 1992

BILLY MARTIN'S BASEBALL LIFE, at once lurid and monotonous, wasn't one damn thing after another, it was the same damn thing over and over. David Falkner's meticulously reported biography, *The Last Yankee: The Turbulent Life of Billy Martin*, begins, appropriately, in a men's room in a Texas bar where the sixty-year-old Martin gets into a 2 A.M. brawl and nearly has an ear torn off. Forty stitches repaired the ear. Nothing could repair his career, which had long since been hurtling out of control.

Mr. Falkner, the author of *The Short Season* and *Nine Sides of the Diamond*, subscribes to the "as the twig is bent" school of biography. Martin was born in 1928 into a brawling family in working-class Berkeley, California, and was reared in a milieu of domestic violence, pugnacious ignorance and alcoholism. Some years later, Casey Stengel, then managing in the minor leagues, took a shine to Martin and, after becoming manager of the Yankees, brought him to New York. There Martin, a marginal player on a team brimming with talent, became obsessed with Yankee glamour. But eventually he became emblematic of the team's decline.

It is fitting that as a player Martin is most famous for saving the seventh game of the 1952 World Series by catching a windblown infield pop-up that, if it had dropped, would have given the Dodgers the lead. It was not a deed on a heroic scale, but it was useful. A .257 career hitter, he hit .333 in five World Series. Adrenaline and fury could carry him to heights where he really

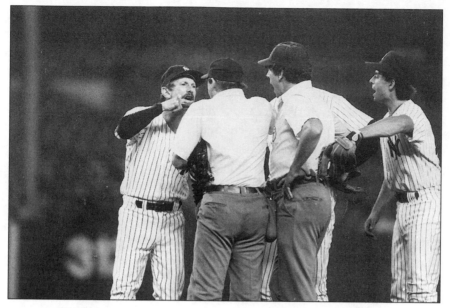

Yankee manager Billy Martin exercising his right of free speech.

didn't belong. Similarly, as a manager he could briefly energize his teams, eliciting bursts of success. But they were not sustainable.

Martin became the chimerical solution for various owners (such as the Oakland Athletics' Charles Finley and the Yankees' George Steinbrenner) who lacked the patience that is an indispensable ingredient of any franchise's long-term success. Martin was the quick fix for teams in too much of a hurry to rely on the slow, steady development of young players, the formulation of real baseball prosperity.

Mr. Falkner never really explains his book's peculiar title. "The Last Yankee"? In what sense? Martin was indeed among the last people connected with the Yankees' glory years, but that fact is linked with this one: The Yankees fell from glory because they fell into the hands of the buccaneer Steinbrenner, who knows so little about baseball that he thought Martin was a winner.

Martin wasn't, on the field or off. "Turbulent" is altogether too pallid an adjective to describe his life. Try "tawdry," "squalid" and "loathsome." He was an appalling parent, a monster of marital infidelity (the day after his second wedding he flew off to see the woman who would be his third wife) and an infantile boor (he and Mickey Mantle, Mr. Falkner tells us, enjoyed sneaking around to the other's apartment to catch a peek of the other copulating). He became increasingly paranoid and destructive of himself and all those around him. And he was a bad manager.

It is an old baseball axiom that any team will win a third of its games and lose a third of its games, and that the point of the season is to settle the middle third. Actually, even the best team will probably lose more than a third. The average of the best winning percentages in each of the last twenty-five years is .630. In this sport of the six-month season, leaving the field beaten just sixty-five times is excellence. So in order to win you must know how to lose. That is, losing must not destroy the emotional equilibrium, the blend of concentration and relaxation that baseball requires of individuals and of teams that live and travel together from April through September.

Baseball, said a sage, is not a game you can play with your teeth clenched. Martin, as a manager, his teeth, fists and soul clenched, annihilated the poise teams need in order to prosper for more than a short spurt.

Mr. Falkner does not go into much detail about what made Martin distinctive as a baseball tactician. But, then, nothing much did. Martin was a rheostat who could turn up a club's energy level. He enriched his teams' menus of offensive options with bunts, base stealing and other measures that make opponents edgy and error-prone. But he hardly pioneered the revival of such baseball. A decade before Martin became a manager, the plodding, station-to-station game of the 1950s—get two men on base and send a home run hitter to the plate—was passing.

In 1959, ten years before Martin's first managerial job, with Minnesota, the "Go-Go" White Sox won a pennant with an attack, if it can be called that, built around two small middle infielders, Nellie Fox and Luis Aparicio. They lost the World Series to the Dodgers, who were in transition from the muscular 1950s teams of Duke Snider, Gil Hodges, Carl Furillo and Roy Campanella to the Maury Wills-Willie Davis spray-hitting speed merchants.

Martin's tactics did make opponents tense and distracted, but no more so than his personality made his own players. "There is," Mr. Falkner notes, "a numbing sameness to the fate of Billy Martin's teams"—an initial rocketlike surge, but then the burn would falter, "the result of overload, too much stress and strain. The rocket ultimately nose-dived, crashing back to earth. . . . The team seemed to slip away from him, worn out either from having to continually play over its head or from simply having to deal with Billy Martin on a daily basis."

Nevertheless, for years there always was another owner who thought the crashes could be avoided. George Steinbrenner was a slow learner—no, a nonlearner—who hired Martin five times.

Mr. Falkner ends oddly by saying that Martin "was the best manager of his era, possibly of many eras. . . . A manager's job is to win. Billy won. In sixteen big-league seasons, there were only two seasons when teams of his had losing records." Mr. Falkner bases his conclusion, which the rest of his book refutes, on a statistical formula concocted by the number crunchers at the Elias Sports Bureau. The formula purports to reveal which managers' teams won more games than they were reasonably expected to win. Well now.

The Elias Bureau is baseball's Homer, telling the sport's story magnificently in the annual volumes of *Baseball Analyst*. These books constitute a continuing epic. But Homer nods.

In fact, *The Last Yankee* might usefully be made required reading for graduate students in the social sciences and all others who need to be immunized against the seduction of numbers. To read Mr. Falkner's absorbing narrative, and then his wildly discordant conclusion, is to be cured of misplaced confidence in quantification. There are limits—and Mr. Falkner's reporting shows that Elias passed them regarding Martin—to the ability to capture messy reality in tidy formulas. Only the fetishism of numbers, to which all baseball fans are susceptible, leads a good student of the game like Mr. Falkner to contradict his own commonsense findings.

Martin, as Mr. Falkner acutely says, had a "powerful core energy, like the interior of a highly volatile, unstable atom," right up to the moment in 1989 when he skidded to his death in a pickup truck. Staying with the language of physics, I would say that Mr. Falkner has written a memorable account of Martin's long meltdown.

STEVE PALERMO'S GAME
OF INCHES

April 6, 1992

OVERLAND PARK, KANSAS—One of the battery of physical thera-
pists who put Steve Palermo through an average of five hours of pain, five
days a week, says he is the first patient she has had who, looking back on the
episode that broke his body, insists he would do it again. Of course he would.
He was just enforcing the rules. He is, after all, an umpire.

Is, not was. As he does laborious leg lifts in a heated pool, a gold number
14—umpires, too, have numbers—glistens on a chain beneath his face,
which at this moment is ashen from fatigue and pain. Inch by inch he is push-
ing away the possibility that his career ended last July on a Dallas sidewalk.

His baseball story began, as baseball stories should, with a scout spotting
raw talent on a sandlot. Palermo first umpired in Little League games, the
year he became too old to play them. He was thirteen, earning $2 a game.
After a five-year hiatus he was asked to umpire a Little League all-star game in
his hometown of Worcester, Massachusetts. An umpire scout saw him. Six
years later Palermo worked third base at Fenway.

Baseball's small community is a severe meritocracy. Umpires, like players,
earn, from the discerning, unsparing assessments. In the sport of the long season, talent, or lack of it, tells. Palermo is one of the two or three best. In a
game thickly coated with clichés, this is one of the most familiar: Baseball
success is inseparable from a lot of failure. The World Series winner is likely to
be beaten about seventy times on the way to glory. Any batter who fails, say,
only two-thirds of the time for a dozen seasons goes to Cooperstown. But
umpires are supposed to be perfect and anonymous. An old umpire once told
the young Palermo that even a good umpire will miss 12 ball-and-strike calls
in a game (of perhaps 260 pitches). Maybe so but, if so, good is not nearly
good enough for Palermo. Twelve a month, he says, would be intolerable.

Once when the Yankees' Lou Piniella was batting he questioned a Palermo strike call. Piniella demanded, "Where was that pitch at?" Palermo told him that a man wearing Yankee pinstripes in front of 30,000 people should not end a sentence with a preposition. So Piniella, no dummy, said, "OK, where was that pitch at, asshole?" What Palermo calls the umpire's "challenge of trying to do something humanly impossible—to get everything right," perhaps should not extend to matters syntactical.

But it is natural that someone who strives for excellence admires it in others. For Palermo, part of the joy of his job is that it is a pretty good place to watch the game. He says that the most professional of the players—men like the Brewers' Paul Molitor and the Twins' Kirby Puckett—are the least likely to complain about umpires' calls. And Palermo's voice fills with an aficionado's enthusiasm when he says he likes to be working first base when the Brewers' Robin Yount gets on base, it is such a pleasure watching Yount on the base paths doing the small things right, the things seen only by the game's initiates.

Palermo's high standards—what society needs, Americans crave and umpires embody—brought him to the rehabilitation hospital here. He and some friends were finishing a late dinner after a night game in Dallas. The restaurant—Italian, of course—was closing when two waitresses were attacked in the parking lot. Palermo and friends chased and captured one of the assailants. Then three others drove up. Five shots were fired. One passed through Palermo's torso at waist level, nicked a kidney, fractured a vertebra and frayed his spinal cord.

Baseball is, as the saying goes, a game of inches—often the difference between a ball and a strike, or a runner safe or out. Good umpires earn their reputations being right about inches in the heat and blur of action. Palermo's life was saved by a millimeter. If the bullet had been that much thicker, he would have died. Instead, he was paralyzed from the waist down. The twenty-three-year-old who shot him has been sentenced to seventy-five years in prison. Palermo has been sentenced to a spring in which the rhythms of baseball quicken again, but without him.

His wife, Debbie, a bride of five months when he was shot, has a mantra: "Inch by inch, life's a cinch." But every inch hurts, as hamstrings are stretched, and muscles cramp because they are no longer controlled by healthy nerves, and terrible burning sensations sear the paralyzed portions of the body that served him so well in a profession both serious and strenuous.

Baseball, said Bart Giamatti, has no clock and indeed moves counterclockwise, thereby asserting its own rhythms and patterns. But because base-

American League umpire Steve Palermo
is greeted by homeplate colleague Don
Denkinger after throwing out the first pitch
at Game 1 of the 1991 World Series.

ball's severe independence includes independence from clock time, the keeper of its especially autonomous rules—the umpires—have special dignity. They represent the human hunger for coherence, which requires rules. Furthermore, sport presupposes equality for the purpose of establishing inequality—a level playing field on which some will achieve the preeminence of the highest attainment. Sport, said Giamatti, replicates the challenge of freedom, which is to combine energy and complex order. And baseball mirrors the conditions of American freedom: We freely consent to an order that enhances and compounds freedom even as it constrains it. Umpires, the constrainers, make it possible.

Next time you go to a game, give yourself a connoisseur's treat. Watch the people who do not want to be noticed. Watch the four umpires' gestures and movements. By the vigor of their gestures they impart authority to their decisions and communicate information to spectators. By their coordinated movements—sprints, often—they get into positions to monitor the various vectors of the ball on particular plays.

Palermo, a slender 6 feet 2, was mobile and graceful. Because he is determined to be so again, his spring training began last July, when he could move only two toes on his right foot. Three months later the world watched him walk. In last October's humdinger of a World Series, one of the most stirring moments occurred before the first batter stepped in, when Palermo walked, with the help of hand crutches and leg braces, to the Metrodome mound to flip the ceremonial first pitch. Today canes have replaced the crutches and one brace has been put away. Some April—not this one, but there is one every year—Palermo may be back where he belongs, looking at pitches from the other end of the delivery. He is still many inches away, but they are all just inches.

BASEBALL'S BASIC DILEMMA

September 21, 1992

IF YOU LIKE MAJOR LEAGUE BASEBALL, you had better take yourself out to the ballpark this month. You may not get back there until 1994. At twenty-eight parks, 1993 may be a silent spring. And summer, and fall. There are twenty-eight teams, counting the new Miami and Denver expansion franchises. Those two may participate in a lockout of players (they do not yet have any) before they play their first game.

Baseball's owners can reopen negotiations on the basic labor agreement this winter, a year early, and another fight over fundamental rights will begin. If, as is probable, it is not settled by the time spring training is supposed to begin, the owners may do what they did in 1990—lock out the players. In 1990 opening day was merely delayed. But the owners' aims were less aggressively ambitious than they now are, at least among those who participated in the downsizing of the commissioner's office.

Some of these owners may be less ardent for confrontation after they have conversations with their bankers. Some owners are, in effect, batting with an 0–2 count, financially. The Major League Baseball Players Association, the union, has a huge—upward of $100 million—emergency fund from licensing revenues (baseball cards and lots of other stuff). Furthermore, in their battles with the union, the owners' won-lost record is worse than that of the 1899 Cleveland Spiders (20–134, .130). Yet today's owners still hope to break the will of a union that has almost never lost and has seen the compensation of its members increase 1,823 percent since 1976.

Baseball's last commissioner: Fay Vincent.

The easiest question to answer about the owners' bidding up of players' salaries is: When will it end? The answer is: When the money runs out. For many teams—perhaps most (but a few may be fibbing)—it pretty much has. And the next national television contract may be half the size of the current one that gives each team $14 million a year. As an industry, baseball is profitable, but very unevenly, and at some point unevenness becomes ruinous to individual teams, and hence to the industry. If twenty-eight widget makers are competing, each hopes to drive some others out of business. But baseball depends on competitive balance.

Baseball's basic dilemma is this: The price of players is set by a national market, but teams' revenues reflect local disparities, the biggest being local broadcasting revenues. Revenue disparities mattered less when broadcasting mattered less, and when players were chattel. Players were among the last American employees to win the elemental right to negotiate terms of employment. Until the mid-1970s a player was owned by a team until it, at its unfettered discretion, traded, sold, or released him. In 1974 players began to accumulate serious rights—to become free agents and to go to salary arbitration. (In arbitration a player demands a sum X, his team offers Y and the arbitrator must pick one sum or the other.)

222

Owners predicted that player mobility would mean the perpetual domination of both leagues by a few rich big-market teams. But free agency has coincided with unprecedented competitive balance. There are six teams in the three largest markets—New York, Los Angeles, Chicago. Only two (the 1986 Mets and the 1988 Dodgers) were among the twenty teams that appeared in the World Series in the last decade. Impecunious but intelligent management (the Twins won two World Championships in five years) can beat rich dolts. (The Yankees get about fourteen times more local broadcasting revenues than the Twins.) But at some point money can overwhelm mind in baseball.

Baseball's fundamental need is a new constitution. It needs government, which human beings find necessary because individuals and their factions are partial to themselves. Good governments produce compromise and look after the general good—the collective interests of the community. Baseball today is anarchy leavened by furious factional strife. Of the twenty-eight owners, nine (ten if the sale of the Giants is consummated) have been in baseball fewer than five years. Baseball's institutional memory is weak. The union has rarely recognized any responsibility to baseball beyond maximizing players' earnings, and owners have rebuffed the union's tentative suggestions for a more collaborative role. And remember—the players certainly do—that the owners' most resourceful response to the players' new rights was illegal. It was collusion against free agents, and it got the owners a $280 million fine.

The owners, with very valuable assets at risk, resent it when a commissioner they hire uses his power to act independently "in the best interests of baseball." They say: We pay him; he should obey our collective will. But they rarely have such a will because their interests are as diverse as their local situations. (Go ahead, try to get the Yankees and Twins to agree on pooling local broadcast revenues.) A suggestion: The union, because it has a huge stake in a healthy industry, should consider amending today's compensation system, which puts many teams in peril. In exchange, and for the same reason, the owners should consider more revenue sharing under a common salary cap, and with a salary floor, for all teams. Otherwise there may be Armageddon next April.

Between the foul lines the national pastime is emblematic of the nation in many nice ways. But off the field it mirrors many of the causes of our current discontents—angry factions loudly invoking the language of "rights," and not even one small voice articulating the community's collective and long-term interests. In the past, commissioners have done that, but only delicately and rarely, husbanding their "best interests" power, like the best wine in the cellar, for extraordinary occasions. However, Fay Vincent may have been the last real commissioner. Sure, someone will be called "commissioner." But as Lincoln liked to say, if we call a tail a leg, how many legs does a dog have? Five? No, calling a tail a leg does not make it a leg.

Subsequent commissioners may have the prominence of a ship's figurehead but little to say about the serious business on the ship's bridge. Today some mutineers among the owners, having put Captain Bligh (as they think Fay Vincent was) overboard, want to steer the ship into the iceberg dead ahead. Fans had better brace themselves.

FIFTIES BASEBALL: NOT LONG ON NUANCE

1992

> Guiltlessness. Our fat fifties cars, how we loved them, revved them: no thought of pollution. Exhaust smoke, cigarette smoke, factory smoke, all romantic. Romance of consumption at its height.
>
> —JOHN UPDIKE,
> "When Everyone Was Pregnant"

IN THE 1950s, America was at the wheel of the world and Americans were at the wheels of two-toned (and sometimes even more-toned) cars, tail-finned, high-powered, soft-sprung rolling sofas. One car was the most fiftyish of them all. A Buick had those—what?—gunports along the hood, and a grille that looked like Teddy Roosevelt's teeth when he was in full grin over some whomping big-stick exercise of American might.

But big muscular Buicks and other fat fifties cars (for which Ike launched the biggest public works program ever, the Interstate Highway System) were not the best symbol of an American decade of pent-up energy busting loose. Remember Ted Kluszewski's biceps, those huge ham hocks erupting from the then-sleeveless uniform jerseys of the Cincinnati Reds? (Or as that team was called for a while in that Cold War decade, the Redlegs.) Baseball in the fifties carried a big stick.

Even shortstops, who once upon a time had been considered inoffensive little guys, got into the act: The Cubs' Ernie Banks won two consecutive MVP awards for seasons (1958, 1959) in which he hit a total of 92 home runs.

The Baseball Encyclopedia says Kluszewski was 6 feet 2 and 225 pounds. That was mighty big then, but not anymore. Arguably the most striking change in baseball in the four decades since then is the sheer scale of the players. In 1953 the Indians' Al Rosen had a monster season—.336, 43 home runs, 145 RBIs. He missed a triple crown by .001, to the Senators' Mickey Vernon. Rosen was considered a "burly slugger." He was 5 feet 10½ inches and 180 pounds. Baseball is still, as Bill Veeck said, a game unlike others because to play it you do not need to be either 7 feet tall or 7 feet wide. But by 1987 Nolan Ryan (6 feet 2, 195) was smaller than five teammates on the Astros' pitching staff.

In Kluszewski's torrid seasons, 1953–56, he hit 171 home runs, a four-year total rarely matched. But what looks most remarkable from the perspective of later decades is that in those four years he struck out only 140 times. (In 1987, when Mark McGwire set a rookie record with 49 home runs, he struck out 131 times, and his teammate Jose Canseco, who hit 31 home runs, had 157 strikeouts.) In the fifties, when clubs had as many as sixteen minor league teams, it took more time for a player to claw his way up to the major leagues, and by the time he got there he was apt to have learned a thing or two, such as the strike zone, and to have acquired some polish.

The fifties had the two most famous pitching performances in baseball history. One was Don Larsen's perfect game for the Yankees against the Dodgers in the 1956 World Series. The other was Harvey Haddix's heartbreaker, the twelve perfect innings he pitched for the Pirates in Milwaukee. The Braves won in the thirteenth. They got one hit. The winning pitcher, Lew Burdette, gave up twelve hits.

The decade included baseball's most storied home run (Bobby Thomson's that won the 1951 playoff for the Giants) and the most famous catch (Willie Mays' over-the-shoulder gem in the 1954 World Series). Both occurred in a park, the Polo Grounds, that would echo with emptiness by the end of the decade.

Images of the fifties:
The fins on a Buick Roadmaster, and the biceps on Ted Kluszewski.

Fifties baseball had the best player who is still not in the Hall of Fame. A quiz: Who had the most hits—1,875 of them—in the decade? If you guessed Williams or Mays or Mantle or Aaron or anyone other than Richie Ashburn, you are mistaken. If Ashburn had played in any other decade, his achievements almost certainly would be spelled out in bronze letters in Cooperstown.* They *are* spelled out in the record book. Check the list of the top ten single-season putout totals by outfielders. Six of the ten best were Ashburn's. On the list of the top ten seasons by outfielders in terms of chances, five of the seasons are his. He had a higher career batting average (.308) than Mays (.302) or Mantle (.298), higher than the averages of a dugout full of Hall of Famers. His career on-base percentage was higher than Mays' (.397 to .387) and he averaged more doubles per year than Mantle (21 to 19). He averaged 88 runs per season, just behind Mays' 94 and Mantle's 93. So what is the flaw that supposedly disqualifies him from the Hall of Fame? He hit just 29 home runs in his entire career, the heart of which spanned the home run–obsessed fifties.

Ashburn had one other handicap that in subsequent decades would not have mattered: he did not play in New York. Not, that is, until 1962, when he was a member of the expansion Mets. When he was named MVP as the Mets lost 120 games, he said, I wonder what they meant by this. And then he retired. The fifties were the last decade in which America suffered from the defect of vision known as New York–centrism. New York seemed to be the center of the universe in culture generally and baseball especially. The nation's gaze was about to turn, south toward Washington, and west, where the course of empire was taking the population—and a couple of New York's baseball teams. But in baseball, until 1958, the fifties belonged to three boroughs—the Bronx, Manhattan and Brooklyn. Yankee Stadium, the Polo Grounds and Ebbets Field seemed to have cornered the market on glory.

In 1951 all three New York teams finished the regular season in first place. In the early fifties New York had center fielders named DiMaggio, Mantle, Mays and Snider. In the fifties, fourteen of the twenty pennants and eight of the ten World Series were won by New York teams. Eleven of the twenty MVP awards were won by New York players. (In the thirty seasons between 1963 and 1992 only three New York players were MVPs.)

The decade that was to end with a rarity—the White Sox in a World Series—began with a rarity: The Phillies won a pennant. That had never happened since 1915 and would not happen again for thirty years. And one thing

---

*This injustice was rectified in 1996.

about the 1950 Phillies was a harbinger of what soon would become baseball's biggest on-field change since the advent of the lively ball. It was the rise of the relief pitcher. The Phillies' Jim Konstanty became the first relief pitcher to win an MVP award. Thirty-three and peering toward the plate through wire-rimmed glasses, Konstanty won 16, lost 7 and had an ERA of 2.66. Those are nice numbers, but not the ones that were then startling: He pitched only 152 innings but appeared in 74 games.

Two years later a twenty-eight-year-old rookie, Hoyt Wilhelm, would be called up to the Giants to begin a twenty-one-year career that would take him to seven other teams and then on to the Hall of Fame, the first relief pitcher to get there. Many pitchers have pitched more than his 2,254 innings but no one has pitched in more games: 1,070.

The basic criticism of fifties baseball is that it was a one-dimensional, station-to-station, stand-around-and-wait-for-lightning-to-strike game. The basic, and often the only, strategy was to get a couple of runners on base and get Godzilla to the plate to blast the ball into the next postal zone (in those days before ZIP codes). The criticism is correct.

In 1950 the Red Sox won 94 games and finished just four games behind the Yankees in spite of a pitching staff with an embarrassing ERA of 4.88. Discerning fans had an anticipation of fifties baseball: "This isn't going to be pretty—but it's sure going to be fun." Loads of fun, but the somewhat limited fun of a long fireworks display—lots of flash and crash, but not long on nuance. After all, in 1950 the Red Sox's Dom DiMaggio led the league in steals with a measly 15, the lowest league-leading total ever. No one would steal more than Willie Mays' 40 in 1956—no one until 1959, when Luis Aparicio stole 56 for the White Sox. He and that team were signals that the game was going to be different in the next decade.

Luis Ernesto Aparicio, who for two years was a White Sox teammate of Saturnino Orestes Armas "Minnie" Minoso from Havana, Cuba, was the second Venezuelan to play shortstop for the Sox. Aparicio followed Chico Carrasquel and has in turn been followed into the major leagues by a long line of Latin American players, often middle infielders, who have made baseball more "multicultural" and, more to the point, better. At 5 feet 9 and 160 pounds, Aparicio was well-matched with second baseman Nellie Fox (5 feet 10, 150 pounds) on the "Go-Go" Sox. That team's attack, such as it was, consisted in no small part of those two pesky people spraying singles, hitting-and-running and stealing bases. Together they took the Sox to the 1959 World Series, and took baseball back to the future.

Playing shortstop for the Dodgers in that Series, which the Dodgers won in six games, was a whippetlike rookie named Maury Wills. He had stolen only 7 bases in 83 games in 1959, but in 1960, when America elected a young president pledged to "get America moving again," Wills helped get baseball moving again, stealing 50 bases. In the first seven years of the fifties, not one of the 16 *teams* had stolen 100 bases. In 1962 Wills stole 104.

In the 1950s Americans were on the move. The first McDonald's and the first Holiday Inn were opened in the fifties. One of the decade's most famous literary works, supposedly a work of alienation and protest, was in fact an almost ecstatic travel book—Jack Kerouac's *On the Road,* published in 1957. Baseball franchises, too, were on the road.

After the 1901 season the American League's Milwaukee Brewers became the St. Louis Browns. In 1903, Baltimore of the American League moved to New York, where they became the Highlanders, and then the Yankees. No other franchises moved until 1953, when the Boston Braves became the Milwaukee Braves. By 1958 five of the sixteen franchises had relocated.

In 1954 the Browns became Baltimore's Orioles. In 1955, the year before the Philadelphia Athletics' manager of fifty years, Connie Mack, died at age ninety-three, the Athletics began their two-stage westward march to Oakland, stopping in Kansas City until 1968. In 1958 New York lost two-thirds of its baseball as California got the first two of its eventual five teams. Technology—the jet airliner—had made another mark on Major League Baseball.

But the best and most profound mark made on baseball by the fifties was the inclusion of black players, without whose subsequent participation baseball would have been a pale shadow of itself. It is commonly said that in 1947 baseball was integrated. Not quite. Three teams fielded black players that year—the Dodgers' Jackie Robinson ("Ty Cobb in Technicolor") and Dan Bankhead, the Indians' Larry Doby and the Browns' Hank Thompson and Willard Brown. Not until the Giants got Thompson from the Browns in 1949 was a fourth team integrated. The Phillies did not field a black player until 1957, the Tigers until 1958 and the Red Sox until 1959.

One way to gauge the caliber of baseball in a decade is to pick an All-Star team from those who played a significant portion of their careers in it. Here it goes:

CATCHER: Roy Campanella, Yogi Berra
FIRST BASE: Stan Musial, Ted Kluszewski
SECOND BASE: Jackie Robinson, Nellie Fox
THIRD BASE: Eddie Mathews, Ken Boyer, George Kell, Al Rosen

SHORTSTOP: Ernie Banks, Luis Aparicio, Phil Rizzuto, Pee Wee Reese
OUTFIELDERS: Ted Williams, Willie Mays, Mickey Mantle, Duke Snider,
  Frank Robinson, Henry Aaron, Richie Ashburn, Al Kaline
PITCHERS: Warren Spahn, Whitey Ford, Robin Roberts, Bob Lemon, Early
  Wynn

Few decades before and no decade since has been so prolific of talent. Perhaps that is one reason why baseball in the fifties, whatever its faults, formed from boys and girls more fans more intensely devoted to the game—I speak with the generational chauvinism of one who was nine in 1950—than were formed by baseball's subsequent decades.

There may be two other reasons why such a rosy glow surrounds baseball in the memories of those for whom the fifties were the formative years. One reason is architectural, the other technological.

To go to a game in Sportsman's Park in St. Louis, or Crosley Field in Cincinnati, or Forbes Field in Pittsburgh, or Shibe Park in Philadelphia was to experience baseball intimately, and to be marinated in a sense of past summers lingering in the atmosphere. That is no longer possible for fans in those cities, or in many others.

Furthermore, the fifties were the years during which America became, in a startling rush, a wired nation. By the end of the decade television offered almost all Americans a new way of experiencing baseball. But at the beginning of the decade, and through most of it, radio, the medium for which baseball's pace and geometry is most suited, was the game's link to fans beyond the stands. By encouraging, even requiring the active engagement of the listener's imagination, radio drew fans deep into the experience of the sport of the long season.

In central Illinois in the 1950s the air was saturated with baseball—with, that is, broadcasts of the Cubs and White Sox and Cardinals and Browns. And the unreasonably black and almost perfectly flat topsoil of central Illinois then as now was wonderfully configured for smooth infields and lush green outfields, one after another, toward the horizon.

One reason for the breadth of baseball's appeal is that we are all failed players. However, some of us fail earlier and more emphatically than others. I did in Little League in Champaign, Illinois. Age has dimmed, or embarrassment has suppressed, my memories of my performances on the diamond. I think I played some second base, but I know I was a born right fielder—someone who was glad to be put out there where the ball is least likely to come. At bat,

I hoped to walk. My ardor for baseball was inversely proportional to my ability, and it drove me to drive my parents into driving the 125 miles to Wrigley Field once a year as my birthday present. There we saw one of those now-vanished treats, a doubleheader. For Cub fans the bargain was two losses for the price of one.

My father, who hailed from western Pennsylvania and thought baseball had pretty much peaked with Honus Wagner, was a professor of philosophy and so was able to be, well, philosophical about his son's obsession. My mother, a briskly practical person who prior to encountering my obsession had no interest in baseball, became a White Sox fan so we could have something to argue about while she washed and I dried the dishes.

Even if your family didn't own a dishwasher, the fifties were a terrific time to be young. Young people had their own novel (*Catcher in the Rye* was published in 1951) and their own music (the anthem of the emerging youth culture was "Rock Around the Clock," popularized by the 1955 movie *Blackboard Jungle*). Bliss it was to be young; to be young *and* a baseball fan, 'twere very heaven.

It is arguable, and so I argue, that baseball has been better—more multidimensional, nuanced and surprising—since the fifties. But baseball has never before or since been more purely American, or more perfectly congruent with an era. With its relentless emphasis on the "big bang" style of offense, baseball was brimming over with energy. And nothing is more characteristic of this ax-swinging, forest-clearing, prairie-breaking, concrete-pouring, skyscraper-raising nation than the exuberant belief that energy, sheer straight-ahead power, is an unmixed blessing and the right approach to most things.

Soon after the fifties ended, domestic turmoil and foreign entanglements made American life seem more solemn and complicated. But before the clouds lowered and America came of middle age, back in the fifties when there still were lots of day games and doubleheaders, the national pastime, like the nation, seemed uncomplicated. As uncomplicated as a Kluszewski shot over the fence toward which the peculiar outfield sloped up in old Crosley Field, a shot over the fence to carom off the sign atop the laundry across the street. Any player hitting the sign won a free suit.

One evening in 1954, the poet Wallace Stevens, driving home to Hartford on Connecticut's Merritt Parkway, was struck by what he later described, in one of his last poems, as "a crush of strength" and "the vigor of glory, a glittering in the veins." Yes, yes, yes. That is how America felt in the fifties. And it is how baseball was.

Andy Van Slyke
and the Present Monetary
Status of Baseball

March 11, 1993

"Put me in, coach, I'm ready to play today. . . ."
—from the song "Centerfield"
by John Fogerty

Bradenton, Florida—Andy Van Slyke, baseball's best center fielder, doesn't look even ready to walk. However, he has just played six innings of the Pittsburgh Pirates' first spring training game, and has run wind sprints along the outfield fence as the game meandered to the ninth inning, and now, in the clubhouse, he has an ice pack lashed to his aching back and another taped to his throbbing knee, and he is doing push-ups, fast. But these exertions do not slow the flow of his State of the Game address.

His three degenerative spinal disks have been partly produced by playing on the plastic-covered concrete of Pittsburgh's hideous Three Rivers Stadium, which he considers one of the architectural contributions to the alienation of fans. On the way to some games last season he stopped at a hospital and was put into traction for twenty minutes. Yet what he calls the "headache in my back" only caused him to miss two games. He is a consummate professional and has standing to speak about the game's standards.

Baseball is, he thinks, like his back: hurting. Owners and players are, he says, so focused on maximizing the gusher of money being generated by the game, and their shares of the gusher, that no one is thinking of nurturing the next generation of fans. In 1992 attendance declined at eighteen of twenty-six parks, and the demographics of baseball's audience are ominous: The most

232

loyal fans are elderly, and youngsters just want to be like Mike—Michael Jordan. Yet rather than sacrifice some revenues by playing some World Series games during the day, when tomorrow's ticket-buyers are not asleep, those games start late and often end after midnight.

Does baseball have money problems? Yes, but of a strange sort. In 1976, at the dawn of free agency for players, the average salary was $51,501. Last year, the average was more than $1 million. This year, the Giants' Barry Bonds will make about $45,000 per game. But franchise values also have soared. The value of the Baltimore Orioles franchise has increased about tenfold in the fourteen years since it was sold for $12 million.

There is lots of money in baseball but the uneven distribution of it is not conducive to the game's health. Last year six teams had payrolls larger than the gross revenues of six teams in small markets.

Still, on the false assumption that baseball's health necessarily improves as the quantity of money generated grows, plans are afoot for radical changes that may generate more money by manufacturing more September excitement. Excitement, that is, for fans not excited by the sort of pennant races that have always excited real baseball fans.

In addition to limited interleague play, both leagues would be split into three, instead of today's two, divisions. There would be an extra layer of playoffs, involving eight teams— the six division winners and two "wild card" teams, those with the best second-place records in each league.

So eight of today's twenty-eight teams would get into postseason play. That is not as ludicrous as the NFL (twelve of twenty-eight) or the NBA (sixteen of twenty-seven) or the NHL (sixteen of twenty-four). Nevertheless, it is a format foreign to baseball's essential tradition, the stern ethic that second place doesn't mean a damned thing.

"Put me in, coach . . . "
Andy Van Slyke.

All this would damage irreparably the rhythm of pennant races. They should be long gatherings of summer heat, punctuated by a single clap of October thunder—the World Series.

Van Slyke, who knows and cherishes baseball's traditions, plays surrounded by tunnel-vision athletes who are, he says, so "self-absorbed" that all they know of Hank Aaron is that he could hit, long ago. They think Cy Young is the name of an award, not a pitcher. However, Van Slyke is so worried about baseball's wavering audience, he favors the contemplated changes.

And yet, and yet. As Van Slyke acknowledges, Major League Baseball is unlike, say, professional basketball in that the pleasure of being a baseball fan is bound up with knowledge not only of the game's nuances but also its history. Baseball's hold on America depends on the fans' immersion in the long stream of the game's traditions, one of which is the stately and mesmerizing crescendo of the long season. The cords of affection that bind serious fans to the traditional game cannot be cut and then rewoven. And those cords depend on baseball's continuities.

In the first half of this century there was in baseball only one radical disjunction. It occurred around 1920, when the lively ball replaced the dead ball. Then during the 1950s change erupted. In a span of six years, five of the sixteen franchises relocated. In 1969 the two leagues were split into two divisions. In 1973 the American League adopted the designated hitter.

Baseball had better think hard before it sheds still more traditions, and more fans.

BILL RIGNEY:
BASEBALL'S FAVORITE UNCLE

April 5, 1993

IF YOU WANT TO KNOW everything important about baseball—meaning everything about baseball; there is nothing unimportant—you can memorize the 2,857 pages of *The Baseball Encyclopedia*. Or you can go sit next to that elderly but sprightly man in the broad-brimmed straw hat, down there behind the screen back of home plate at the Oakland A's spring training camp in Phoenix. Bill Rigney, seventy-five, is working, but he can work and conduct a tutorial at the same time.

Spring training—pure oxygen for a fan's fires that have been banked all winter—is scrumptious everywhere, but is best in Phoenix. Florida's sunshine is fine, but Arizona's seems tactile, drenching the diamond. Tactile and audible, filling the dry air with a hum of energy. In or around audacious Phoenix—a sprawling city making itself at home in a desert—six teams (the A's, Cubs, Giants, Angels, Mariners and Brewers) train, and two others visit (the Rockies from Tucson and the Padres from Yuma). Baseball's annual family reunion, with Rigney presiding as everyone's favorite uncle, is in full swing around Arizona batting cages, and in steak joints like the Pink Pony and Don and Charlie's in Scottsdale.

At that table yonder, the ample man doing vigorous justice to a plateful of red meat is Hank Sauer. Today he scouts for the Giants. In 1952 he won the National League's Most Valuable Player award playing for the Cubs. (In the eight seasons from 1952 through 1959, Cubs players won three MVP awards—Ernie Banks won in 1958 and 1959—but the team lost 139 more games than it won and never finished higher than fifth. Go figure.) And that slab of a man across the room, who looks like he wandered away from Stonehenge, is the Bull, Greg Luzinski, retired slugger, currently the A's hitting coach. He is also the father of Ryan, a Dodger minor leaguer whose substantial architecture and talent are both tributes to the diligence of DNA. And speaking of family values, the Mariners' second baseman, Bret Boone, twenty-four, is the major leagues' first third-generation player. His father is Bob, the catcher, and his grandfather is Ray, the infielder.

If you remember Ray—he played until 1960—you have been around for a while, but probably not as long as that guy wearing the big black-rimmed glasses: It might be . . . it could be . . . it is—Harry Caray, the Cubs' broadcaster. Forty-nine spring trainings ago he started in St. Louis on "the Griesedieck Brothers [a brewery] baseball network." Back then St. Louis was baseball's western frontier and Caray's voice, crackling over the Ozarks and across the prairies, poured out of Philco and Emerson radios in living rooms in Oklahoma and Nebraska. Caray was for many fans their only link with Major League Baseball.

Rigney probably heard Caray when Rigney was playing for the Topeka Owls, which he did before he made it to the Oakland Oaks, and after he had played for the Spokane Hawks, the Vancouver Capilanos and the Bellingham (Washington) Chinooks. Today Rigney is the reservoir of all-purpose wisdom for the A's. But fifty-seven springs ago he was in Brawley, California, an eighteen-year-old trying to get a grip on the slippery first rung of what then was baseball's long ladder to the big leagues. In 1936 most teams had sixteen or more farm clubs. Even at the end of the second world war there were still fifty-one minor leagues. It was quite a climb from the bushes to the Show.

Rigney is hardly the senior camper in Arizona. The Angels' Jimmy Reese, a coach, in fact the conditioning coach, still suits up and hits fungoes—sometimes several hundred in a day—at ninety-one. Now in his seventy-sixth year in organized baseball, he once roomed on the road with Babe Ruth. Or, as Reese puts it, he roomed with Ruth's luggage. The great man kept vampire's hours when he was on what Satchel Paige called "the social ramble." But I digress, as baseball people are wont to do.

When Rigney was a Giants rookie in 1946, the Giants and Indians settled into Pullman sleepers and played their way north from spring training, stopping in places like Danville, Virginia. Baseball was hard work but handsomely rewarded. Rigney earned $8,500 in 1946. On opening day that year, in New York, he played in the first major league game he ever saw. He had never seen New York before. Early on game day, he walked into the stillness of the vast Polo Grounds, where he would play shortstop on ground hallowed by the spikes of Christy Mathewson and Babe Ruth. He said to himself: "If there's a God in heaven, let someone quickly hit a ball to me and get it over

Jimmie Reese, the Paderewski
of the fungo bat.

Bill Rigney, "a reminder
that mind as well as money
matters in a game chock-full
of telling details."

with." The Phillies' leadoff man, Skeeter Newsome (Rigney forgets *nothing*), hit the first pitch of the game through the box. "I sucked it up," Rigney says, still savoring the forty-seven-year-old feeling. (It was going to be that kind of season—a .232 season—for Skeeter.)

What does Rigney remember about his first at bat? I'm telling you, baseball people remember *everything*. He struck out swinging on a 3-2 screwball from Oscar Judd. He is still muttering about it: "Can you believe he threw a screwball, 3–2?" Never mind, the Giants beat "the Philadelphias." (Rigney occasionally lapses into such pleasing archaisms as, "Back in '50, when we were playing the Bostons . . .") The score was 8–2. The Giants' pitcher was Bill Voiselle, from the hamlet of Ninety Six, South Carolina. Guess what number he wore.

Baseball players play as long as they can, then they take up talking about it. The late Bart Giamatti, watching baseball talk boil up in a St. Louis hotel lobby (a lobby, said Giamatti, is "the park of talk . . . baseball's second favorite venue"), marveled at "all the crosscutting, overlapping, salty, blunt, nostalgic, sweet conversation." He concluded that baseball is a narrative, an unending one, and that explains the game's seamless, cumulative character. As a conversationalist, Rigney rounds into midseason form early in spring training.

His nicknames, he says, were Specs (he wore glasses even then) and Cricket. This last was because fans could hear his chatter in the stands. Cricket is a middle-infielder sort of name. When Rigney was playing shortstop in New York City, so were Pee Wee and Scooter. But Rigney roomed on the road with a future Hall of Famer, Johnny Mize, whose muscles had muscles. "Our room hit sixty-eight home runs that year," says Rigney. Mize hit fifty-one of them.

Rigney has done well for a fellow who did not make his high-school team, and who played in only 654 games over eight major league seasons. (One game was a beaut. In the final game of the 1951 Giants-Dodgers playoff, Rigney was one of the three victims when Don Newcombe struck out the side in the eighth inning. In the ninth the Dodgers' Ralph Branca pitched to Bobby Thomson. . . .) Rigney had an eighteen-year career managing several teams. He spent many years on the field and in the dugout with a guy who, baseball people say, they "would pay to see." Rigney remembers what a Giants scout said about that young man when he was in Birmingham, Alabama: "What I've seen today I can't believe!" He had seen Willie Mays.

Like a lot of players not long on talent, Rigney honed a sharp baseball mind. That from a former professor of poetry. Today Rigney, his eyes crinkled against the desert glare that makes the red dirt of the infield glow, is at work for the A's, who are playing the Cubs. As he chats and comments and greets old friends and answers questions, he doesn't miss a nuance, and after the game he will be able to tell A's officials how each pitcher did, pitch by pitch, and if he is asked (which he is apt to be) whether a player was positioned too far off the foul line in the late innings, he will know, and without having taken a single note.

Rigney is a pleasant face of a sport that too often turns to the public only the flinty face of avarice. Consider this: Of the four teams with the highest payrolls last year, only the world champion Blue Jays had success. The Red Sox, Dodgers and Mets finished last, last and next to last, respectively. Rigney is a reminder that mind as well as money matters in a game chock-full of telling details.

In an era of constant rumbles between players and owners, Rigney is an incarnation of the game's continuity, its organic life and capacity for renewal. He worries that today's players, fiercely focused on careers that are lucrative beyond the dreams of Rigney's contemporaries, will aggravate baseball's loss of institutional memory. Many of them will, indeed, pass through baseball without pausing to appreciate the privilege of their passage. Baseball suffers, as the larger society does, from cultural amnesia, but Rigney is a keeper of the flame. He understands this paradox: Each player's dignity is enlarged because each player is a small part of a long and lengthening tradition of craftsmanship and companionship across the generations.

And surely in late winter fifty years from now, a few of the men who were young and lithe in 1993 will come south again, bringing their autumnal memories of baseball's many springtimes.

Coming Back to Clark
and Addison

October 1993

The first time I went to Europe I traveled by ship. A good thing, that. It meant that I did not first set foot in the Old World in the antiseptic glass and stainless steel corridors of an airport that could as well be in Los Angeles as London. Rather, I stepped into England through the old port of Southampton, and so experienced with full force a particularly American wonderment: How many shoes have trod upon these stones? And if these stones could speak, how many generations would they speak of?

Now, ask yourself this. Where, here at home, can we Americans have a similar sensation of mingling with the shades of many generations? In a few of the older neighborhoods of our older cities, neighborhoods that have eluded the heavy tread of Progress and not been transformed many times. And perhaps in some rural communities, particularly out west. But it is a lovely fact, and one that speaks volumes about the interweaving of the national pastime with the national experience, that we can experience the sense of mingling with the generations—the almost palpable presence of the past—in a few ballparks. And nowhere more than in Wrigley Field.

In Wrigley Field's first eighty seasons, through 1993 (although Wrigley opened in 1914, the Cubs did not play there until 1916), about 85 million people attended baseball games there. That is a crowd not much smaller than the population of the United States (99 million) in 1914, when what is now known as Wrigley Field was brand spanking new.

If grandparents brought grandchildren to the park in 1914, as surely some did, then there may today be some seventh-generation Cub fans in the grandstands. A grandfather in 1916 could have been a Civil War veteran. And a youngster in the Wrigley Field bleachers today may bring grandchildren here when this nation celebrates its Tricentennial in the year 2076.

240

Wrigley Field, so saturated with memories, is cherished by a nation too often enamored of novelty. The nation, or at least its baseball fans, may have learned a stern lesson. As someone—Oscar Wilde, I think—once warned, people should be careful not to be too modern; they run the risk of quite suddenly seeming old-fashioned. Fans in Philadelphia, Cincinnati, Pittsburgh, Atlanta, Oakland, San Diego and St. Louis can ruefully confirm that. Not long ago they were given up-to-date, state-of-the-art "multipurpose" stadiums. And today those stadiums look like young relics—like bell-bottom slacks and platform shoes. Or perhaps even more like another fad from the silly seventies—pet rocks.

These misbegotten stadiums were designed to accommodate both baseball and football, which makes about as much sense as designing a building to be both a library and a foundry. The question of the proper setting for watching a football game seems to me utterly unimportant. I mean, how important is the venue of a train wreck? Football should be watched, if at all, on television, so the camera can bring the spectator close enough to the carnage to make sense of the piles of bodies. But baseball, the most observable of team sports, should be played as close to the observant fans as possible—so close that even fans far back in the stands can hear the infielders' chatter. Cub fans can hear it.

The people who perpetrated the "multipurpose" edifices forgot a funda-

Form following function: Wrigley Field.

mental principle of design, the principle that explains the beauty of, for example, the old clipper ships. The principle is that function should dictate form. That simple notion explains the timeless beauty of, and unfailing satisfaction given by, Wrigley Field and a few other old parks. When the state of Maryland built Oriole Park at Camden Yards in Baltimore, it aimed not to break new ground but to recapture lost ground. And the resounding success of Camden Yards is confirmed every time a fan exclaims, "It reminds me of Wrigley Field!"

With the new parks built in Cleveland and Texas, baseball's quest continues, the quest to capture at least a portion of the perfection that Cub fans rightly consider their birthright. It is altogether proper that as baseball ends the long detour that took it away from its best architectural heritage, baseball finds itself striding, as it were, toward the corner of Clark and Addison.

JOHN OLERUD: NOT NEON

March 17, 1994

DUNEDIN, FLORIDA—In the cacophony of the Toronto Blue Jays clubhouse John Olerud is a fjord of Norwegian calm. He is a high-impact player with a low-intensity personality, an agreeable combination in an era when many athletes in other sports combine the opposite traits.

When he was elected to play on last year's All-Star team he was asked if he would be nervous. "Yes," he said. He was asked how it would show. "It won't," he said. He is as angular and unprepossessing as the young Jimmy Stewart and as laconic as the young Henry Fonda. But when he turns on a pitch, another comparison comes to mind: the young Ted Williams.

Like Williams, Olerud is a tall (6 feet 5, two inches taller than Williams) left-hander who wears number 9 and is fastidious about what he swings at: He is just the twentieth player in this century to get 200 hits and 100 walks in a season. But Williams was frequently moody and occasionally volcanic. Olerud, who has recorded an at-rest pulse rate of 44 beats per minute, is described as "just north of comatose."

At Washington State University he pitched, too, but Nature had a first baseman in mind when making him left-handed and long enough to gather in errant throws. Besides, first base is a sociable position, with lots of runners to chat up, should loquaciousness overcome Olerud. And it keeps a fellow's mind in the game because it is a busy place. (Usually. On April 27, 1930, White Sox first baseman Bud Clancy played the full nine innings against the Browns without making a putout or an assist. You can look it up.)

At Washington State he suffered a brain aneurysm requiring surgery. It kept him out of competition only seven weeks, and fortunately the weak spot on his skull, where the surgery was, is on the left side, away from the pitcher.

He never played an inning in the minor leagues, jumping from campus to the pennant race in 1989. In his first three full seasons he hit .265, .256 and .284. But last year in spring training he hit .433 and then got hotter.

He hit .450 in April. Eleven times during the season he fell below .400, ten times he came back up, the last time on August 2. He finished with a league-leading average of .363. In what is for him something of an extended soliloquy, he explains his improvement: "I made a few adjustments. Nothing major."

Well. When a fastball leaves a pitcher's hand with an initial velocity of 97 mph it crosses the plate 0.4 seconds later. Batters don't have much time to brood about pitches. They

A metabolic rate "just north of comatose." John Olerud of the Toronto Blue Jays.

have about 0.17 seconds to decide to swing. If they swing 0.0005 seconds too soon, they will not have maximum bat velocity. (Says who? Says Robert Adair, Sterling Professor of Physics at Yale, in his book *The Physics of Baseball*.) So even minor adjustments are major.

Olerud's adjustments included making his swing slightly more compact, and swinging at more first pitches. Pitchers, who have bad experiences if they don't have good memories, knew he was taking too many pitches, and he found himself too often behind in the count. But last year his batting average on the first pitches that he put into play was .500.

Having chased .400 so far into the summer, he is now in the pleasantly awkward position that a merely superlative season may be considered slightly disappointing. However, hitting .400 is like balancing the federal budget: It has been done in living memory (Williams hit .406 in 1941; the budget was balanced in 1969, the year after Olerud was born) but decades pass without anyone doing it. The closest anyone has come since 1941 was George Brett's .390 in 1980, Rod Carew's .388 in 1977 and Williams' .388 in 1957. Williams, Brett and Carew fell five, five and eight hits short, respectively, but as baseball people say, close only counts in horseshoes and hand grenades.

Olerud emphasizes the advantage he has playing on artificial grass in Toronto's Skydome: "The ball definitely does get through the infield a lot quicker. Places like Detroit that have the grass longer and the infield slow kill me because I'm not going to beat out many infield hits." But who is killing whom? His career average in Tiger Stadium—.418—is higher than in any other park, which shows that Tiger pitching is so crummy that not even creative groundskeepers can do much about it.

Because baseball is, as Michael Jordan can testify, so difficult, the best practitioners are usually the most understated. There still are, mercifully, few of the flamboyant types who nickname themselves "Neon" and make careers making shoe commercials and mediocre baseball. And fans of this sport of the long season and long careers can anticipate savoring a decade or so of Olerud plying his trade just north of comatose and just south of perfection.

A Stupendous Mystery

May 16, 1994

I₣ ₛₒₘₑₒₙₑ surreptitiously took everything but ESPN from my cable television package, it might be months before I noticed. But I am up to speed on the subject du jour: Why are so many baseballs flying over fences? Players and fans who share Flaubert's flair for *le mot juste* say the ball has been "juiced." Must be a conspiracy. Or not.

In 1987 a sudden increase in home runs produced the "Happy Haitian" explanation: Baseballs were then manufactured in Haiti and the theory was that the fall of the Duvalier regime so inspired Haitians that they worked with more pep, pulling the stitching tighter, thereby flattening the seams—and flattening curveballs. The smoother balls had less wind resistance to give them movement when pitched, or to slow their subsequent flight over outfielders. Baseballs are now made in Costa Rica for the Rawlings company, which stoutly denies that its exacting specifications have changed.

If, say, the yarn were wound tighter, the ball would either be smaller or would weigh more. It isn't and doesn't. At issue is the ball's "coefficient of restitution," which is what folks in the bleachers mean by the ball's tendency to land in the bleachers—"liveliness." COR is measured by firing balls from an air cannon at a slab of wood and measuring the rebound. Let's not do that, lest scientific information inhibit an argument that is jolly fun. But let's sift *some* evidence.

Time was when baseball was a seven-month profession. Most players were poorly paid, so they spent their winters operating bowling alleys or tending bars—and sampling the suds. But today long careers are lucrative, so players pump iron year-round and watch what they put into their sculptured bodies so they can produce big offensive numbers that pay off in salary arbitration and free agency. A major league locker room looks like Muir Woods—a lot of towering redwoods. When people say the ball must be different because even itsy-bitsy players are crushing home runs, remember: Itsy-bitsy is a relative concept. Willie Mays (5 feet 10½, 170) and Mickey Mantle (5 feet 11½, 195) would be little guys on today's teams, which are chock-full of players at least four inches taller and twenty pounds heavier. These Paul Bunyans need a livelier ball? They could hit Jell-O 400 feet.

Bulked-up batters whipping thin-handled bats produce terrific speeds of the batheads through the strike zone, or what is left of it. Disregard the rule book—umpires do. That book says the strike zone extends from the top of the knees to the midpoint between the top of the pants and the shoulders. But today any pitch above the belt is apt to be called a ball. Thus more pitchers are throwing more pitches, and are working behind in the count, and are getting hammered. And assaulted.

Lately there has been a lot of testosterone spilled on infields by batters who prove their manhood by charging the mound when pitchers have hit them or even thrown uncomfortably inside. Lots of pitchers are not skillful at pitching inside, not having done much of that when young. They grow up pitching to aluminum bats. Those bats don't break when the ball hits on the handle. In fact, aluminum bats can punch inside pitches over infields. So pitchers specialize in pitching outside. As fewer pitches come inside, more are left hanging over the middle of the plate. Furthermore, umpires are among Nature's conservatives: They want order, so they dislike pitchers coming inside. The result? More balls are being hit long distances.

And distances aren't what they were. The newer ballparks in Baltimore, Cleveland and Texas are hitter-friendly: The outfield fences are closer. These parks also are fan-friendly: Fans sit closer to the action, so there is less foul territory, so fewer pop fouls get caught, so batters get more swings. Also, this April was unusually warm in some places. And Ray Miller, the Pirates' pitching coach and my guide to baseball's deepest mysteries, says Houston may be keeping the temperature in the Astrodome higher. Everybody knows balls

Formerly made in Haiti.

246

fly farther when the air is warm. (How does everybody know this? Don't ask me. Or, in the words of Ring Lardner, "'Shut up,' he explained.")

Given all this, what of the Conspiracy-to-Juice Theory? Many conspiracy theories, like those surrounding the assassination of President Kennedy, are insulated from reality by a mind-bending idea: An utter lack of evidence for a conspiracy proves how diabolically vast and clever the conspiracy was. But most conspiracy theories can be dissolved by a cold splash of common sense. Consider the theory that JFK was killed by a conspiracy involving the FBI, CIA, military, Secret Service, etc. That theory assumes that our government, the one that can barely deliver the mail and can't abolish the World War I–era helium reserve (it was for blimps), can bring off a conspiracy of exquisite complexity in perfect and perpetual secrecy.

Now, if today's baseball has been tampered with, that must have been ordered by conspiring owners. But they can't agree on *anything*. And they have been fined $280 million for their last conspiracy—collusion against free agents in the 1980s, a conspiracy that was about as secret as a steam calliope.

Here's a thought. Perhaps hitters are thriving because, for no big reason, we are going through a bad patch of pitching—the reverse of 1968. In 1968 pitching was so dominant that the highest American League player's average was .301, the Yankees batted .214 and 21 percent of all games were shutouts. But no one then suggested that the ball had been deadened. Instead, the pitcher's mound was shaved from 15 inches to 10, five teams moved their fences in and hitting revived.

Peter Gammons, who knows everything worth knowing about baseball, which is almost everything worth knowing, says that almost 30 percent of the pitchers on major league rosters in April had been released by a team at some point in their careers. See, you'd know this stuff if you would quit watching MacNeil-Lehrer and Brokaw and that bunch and instead tuned in ESPN's "Sportscenter" every evening like the rest of us who are abreast of current controversies.

Tony Gwynn,
Union Man

August 22, 1994

Tony Gwynn, baseball's best pure hitter today, stood in the Padres' dugout in San Diego listening to a friend talk about Ted Williams. The friend said that when Williams hit .388 in 1957, his thirty-eight-year-old legs probably cost him at least the five hits that would have given him a .400 average. Gwynn replied that his own sore knee—it has been drained three times this season—has already cost him at least six hits.

If so, he would have been hitting .408 when the strike began. Even playing with that knee, and in a lineup so weak opponents pitch around him, Gwynn is hitting .394. Only the strike stands between Gwynn and pursuit of baseball's most magical number. No one has hit .400 since Williams' .406 fifty-three years ago. No one has even hit .390 since George Brett in 1980. Gwynn (whose average between July 1, 1993, and June 30, 1994, was .399) could mesmerize the nation this September. He knows how much immortality as well as salary he stands to lose from the strike, but he loses no sleep over standing with his union. He remembers Walla Walla, Washington, in 1981. He was a minor leaguer fresh from college when that summer's fifty-day strike began and the Padres' manager, Frank Howard, a former player, came to see him. Gwynn asked what the strike was about. Howard said, "Son, it's about people trying to make things better for young guys like you."

Ballplayers are not natural trade unionists. Temperamentally, they are individualists. They play the most individualistic of team games—it revolves around a one-on-one struggle between pitcher and hitter—and they rise or fall on their own performances. So how did they acquire such solidarity? By experiencing the owners' unchecked power before the players' right of free agency was firmly established. It is a story told in John Helyar's book *Lords of the Realm.*

Jimmie Foxx and Lou Gehrig won triple crowns (home run, RBI and batting championships) and yet had to battle pay cuts. Ralph Kiner's pay was *cut* 25 percent after he led the league in home runs in 1952 for the seventh consecutive season. So it was when players were chattel, until 1976.

Baseball has too many such memories, and too little institutional memory. Eight of today's twenty-eight owners have come to the game since 1990, eleven others since 1980. Today the owners, who have been warning of bankruptcy constantly during baseball's twenty-five-year boom, say nineteen teams are losing money. Or fourteen. Or twelve. The players do not trust the owners to portray the problem honestly, and refuse to be required to solve the problem, whatever it is.

Tony Gwynn, baseball's best pure hitter.

Players and owners agree that the industry's revenues are not optimally distributed, principally because of huge disparities in local broadcast revenues. There agreement ends, and today's trouble begins. The trouble is less between the owners and the players than between the small- and large-market owners. The large-market owners will not increase revenue sharing sufficiently to ensure the long-term viability of baseball in markets like Milwaukee and Pittsburgh, and will not agree to increased revenue sharing that the players do not largely pay for.

The owners reopened the collective bargaining agreement a year early, then took 554 days to produce a proposal. It involved only a modest increase in revenue sharing among the clubs, and made even that contingent on the players' accepting an old idea, a salary cap. Players say a cap would have four baneful effects. It would give owners an excuse for not fielding stronger teams. It would curtail competition for talent, limiting player mobility and making free agency a nullity. It would set the aggregate compensation of players below what compensation otherwise would be. (The owners talk of wanting only "cost certainty," but they would not want a cap unless they were certain it would mean lower labor costs.) And by linking the cap with revenue sharing, the owners want the players to recompense the big-market teams for the additional revenues they share with small-market teams. The cap is what owners mean by "partnership" with the players, who know a euphemism when they hear one.

They also know the owners are almost infallibly wrong in their gloomy forecasts. For example, the owners said free agency would ruin competitive balance: The best players would be signed by the rich teams in the biggest markets. Well. There are six teams in the three largest markets—New York, Los Angeles and Chicago. Of the thirty teams that have appeared in the last fifteen World Series, only four have been from those three cities. In these last fifteen years twenty-three different teams have won divisional titles, and a majority of the Series have been won by small-market teams from St. Louis, Baltimore, Pittsburgh, Minnesota (twice), Kansas City, Oakland and Cincinnati.

When a hitter is in a slump, friendly broadcasters say he is "overdue." The owners are overdue to be right about something, and perhaps they are concerning what they say is the parlous condition of some clubs. Bud Selig, struggling to keep his Brewers solvent in Milwaukee, is believable when he says his distress is severe, and he is right when he says that migrating franchises are not the best answer to such distress. Surely part of the answer is this: Large-market teams are not making money selling intrasquad games. They are selling Major League Baseball, which is a community that deserves to receive and distribute a larger share of the large-market revenues.

Meanwhile let us keep perspective. Back in what silly sentimentalists call baseball's good old days, the Boston Braves had to buy Henry Aaron on the installment plan because they could not scrape together the full $10,000 price asked by the Indianapolis Clowns of the Negro League. In the good old days the Yankees won twenty-two pennants in twenty-nine seasons (1936–64). The St. Louis Browns drew fewer fans in a season (1935) than Colorado's Rockies drew on April 9, 1993—82,227. Forty years ago the Browns became Baltimore's Orioles. This year the Orioles drew more fans in their first twenty-four games than the Browns drew in the entire decade of the 1930s (1.18 million).

Earth to baseball: The good old days were never nearly as good as today.

Now, while you are trying to get the numbers straight, let's get Gwynn back at bat, chasing the number .400.

THE 14 MILLION, AND THE 276 MILLION

September 4, 1994

THIS YEAR Major League Baseball's owners revamped the two leagues into three divisions, adding "wild card" teams to an extra round of postseason play, so more teams would play meaningful September games. Said one owner, "Before, in September, Michigan played Notre Dame and baseball was relegated to the back of the sports section."

The owners fixed that. This Saturday Notre Dame plays Michigan and baseball is not in even the back pages. It has disappeared.

Both owners and players are broadly disdained by fans who are increasingly disinclined to regard baseball as oxygen—essential. But fans, at first marginally partial to the owners' side, increasingly understand that the owners, or a controlling cabal of them, are the aggressors, demanding large changes in the status quo of baseball's compensation system, and that the players struck defensively to avoid unilateral imposition of changes by ownership.

The owners say their straitened circumstances justify demanding that players accept a "salary cap." But since the strike started the owners have been unable to agree among themselves about how many teams are losing money, or to argue plausibly that baseball as a whole is. Baseball's last expansion fee was $95 million per team, and will be higher next time. To speak as economists do, that sum represents the discounted present value of the anticipated profits stream, which can hardly be negative.

The players see the salary cap as injurious to a hard-won right, that of free agency. By striking, they are absorbing financial losses they will never recoup, in order to protect the future earnings of subsequent generations. The owners have overworked one pedal on their organ—the fact that the average major league salary is $1.2 million. But the median salary is $410,000, and because there are seven times more minor leaguers than major leaguers (the minor league minimum salary is $700 a month for a five-month season), the median salary of professional baseball players probably is less than $10,000 a year.

The owners, having waited until late to submit the provocative—and shopworn—salary cap idea, and having changed their internal rules to allow any eight owners to block a settlement, evidently want a long strike. But what then? Here's what.

This season and postseason probably are lost. Advertisers and fans are finding other interests. The off-season, with its trades and talk, is more important to baseball than to any other sport. It is called the "hot stove league" because it contributes to the conversation that is so central to the baseball fan's fun. This winter the stove will be stone cold. Baseball is completing its ruinous transformation into just another entertainment option. Note the word that is the root of the word "optional."

The national pastime is partaking of the national carelessness about the conservation of institutions. Baseball's travails are not as important as the abuses of, say, courts and universities, but they are illustrative of a generic frivolousness.

Columnist Leonard Koppett, one of baseball's wisest chroniclers, notes this attention-getting arithmetic: Assume, somewhat optimistically, that baseball sells 70 million tickets a year, and assume, conservatively, that the average customer makes five ballpark visits. That means 14 million North Americans actually go to games—and 276 million don't.

Some entertainment, such as major television programming, is of potential interest to the general population. Baseball isn't. It is supported by baseball fans, who are sustained by their sense that baseball is special. That sense is rooted in the feeling that although the sport is a business, it also is part of the rhythm of their lives and the fabric of their nation's history. This is why the involvement of baseball fans with their sport is different, in kind and intensity, from the involvement of people with professional football and basketball.

Bob Costas of NBC, who should be baseball's commissioner, understands. Baseball, he says, is a pastime, not a spectacle. You can watch an NFL or NBA game for the sheer self-contained spectacle. But in baseball, the sport with the most history and continuity, and in which both of those matter most, enjoyment is to a considerable extent contingent on that special kind of caring, which derives from the sense of the sport's specialness as an institution. (Speaking of continuity, Costas suggests, half-whimsically, letting the strike run to next August 12, and picking up the 1994 seasons then, with Matt Williams at 43 home runs and Tony Gwynn at .394.)

Baseball's connection with its fans has been remarkably durable, but is not indestructible. As Costas says, previous discontinuities have bruised the connection, but this one may rupture it.

BABE RUTH,
REPLACEMENT PLAYER

February 6, 1995

IF BABE RUTH were living he would be a hundred next Monday and might be a "replacement player" on April 2. That could be opening day of a Distinctly Not Major League Baseball season. The Bambino at one hundred would be a tad out of shape, but, then, he never was a martyr to strict training rules, even when he was rewriting the record books. "Ruth," writes biographer Robert Creamer, "was one of the great natural misbehavers of all time." Yet in 1935, five days before retiring, he hit home runs 712, 713 and 714, including the longest ever hit in Pittsburgh—the first ever hit over Forbes Field's right-field roof. A hundred-year-old Ruth probably could take Phil Niekro deep. The Braves reportedly were interested in Niekro as a replacement player. Niekro demurred. He is fifty-five.

Some of the guys playing slow-pitch softball for Edna's Bar & Grill may be heading for tryout camps. Hold 'em and they will come. The Blue Jays reportedly held three camps, saw more than 600 players, signed one—a pitcher whose Northern League ERA last year was a comical 7.71. Imagine watching has-beens and never-will-bes without even the consolation of cold beer. Will unionized truck drivers deliver the beer to games played by strikebreakers?

Ontario law forbids the hiring of replacement workers, so the Blue Jays might have to make a 162-game road trip. Canadian law bars the immigration of non-Canadian citizens as replacement workers, so Montreal's Expos might have to cobble together two teams, one of Canadians for home games, another of Americans and Latinos. And then there is the basic flaw in the replacement player idea: When, say, tractors are made by replacement workers, customers do not care, if the product is good. But in baseball the workers *are* the product.

Ruth, and the livelier ball, rejuvenated the game after the Black Sox scandal of the 1919 World Series. When Ruth reached the Red Sox at nineteen, in 1914, the baseball statistics published in Sunday newspapers included batting averages, sacrifices and stolen bases, but not home runs, which were not a significant part of the game. The American League leader that year, "Home Run" Baker, hit 9. In 1920 Ruth hit 54, more than any other American League *team* that year. Between 1926 and 1931 he averaged 51 a season. His appetites, like his talents, were prodigious, and suited him to the roaring twenties, when broadcasting, movies and the new arts of ballyhoo ushered in the age of celebrity. Furthermore, he was one of Nature's democrats, whether chatting up President Harding ("Hot as hell, ain't it, Prez?") or Marshal Foch ("I suppose you were in the war").

Back then, baseball had no serious competition for the title "national pastime." Today? Well, the California Avocado Commission says that on Super Bowl Sunday Americans scarfed down 8 million pounds of guacamole. Bill Plaschke of *The Los Angeles Times* notes that the average NFL regular-season game has a bigger television audience than baseball's postseason games. A Harris poll finds that 25 percent of respondents call NFL football their favorite sport. Baseball comes in a distant second with 11 percent. Baseball's demographics are ominous: Among young people, it is behind NBA basketball, too.

But baseball was back in a strong ascent last year, flourishing commercially (as measured by rising attendance and franchise values) and artistically. Indeed, history may conclude that baseball's long trajectory was at its apogee last August 12, when the strike began. The Padres' Tony Gwynn was flirting with .400. The Astros' Jeff Bagwell, the Giants' Matt Williams, the Mariners' Ken Griffey and the Braves' Greg Maddux were putting up numbers that could reasonably be called Ruthian. (Yes, Maddux is a pitcher. So was Ruth, of Cooperstown caliber, until his bat made him too valuable to play only every fourth day. Of all his records, the one of which he was most proud—it

Replacement players watch Texas Rangers' minor league coach Bump Wills.

lasted forty-three years, until Whitey Ford broke it—was pitching 29 consecutive scoreless World Series innings, one more than Christy Mathewson.)

Never mind the tangle of conflicts and animosities that produced the strike. Today the players believe—and many on management's side, including some owners, agree—that the minority of owners currently controlling baseball do not want a negotiated settlement. They want to feign an impasse, impose a new contract and break the union. (The only purpose of replacement players is to provide a setting for real players to abandon the union.) Having won in eight consecutive negotiations with the owners over a span of twenty-two years, the players have since August 12 made substantial concessions. They have agreed to the owners' demand for an end to the arbitration process that has ratcheted up salaries. They have agreed to the owners' idea for a "secondary" or "luxury" tax on all spending by teams over a level to be negotiated. Such a tax would penalize high-spending clubs, thereby exerting a drag on players' salaries. When the players proposed such a tax in December, the owners bolted from the negotiations. The owners seemed to understand that the two sides were now in the realm of splittable differences, and they had to hide to avoid reaching a settlement.

A strike always is a test of each side's capacity for absorbing pain. Both the players and the owners have proven themselves gluttons for punishment. But the game can take only so much. If the 1995 season is made ridiculous by beginning with replacement players, or if it is otherwise truncated or blemished, baseball will go from 1993 to 1996 without a proper season. If so, two of Major League Baseball's most attractive attributes, its continuity and its dignity, already much diminished, will be squandered. So will be the value of what the owners own. And the owners had better not count on baseball being rescued by another Babe Ruth. Nature is parsimonious of such prodigies.

Fortunately, there is plenty of talent in the game today, as real players will resume proving when the owners give them a chance. In the negotiations that resume this week, the players, whose professional ethic is maximum effort for maximum victory, must steel themselves to define victory as the making of merely modest concessions. And the moderate owners must tell their immoderate colleagues to learn to take "yes" for an answer.

THE STRIKE:
A POSTMORTEM

April 6, 1995

THE ANSWER IS: John Fishel. The question is: What California Angels replacement player was arrested in Arizona during—yes, during—a spring training game and charged with failure to pay child support?

Aside from such enrichments of baseball trivia quizzes, did any good come from the strike that cost the players $230 million in salaries, cost the owners $700 million in revenues, and will continue to reduce the revenues and status of the sport below what might have been were it not condemned to go from 1993 to 1996 without a full season? Actually, yes.

It is not true that the owners suffered yet another total shellacking from the players' union. The players have accepted the principle of a luxury tax—a tax on team payrolls over a certain threshold—to exert some drag on the growth of their salaries. The owners have acknowledged to each other the need for improved revenue sharing, largely to compensate for huge disparities between teams' local broadcast revenues. And there may be an end to the imprudence of having an owner, Bud Selig, serve as commissioner—the imprudence compounded by the owner being from a low-revenue team, the Milwaukee Brewers.

The owners engineered the strike, and made sure it would be a long one. They fired Commissioner Fay Vincent, instituted rules by which any eight owners could block a settlement, reopened the contract a year early, waited 554 days to make a proposal—then proposed something the players had repeatedly and emphatically rejected before, a salary cap.

The owners have an unenviable record of misplaced certitude over the years. They wrongly thought radio and television broadcasts of games would kill attendance. They wrongly thought free agency for players would ruin competitive balance and fan loyalty. They wrongly thought they could get away with illegal collusion against free agency.

During this strike the owners were confident that a significant number of players would break ranks and come to spring training. Not a single player did. The owners thought that fielding teams of replacement players would put pressure on the real players. Actually, the implausibility of those teams put pressure on the owners. However, most of the owners would have opened the season with the travesty of replacement teams if the owners had not been wrong about what they could do under federal labor law.

The union, too, has been too confident about some judgments. The negotiations might have been less bitter if the union had not taken such a dark view of the dampening effect a luxury tax would have on competition for talent. The owners underestimated, again, the athletes' competitive passion for winning at the negotiation table as well as between the white lines. However, the players' union may have underestimated the owners' animal spirits. Even a luxury tax of 50 percent on spending over $44 million—the rate and threshold in the owners' last proposal—might have a negligible effect on the spending of owners who become convinced that they are just one player away from making the playoffs.

Last month the owners, taking time out from lamenting baseball's supposedly parlous financial condition, charged investors from Phoenix and Tampa-

St. Petersburg a total of $310 million for the privilege of entering the baseball business with expansion franchises. Obviously, the owners—the twenty-eight old ones and the two new ones—think baseball is a good investment. Yet the owners continue telling their customers, the fans, that their products, the players, are greedy and overpaid. The supposed evidence of the greed is that players have taken the salaries that owners have offered in competitive bidding for talent, and the fact that players have been reluctant to negotiate limits to such competition for their services.

But the players' strike contained a large ingredient of the opposite of greed—sacrifice for the benefit of strangers. Many players who struck absorbed financial losses they will never recoup. They did so to preserve a compensation system—a system won for them by the sacrifices of earlier strikers—many of the benefits of which will accrue to players who are not yet in the major leagues, or even professional baseball.

"I've never been able to afford one of those Gillette Sensor shavers," said a replacement pitcher for the Dodgers. "But I come here [to the Dodgers' spring training camp] and they got those things lying all over the bathroom for free. I'm telling you, the big leagues are unbelievable." Much of what has recently been said and done in baseball has been, in one way or another, unbelievable.

A GROWN-UP

September 3, 1995

BALTIMORE—When Jeff Yates began his thirteenth NFL season, a teammate with a flair for parsimony in explanations said, "The thing that's kept Jeff around is his longevity." What has kept Cal Ripken playing baseball without interruption since the middle of the Falklands War—May 30, 1982—is that since then he has never come to the ballpark on a day when the

The Orioles' shortstop shows up for work for the 2,131st consecutive time,
September 6, 1995.

Orioles had anyone who could play shortstop better than he can. Even if he didn't enjoy playing, which he does, he would do it anyway, every day, because that is what responsible grown-ups do: their jobs.

So, is it worrisome that many Americans think that what Ripken has done is exotic, even weird?

What he has done is work so regularly that on Wednesday he will cruise past Gehrig's record of 2,130 consecutive games, heading for 2,500 (in late April 1998, if you plan to be there) and beyond. Someone probably will surpass DiMaggio's 56-game hitting streak—an "unbreakable" record—before anyone comes close to breaking the one Ripken is writing. (The closest current streak is fewer than 240 games.)

People who don't know baseball as big leaguers experience it say: How lucky for Ripken that he was never hurt. Actually, he has been hurt every year, but not hurt enough to justify, in his mind, taking a day off. What defines Ripken is his definition of "enough."

The ball is hard and is thrown hard. The ground is hard and players throw themselves on it, hard. (In 1982 Rickey Henderson stole 130 bases and was caught stealing 42 times. Imagine throwing yourself 172 times from a car traveling 20 miles per hour.) Baseball is a game of severe torque on the torso and arms, and sudden explosive accelerations. In a season of 1,458 innings, hurts accumulate and players play with pains that would prevent many sedentary moralists from picking up their paper off the porch so they can read the sports section and complain about the character of today's players. Loud-mouths in the bleachers would not walk to the concession stand on knees that hurt as much as those that may be carrying the Padres' Tony Gwynn to his sixth batting title.

People who do not know Ripken wonder whether in recent years he has protected his streak by protecting himself. Such people should ask Terry Steinbach, the Oakland A's catcher.

On June 9, 1993, an A's pitcher hit Ripken, who was not amused, but neither was he theatrical. He did not glare at the mound or otherwise "share his feelings" like a Nineties Man. He trotted to first base and the next batter moved him to second, at which point Steinbach must have thought: "Please, Lord, don't let this next batter get a hit that produces a play at the plate."

The next batter singled to the right fielder, who came up throwing toward Steinbach, who had to look toward right while Ripken roared in on his left. There was a majestic collision. Steinbach held on to the ball. Ripken was out. But Steinbach had to be taken out of the game to recuperate from this meeting with a man more interested in winning that night's game than in breaking records.

Ripken runs the risk of being remembered more for his work ethic than for the quality of his work. That happened to Gehrig, who is considered a kind of machine, more remarkable for mere durability than for driving in at least 150 runs seven times (no one has driven in 150 even twice since 1940), hitting 23 grand slams and being one of just three players (the others are Ruth and Williams) who rank in the top fifteen in career home runs, RBIs and batting average.

For connoisseurs of the craft of baseball, Ripken's most memorable number is not 2,131 but 3. That is the number of errors he made in 1990 when he had 680 chances and set a major league fielding record of .996. From 1989 through 1994, when he had 4,243 fielding chances, Ripken made 58 errors, the lowest six-year total by an everyday shortstop in baseball history. Shortstop is the most exacting position in fair territory (give catchers their due) and Ripken's rival for the starting shortstop position on baseball's all-time team retired in 1917 (Honus Wagner).

Cal Ripken was born and bred in baseball—his father coached and managed in the minor and major leagues—and no one, player or manager, knows more about this game, about which there is so much to know. "Competence, indeed, was my chief admiration, then as now," said a Baltimorean who worked a few blocks from where Ripken does, "and next to competence I put what is called being a good soldier—that is, not whining." H. L. Mencken could have had Cal Ripken in mind.

Brett Butler,
Human Bunt

March 31, 1996

Vero Beach, Florida—It is one of the little civilities that soften life. At end-of-the-season high-school sports banquets, coaches always say something nice about everyone, even scrubs. But at Brett Butler's high-school baseball banquet in Libertyville, Illinois, this is what his coach said about him: Butler couldn't play for me and he thinks he's going to play for Arizona State.

Monday in Houston, Butler will dress in Dodger blue and play in his 2,075th major league game. It is opening day. Twenty-eight teams are unbeaten and it is possible to think that anything is possible, so in the spirit of the season, consider the unlikely career of a ballplayer's ballplayer.

Most of the men who make it to the big leagues these days are big—human home runs. Butler is a bunt—5 feet 10 inches, 160 pounds. At age thirty-eight he is entering his sixteenth season and if he plays a few more he will have put up numbers that should get him considered for Cooperstown. Not bad for someone who as a high-school freshman was 5 feet tall and weighed 89 pounds.

As a senior he wrestled at 119 pounds, then gained about 30 pounds in ten days for baseball. For little advantage. He was played sparingly. But having decided he was going to be a major league player, he decided to go to the university with the best baseball program, which in the mid-1970s was Arizona State.

At ASU, Butler and 207 other dreamers tried to get into the program as nonscholarship "walk-ons." Butler was one of eight the coaches kept. He played junior varsity his freshman year and was told that by his junior year he might get a scholarship. But he was out of money so he had to leave school.

Back in Illinois he was playing in a fall league when someone from Southeastern Oklahoma State saw him and urged the baseball coach there to give him a scholarship. When Butler arrived on campus the coach took one look at him and asked, "This is the guy you recommended—this little guy here?" That little guy became a two-time all-American. Still not getting respect, he was drafted by the Braves in the twenty-third round, as a favor to Southeastern's coach. In just two and a half years he went from A ball to the big leagues.

Of the approximately 14,600 people who have played in the big leagues since 1876, only 117 have got more hits than Butler's 2,243. If he plays two more seasons he will rank around 70th, ahead of such Hall of Famers as Pie Traynor and Mickey Mantle. A leadoff man, which is what Butler has been most of his career, is supposed to get to first base so the big guys can drive him in, and Butler has walked to first base 1,078 times. But he does not loiter at first. Only sixteen players in major league history have stolen more bases than Butler's 535.

Are you picking up the pattern here? Baseball since Babe Ruth and the end of the dead-ball era has featured power hitters producing runs in bunches. But Butler is a reminder of what elegant fun baseball can be when played 90 feet at a time.

He is left-handed so he starts a step closer to first base than right-handed hitters do. Still, it takes impressive skill to lead the league, as he did last year, in the production of what, to the untutored eye, seems unimpressive—43 infield hits, 19 of them on bunts. He once got 41 bunt hits in a season. He has 280 in his career. That is a season and a half worth of hits without swinging at the ball. He probably has about four seasons' worth of hits that never left the infield. But as baseball people say, in the box scores 100-foot four-hop hits are indistinguishable from frozen-rope line drives.

Recently after playing seven innings of an exhibition game here, Butler spent an hour work-

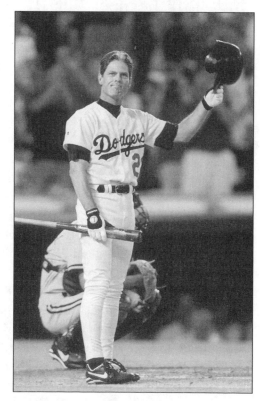

Brett Butler of the Los Angeles Dodgers at his first game since his cancer surgery, September 6, 1996.

ing out, part of the time on his back throwing a medicine ball up in the air. With that kind of dedication, you can make serious money hitting singles. Is this a great country or what? Short hits have brought him a long way from Libertyville, which must have had a heck of a high-school team that couldn't use him.

Butler missed part of the 1996 season because of cancer surgery, but played in 1997, his last season.

The Infield Fly Rule and the Absence of Chivalry

April 1, 1996

THE FIRST WORDS of the Bible are not, as some baseball fans think, "In the big inning . . ." But, then, to serious communicants in the Church of Baseball, the Bible is but one Good Book. Another is baseball's rule book, which begins problematically: "Baseball is a game between two teams of nine players each . . ." Oh? So the National League, pristinely without the tenth player, the designated hitter, is the last redoubt of real baseball? You can get an argument about that.

In prehistoric times (before June 19, 1846, when Alexander Cartwright organized the first game under rules recognizable as the antecedents of modern baseball), Tocqueville wrote, "An American does not know how to converse, but he argues." Small wonder litigation has become another national pastime. And baseball's rules, together with the interpretive Case Book, are rich in lessons about the rule of law, beginning with the fact that a law often exists to promote virtue: "The umpire shall not direct the attention of any person to the presence in the batter's box of an improper batter. This rule is designed to require constant vigilance by the players and managers of both teams."

Sometimes the external restraint of law is required because the internal restraint of morality is missing. A sportswriter once said that professional baseball is "agreeably free of chivalry." Which is why we have the infield fly rule. It begins with a definition: "An *infield fly* is a fair fly ball (not including a line drive nor an attempted bunt) which can be caught by an infielder with ordinary effort, when first and second, or first, second and third bases are occupied, before two are out." When the umpire signals "infield fly," the batter is out regardless of whether the ball is caught. This prevents infielders from letting the ball drop and getting a double play by making force-outs on the runners who must assume the ball will be caught and therefore cannot stray far from their bases.

Before the infield fly rule, the defense could benefit undeservedly—that is, not from skill and speed but from tricky exploitation of a loophole in baseball's laws. As was argued in 1975 in an analysis in the *University of Pennsylvania Law Review*, the infield fly rule's codification of fair play would not have been necessary had the attitude of the amateur, the gentleman, the sportsman—"the British cricket spirit"—prevailed in America. But, then, this would not *be* America if we did not think that the primary point of playing is not just exercise but victory. So there.

As a legal code becomes more complex, the need for Solomonic judgments becomes more common, as was demonstrated when George Brett of the Kansas City Royals hit the shot heard 'round the law reviews. On July 24, 1983, in Yankee Stadium, the Yankees were leading 4–3 with two outs in the top of the ninth when Brett, batting with a runner on, homered. Royals lead 5–4, right? Not so fast. Yankees manager Billy Martin averred, and the umpires confirmed, that Brett's bat had pine tar higher than the permissible 18 inches of handle. The rules say a batter

Home plate umpire Tim McClelland holds the bat used by George Brett to hit the "shot heard 'round the law reviews."

is out when he hits "an illegally batted ball," such as one hit by an illegal bat, such as a bat that does not conform to the rule about 18 inches of tar. The umpires said Brett was out and the game was over, a Yankee win. Brett went berserk and the controversy went to the American League's president, Lee MacPhail.

He, according to an exegesis in the *Fordham Law Review,* practiced what Aristotle called *epieikeia,* putting himself in the legislator's shoes, and applied the rule of lenity, which is that penal statutes are to be strictly construed against the government, which in this case means the umpires. Noting that the rule regarding illegal bats merely provides for banishing the bat from the game, MacPhail said it did not seem logical to add to the infraction the penalty of calling the batter out. Brett's home run counted, and later in the season the last four outs of the game were completed. Royals 5, Yankees 4.

Baseball, like the Republic, is a republic "of laws, not men." In theory. In fact, judges, and umpires, sometimes decide what the law is. Three years before being appointed to the Supreme Court, Charles Evans Hughes said, "We are under a Constitution, but the Constitution is what the judges say it is." So is the strike zone, which the rule book has redefined to bring into conformity with what umpires do.

The strike zone is what each umpire calls it, and that can vary with who is hitting (an umpire is particularly apt to call a pitch a ball if a great hitter like Tony Gwynn does not swing at it) or who is pitching (if a great pitcher like Greg Maddux comes close to the zone, the pitch is apt to be called a strike). But for years all umpires have been lowering the strike zone, rarely calling many strikes much above the batter's belt.

Time was, the zone extended from the batter's shoulders to his knees. Recently baseball's rule-writers tried to enlarge the strike zone by shrinking it. They shrank the zone as the rule book defines it by further lowering the top of the zone. They did this in the hope of enticing umpires to enlarge their strike zone by calling higher strikes—strikes above the belt—in conformity with the new definition. By 1995 the top of the zone was defined as "the midpoint between the top of the shoulders and the top of the uniform pants" (which National League instructions to umpires defined, indelicately, as "the nipple line") and the bottom of the zone was "at the top of the knees." The 1996 rules reflect another surrender to umpires. The top of the zone remains the same but the bottom is "at the hollow beneath the kneecap."

An architect said God is in the details. Umpires, like all judges, know the Devil is in the adjectives. Through them, law can be tantalizingly suggestive, as with the word "unwarranted" in this instruction to umpires: "A player guilty of an unwarranted attack on another player is subject to discipline . . ." Baseball's rules are practical and mostly prosaic, but in the elaborations there are flashes of poetry. The instructions to umpires include seven lyrical words to live by: "Keep your eye everlastingly on the ball." Some of us will do just that for the next seven months.

A SPLASH OF HISTORY
AS A CURE FOR NOSTALGIA

April 7, 1996

NOTHING CURES NOSTALGIA quicker than a splash of history, so:

Major League Baseball's supposed "Golden Age" was from 1903, the year the major leagues really got properly organized, to 1953, the era of stability that ended with the first franchise move in half a century, when Boston's Braves became Milwaukee's. In those years there was no team south of Washington or west of St. Louis, where in all of 1935 the Browns drew barely more fans (80,922) than the Colorado Rockies were to draw in the franchise's first game, in 1993 (80,227). The Rockies drew more fans in their first twenty-one games (1,226,450) than the Browns drew in the decade of the 1930s (1,184,076). In the strike-shortened 1995 season five teams drew more fans than the highest season attendance in the "Golden Age" (Cleveland's 2,620,627 in 1948). Teams from New York won 41 of the 102 possible pennants from 1903 through 1953 and 20 of the 50 World Series (which began in 1903, but did not occur in 1904), while Philadelphia's Phillies and Athletics finished last 35 times and were a combined 1,436 games under .500 in the "Golden Age." There was no major league night game until 1935, fifty-six years after Edison's invention of the incandescent lightbulb and fifty-five years after some people in Hull, Massachusetts, played the first game under electric lighting. The first radio broadcast of a major league game was in 1921, but as late as 1939 none of the three New York teams broadcasted any games. Players worked in such servitude that when in the 1930s the Yankees proposed that pitcher Lefty Gomez, a future Hall of Famer, take a pay cut from $20,000 to $7,500, Gomez, who had no rights other than the right to retire, joked, "You keep the salary and pay me the cut."

Yet it was in the century's first six decades that baseball came to be considered more than just an entertainment. It became the "national pastime." That status today seems perishable, even though baseball enjoys more prosperity and better competitive balance than ever. This puzzle has piqued the curiosity of a historian, G. Edward White, university professor and John B. Minor Professor of Law and History at the University of Virginia, whose many books include a study of John Marshall's Supreme Court and a biography of Oliver Wendell Holmes. In *Creating the National Pastime: Baseball Transforms Itself, 1903–1953,* White, an affectionate but agreeably dry-eyed student of the game, argues that baseball's evolution from a marginal urban sport to an institution with "special cultural resonance" was the result of many factors, many of them fortuitous, including what can be called (although White is too polite to call it this) the fortunate foolishness of many team owners.

"The long-nosed rooters are crazy whenever young [Buck] Herzog does anything noteworthy."

Professional baseball began in the nineteenth century as the rowdy amusement of the brawling working classes of growing cities. It was so tangled up with gambling and drinking that baseball's first task was to attract a better class of fans. This it did by raising ticket prices, banning beer, not playing on Sundays and giving free tickets to the clergy. Most important, baseball replaced wooden ballparks with permanent structures of concrete and steel such as Brooklyn's Ebbets Field, which opened in 1913 with a lobby like an opera house, featuring an Italian marble floor and a large chandelier. Changes in ballparks also reflected changes in how the game was played. In the dead-ball era before 1920, when in-the-stands home runs were rare, most of the action was in the infield, so there was less need for outfield seats, and spacious outfields provided opportunities for crowd-pleasing triples.

Baseball, Mr. White writes, grew up with America's cities, and its leisurely pace and outdoor and afternoon settings "invoked rural and pastoral associations that were particularly evocative to a generation of Americans confronting an increasingly urbanizing and industrializing environment." So baseball's rise to preeminence was served by the owners' "archaic conception of the game." However, that later made them resistant to desirable, indeed inevitable, changes and vulnerable to competition from professional sports less anchored in the past.

The National Agreement of 1903, which brought peace between the American and National Leagues, codified the rules that would govern baseball for the next seven decades. The most important was the reserve clause that bound a player to a club until the club traded or released him. The theory was that this "buyers' monopoly" of talent would depress the price of talent, maintain competitive balance and nurture fan loyalty by preventing player mobility. It did the first. But real competitive balance came to baseball only when the players overthrew the reserve clause, thereby establishing free agency. And there is no evidence that players having rights is inimical to fans' loyalty to franchises.

The American gentry withdrew from the gamy politics of the Gilded Age as urban bosses flourished. Baseball, played in social decorum in architectural settings in which cities could take pride, became, in the first two decades of this century, part of "the gentrification of American culture," of which Theodore Roosevelt's career was emblematic. However, Mr. White stresses the dangers that were to come from baseball's seeming "frozen in time."

Members of the baseball establishment thought nighttime ball was "unnatural." (Until they noticed that Cincinnati paid for its lights with the proceeds from the first two night games in 1935, and drew a third as many fans to that season's seven night games as it drew to the other sixty-seven games.) The owners thought mass transit was everything (some trolley companies helped build early ballparks) so parking was unnecessary. They saw radio, which turned out to be baseball's greatest means of promotion, as a threat. ("Our latest problem," in the glum words of baseball's "bible," *The Sporting News*.) They were slow to recognize that air travel undermined the rationale for baseball's territorial distribution of teams. (In 1950 Los Angeles, with a population of 1,970,358, had no team and St. Louis, with a population of 856,796, had two.)

And then there was the matter of race. White notes that in 1923 *The Sporting News* celebrated baseball's embodiment of democracy: "In a democratic, catholic, real American game like baseball, there has been no distinction raised except tacit understanding that a player of Ethiopian descent is ineligible. . . . The Mick, the Sheeny, the Wop, the Dutch and the Chink, the Cuban, the Indian, the Jap or the so-called Anglo-Saxon—his 'nationality' is never a matter of moment if he can pitch, hit, or field." Well, yes, a species of tolerance reigned, as in this from a 1908 report in *The Sporting News* concerning Charley "Buck" Herzog, a Giants rookie: "The long-nosed rooters are crazy whenever young Herzog does anything noteworthy. Cries of 'Herzog! Herzog! Goot poy, Herzog!' go up regularly, and there would be no let-up even if a million ham sandwiches suddenly fell among these believers in percentages and bargains."

Mr. White is unfailingly interesting about the influence of Hank Greenberg and Joe DiMaggio on American attitudes about ethnicity, or about the business culture of an industry in which competitors also are partners, or about the evolution of the relationship between major league teams and the journalists who cover them, or about the strange career of the blowhard Commissioner Kenesaw Mountain Landis. White's insights are frequently accompanied by fascinating facts, such as: Early in 1954, months before the Supreme Court handed down its school desegregation decision, the city council in Birmingham, Alabama, repealed the city's ban on interracial sports competition so that the Dodgers could play a spring training game there.

Mr. White disappoints only when, in his final chapter, "The Decline of the National Pastime," he suggests that baseball, by shedding many of its anachronistic features, has "engineered its own transition to ordinary status," becoming indistinguishable from other professional sports or, for that matter, other entertainment industries. Actually, baseball is consciously reacquiring some features, which are not anachronistic but retrospective.

Before opening day this year, Jacobs Field in Cleveland is nearly sold out for the season. This is one of the new old-style concrete-and-steel downtown parks which represent the rediscovery by Major League Baseball of the importance of ambience to the fans' experience.

Listen up: Professional football and basketball are extravagances. Baseball is a habit. The slowly rising crescendo of each game, the rhythm of the long season—these are the essentials and they are remarkably unchanged over nearly a century and a half. Of how many American institutions can that be said?

Sure, baseball is a business. But in the relationship between fans and baseball, as in other love affairs, realism need not mean the end of romance. G. Edward White might have mentioned that the reason baseball retains its hold on us is that it remains a remarkably lovely game.

HARD FEELINGS ALONG THE LOWER HUDSON RIVER

June 2, 1996

THIS COULD GET UGLY. Uglier. New Jersey and New York are at daggers drawn over bragging rights as the birthplace of baseball.

Some people think that is something to apologize for, not brag about. Remember the football fan who, told that the American hostages returned from Iran were given passes to major league parks, asked, "Haven't they suffered enough?" Still, the dispute poisoning relations along the lower Hudson River illuminates the problematic nature of our national fascination with pinpointing origins.

The fiercest skirmishing about baseball's birth is in the U.S. Senate, where the heat of passion often is inversely proportional to the gravity of the subject. Frank Lautenberg of New Jersey wants June 19 declared "National Baseball Day." His resolution originally was supported by New York's Pat Moynihan, who at that point was somewhat of a latitudinarian regarding baseball's provenance. Moynihan has since defected to the D'Amato insurgency.

Lautenberg says that 150 years ago on June 19 "baseball's first game was played." That is a bit strong, but as is said in Washington, it's true enough for government work. On June 19, 1846, a team of New Yorkers called the

Knickerbockers invited another team to play a game at Elysian Fields in Hoboken, New Jersey. Lautenberg does not explain how it was that those two teams, and many others, existed prior to baseball's "first game," but never mind.

Never mind that some historians say the Knickerbockers began playing in Madison Square in 1842. Or that Boston and New York versions of base ball—it was two words then—had for several decades been evolving from the British game of rounders. Or that the diary of a soldier at Valley Forge refers to a game of "base." The game Lautenberg calls "baseball's first," played under rules codified by Alexander Cartwright, was recognizably the antecedent of today's game—at least as recognizably antecedent of modern baseball as Cro-Magnon man is antecedent of thee and me.

On June 19, 1846, the bases were still not 90 feet apart, and for several decades pitchers stood 45 feet instead of 60 feet 6 inches from home plate, and threw underhand. Never mind. Who can object to giving Hoboken a claim to fame?

Al D'Amato, that's who. He, now joined by Moynihan, wants September 23 declared "National Baseball Heritage Day" because on that day in 1845 the Knickerbockers began playing regular games on a meadow in Manhattan's Murray Hill section. D'Amato's resolution begins with a bugle blast of New York chauvinism: "Whereas it is universally accepted that the idea of baseball was created by Abner Doubleday in 1839 in Cooperstown, New York, when Doubleday attempted to chase cows out of Elihu Phinney's cow pasture . . ."

Actually, Doubleday spent the summer of 1839 as a plebe at West Point, preparing for a military career that in 1893 earned him a handsome *New York Times* obituary that did not mention baseball. It was not until 1907 that a commission appointed by major league owners concocted the Doubleday story—what one historian

General Abner Doubleday.

calls baseball's myth of immaculate conception—on the basis of one letter from an elderly man who later died in an insane asylum.

Never mind. Moynihan breezily says, "Baseball was born in Cooperstown in 1839. The New York State Highway sign near Doubleday Field outside the Baseball Hall of Fame says so." So there.

Baseball is magnificently brazen about asserting origins. Candy Cummings' plaque in Cooperstown's Hall of Fame says: "Pitched first curveball in baseball history." In 1867. Real baseball fans just flat know that the seventh-inning stretch started because a 300-pound fan, President Taft, finding his seat confining, rose to stretch during one seventh inning, and fans rose out of respect, and have been rising in seventh innings ever since.

Precision about origins is appropriate in the national pastime of a nation that knows precisely when it got going: July 4, 1776. Not that there hasn't been a rhubarb about that. Lincoln at Gettysburg in 1863 made a point of pinpointing the nation's birth fourscore and seven years earlier, at the Declaration of Independence. He did so because some wily Confederates were arguing that the country came into existence in 1789, with the ratification of the Constitution, which was, they said, a compact among sovereign states that therefore retained a right to secede.

Lincoln had sound reasoning and, more important, the bigger army, so his view prevailed. It did so with the help of General Abner Doubleday, who, before he fought at Antietam, Fredericksburg and Gettysburg, fired the first shot in defense of Fort Sumter. So in a sense he really did start something. Just not something as important as baseball.

Explaining the Power Surge: Up from Oliver Stone

June 10, 1996

This year's power surge—high scores produced by barrages of home runs is making pitchers sad and is pleasing those fans who think slugging is a good thing and agree with Mae West that too much of a good thing is wonderful. However, it also is bringing out the Oliver Stone that sleeps, and should not be awakened, in many Americans.

In 1987, two American appetites—for conspiracy theories and populist rhetoric—combined to produce the idea of a scandal called Rawlingsgate. The thought was that the plutocratic owners in their unslakable avarice tried to spur attendance by secretly "juicing" the ole horsehide (which is made by Rawlings and has been covered by cowhide since 1975). In 1996 it seems that America is growing up: There is an agreeable scarcity of the Oliver Stoneish, "The-guy-on-the-grassy-knoll-did-it!" kind of suspicion occasioned by the fact that so many baseballs are caroming off and rocketing over outfield fences.

Granted, the owners are not indifferent to their customers' preferences. After the 1968 season, when pitchers were oppressively proficient (21 percent of all games were shutouts; the major league batting average was .237, the lowest ever; Carl Yastrzemski's .301 led the American League), the owners lopped five inches off the pitcher's mound and shrank the strike zone, and five teams moved their fences in.

Pitchers, who were cultivating the status of victims long before it became fashionable, saw this solicitude for fans as pure persecution. Granted, pitchers are paranoiacs. But as Freud said, even paranoiacs can have real enemies. Pitchers have three categories of enemies—owners, umpires and batters. Owners like scoring. Umpires have produced the incredible shrinking strike zone, so pitchers find themselves throwing more pitches, pitching behind in the count more often and pitching more often from the stretch, with runners on base. And batters have become behemoths.

Because of many factors, from better nutrition to antibiotics, Americans in general are becoming bigger and healthier. But batters are increasingly built like linebackers. The guy the Orioles have at shortstop—a position that used to be played by people with nicknames like Scooter and Pee Wee—is not only more durable than Lou Gehrig, he is bigger than Babe Ruth. The increased power of batters is, to a significant extent, because batters have discovered weight training and teams have hired strength coaches. Put these bulked-up batters in some of the new, more intimate ballparks, and put one of those parks in the thin air of Denver. Then don a hard hat before entering the outfield bleachers.

Not only are batters stronger than they used to be, pitchers' arms are less strong than they used to be, partly because childhood is not what it used to be. Time was, before childhood became overorganized, children had time to kill and many did so by playing baseball from dawn to dusk on the vacant lot down the block. They developed strong arms the only way such arms can be developed—by constant throwing. They grew up to furnish the major leagues with an abundance of what is now a scarcity—pitchers who could consistently throw 90-plus-mph fastballs. Today there are few vacant lots in the suburbs, where children, when they are not at home developing flaccid bodies and barren minds by playing Nintendo, spend too much time being driven to and from soccer or hockey or lacrosse practices. And by the time the few who become serious baseball players get to high school, the pitchers, confronted by aluminum bats, become defensive, throwing breaking balls, not fastballs.

Back in America's more rough-and-tumble past, when it was not considered a casus belli if a pitcher knocked down a batter in order to spread wholesome insecurity, and when the strike zone was bigger than a basketball (and, not coincidentally, when games were commonly forty-five minutes shorter than today's games), back then pitchers commonly pitched complete games and did so throwing fewer than a hundred pitches. This year, in one inning in Texas, Orioles pitchers (and an infielder pressed into service as a pitcher) threw ninety-nine pitches while sixteen Rangers scored. *Sports Illustrated*'s Tim Kurkjian notes that as of last Friday, teams in the American League (the league with the designated hitter and the most hitter-friendly parks) had scored 10 or more runs ninety-six times, and seven times a team had scored 10 runs and lost. Peter Gammons notes in *Baseball America* that no team's pitching staff has had a season ERA over 6.00 since the 1939 Browns, but as of Friday, the Tigers' ERA was 6.92. The major leagues are averaging 10.14 runs per game, the most since the 10.38 average in 1936, and not far behind the 11.1 average of the strange year of 1930, when the entire National League's batting average was .303.

And all this may be the relative calm before the real storm breaks. In 1998 two expansion teams, the Arizona Diamondbacks and the Tampa Bay Devil Rays, begin play. So baseball will need, but will not have, twenty more major league–caliber pitching arms. The record Roger Maris set in 1961, of 61 home runs in a season, has survived thirty-four seasons—longer than Ruth's 1927 record of 60 survived. Maris' record may be broken this year, and the new record may last only two years. Records are made to be broken, but perhaps not so promiscuously.

DRED SCOTT IN SPIKES

November 21, 1993

NEW YORK—Curt Flood, a 165-pound whippet of a center fielder, could outrun most fly balls but it took him twenty-four years to catch up to his 1969 Gold Glove award. His story is rich with lessons about courage, freedom and the conceit that we can predict freedom's consequences.

He had a career batting average of .293 in fifteen seasons, twelve with the Cardinals. But nothing so became him in baseball as his manner of leaving it. Although he played thirteen games with the 1971 Senators, he really left after the 1969 season when the Cardinals traded him to Philadelphia and he said hell no, I won't go.

Black ballplayers have done much to move freedom forward. In 1944, eleven years before Rosa Parks refused to move to the back of a bus in Montgomery, Alabama, a lieutenant in Texas faced a court-martial for a similar refusal on an Army bus: Lieutenant Jackie Robinson. A similar spiritedness made Flood help win for players the elemental right to negotiate with employers their terms of employment.

He was born in Houston in 1938 and played his way up through minor leagues in the South in the 1950s, before public accommodations were desegregated. He received food at the back door of restaurants that served his white teammates and he relieved himself behind the bus on the shoulder of the highway.

In the 1950s and 1960s pitchers were driven to distraction by black players such as Henry Aaron and Frank Robinson who played with an implacable intensity that suggested the controlled venting of indignation stored up during many minor league and spring training experiences in a South in transition. The Cardinals of the 1960s were fueled partly by the fierce pride of four black men who were taking out their anger on the ball and on opponents— Flood, Bill White (who would become president of the National League) and two Hall of Famers, Lou Brock and Bob Gibson, the take-no-prisoners pitcher who once drilled the ribs of a rookie (Steve Garvey) who had the impertinence to hit a long foul off him.

In the 1950s there was a lot of social learning going on in major league clubhouses, as whites and blacks, often in advance of the rest of the country, got used to getting along. There was, for example, the day a white teammate, who was Curt Flood's friend and Bob Gibson's friend, said to Gibson as he was about to leave the clubhouse, "There's a colored guy waiting for you."

"Oh," said Gibson, dryly, "which color is he?"

There was poetry and portent in the fact that Curt Flood's career blossomed in St. Louis, the city where Dred Scott had taken his case to court. In 1966 the Cardinals moved into a new stadium that is located just a long fungo from the courthouse

"I am pleased that God made my skin black, but I wish He had made it thicker."
Curt Flood.

where Scott, a slave, argued that he had lived on free soil and therefore should be free.

Talk about lighting a long fuse. That one led straight to four years of Civil War. Scott's case went all the way to the United States Supreme Court, which ruled against him and thereby against the strong-running tide of history. It was not the last time that the Supreme Court would blunder when asked whether a man can be treated like someone's property.

That is the question Curt Flood posed when the Cardinals tried to trade him. They said he had to go wherever they decided to send him. It had always been so, and always would be. He said, well, we'll just see about that. He rose in rebellion against the reserve clause that denied baseball players the fundamental right to negotiate terms of employment with whomever they choose. He lost the 1970 season and lost in the Supreme Court, but he had lit a fuse.

Six years later—too late to benefit him—his cause prevailed. The national pastime is clearly better because of that. But more important, so is the nation, because it has learned one more lesson about the foolishness of fearing freedom.

In 1975 the clause was overturned by an arbitrator. Loud were the lamentations predicting the end of baseball's competitive balance and a decline of attendance. Well.

The decade 1978–87 was the first in baseball history in which ten different teams won the World Series. Until 1990 there had been no "worst-to-first" volatility in this century—no team won a pennant the year after finishing last. The Twins and Braves did in 1991 and the Phillies did in 1993. The 1993 A's were the first team since 1915—the A's Philadelphia ancestors—to finish alone in last place the year after finishing first.

In 1993 the team with the worst attendance—the Padres with 1,375,432—drew more fans than the St. Louis Browns drew in the entire 1930s (1,184,076). The Orioles' lowest attendance for two consecutive regularly scheduled games was 83,307—more than the Browns (who became the Orioles in 1954) drew in all of 1935.

In 1954, the year Jacques Barzun wrote that anyone who would know America must know baseball, the average attendance was 13,000. This year the Padres averaged 17,191 and the major league average was 31,337. The Rockies drew 4,483,350, more people than live in Minnesota or thirty-one other states. Major league attendance was 70,257,938, more than the combined population of thirty-two states.

But no one last year bought a ticket to see an owner. Because of what Flood started, the players, who largely create baseball value, now receive their share of that value. In 1969 the players' average salary was $24,909. In 1993 it was $1.1 million, much more than Flood earned in his entire career.

It would be a disservice to Curt Flood's memory to honor him exclusively for what he did off the field. The lyrics of John Fogerty's song say, "Look at me, I can be, centerfield." Center field is not for the shrinking violets. It is a big place, a big responsibility, and when you run out of room you run into walls. And what was once said of another player could have been said of Curt Flood: Two-thirds of the Earth is covered by water and the rest was covered by Curt.

Beneath the strife and turmoil of the baseball business, the game—the craft—abides. It is a beautiful thing, the most elegant team sport. And few have ever matched the grace and craftsmanship Curt Flood brought to it as a player. However, none has matched what he did for the game as a citizen.

Rawlings Gold Gloves are awarded annually to the nine players in each league voted best defensively at their positions. Flood won in 1969, but in the turbulence of his rebellion he never collected his glove. He got it here last week at this year's award ceremony.

He once said, "I am pleased that God made my skin black, but I wish He had made it thicker." Friends of baseball, and of freedom, are pleased that He didn't.

LEYLAND IN TEAL

March 23, 1997

VIERA, FLORIDA—His spikes echoing in the concrete runway under the stands, Jim Leyland heads for the field, a fungo bat in one hand and a Marlboro in the other. He is basic baseball and what brought him here to the Florida Marlins training camp tells much about baseball today.

Build it and they will come? Developers seem to have built a ballpark here to attract not just fans but a town. A sign on the center-field fence says Viera is a neat place to live. But except for the ballpark, Viera is pretty much hypothetical. Well, first things first.

Which is fine with Leyland. Other baseball people consider him one of the premier managers, even though he is 12 games under .500 (851–863) in his eleven-year managerial career. He made his name wearing Pittsburgh black, but the ink was not black there, so today he is wearing Marlins teal.

The Pirates resemble what the Marlins were four seasons ago, an expansion team. Their twenty-five players will be paid a total of about $10 million this year, about $1 million less than the Giants' left fielder, Barry Bonds. Leyland will be paid about $1.5 million, more than the combined salaries of at least three of the Pirates' eight starting position players.

After last season, when the Marlins' attendance declined for the third consecutive season (to 1.6 million; the Rockies have already sold more than 3.4 million tickets for this season), Marlins ownership, which is rich, decided to build the team the new-fashioned way, and see if fans will come. The Marlins spent $89 million on multiyear contracts for six big-name free agents. However, Leyland, who was weary of scuffling for victories in Pittsburgh, baseball's Bangladesh, was the Marlins' biggest catch.

Baseball has finally figured out how much managers matter. Baseball is so hard to play, only a few players—Bonds, for one—can do everything. The rest can do some things, and a manager's job, in making out the day's lineup and during the game, is to have the right player in the right spot at the right time.

Like most of the best managers (recently Tony La Russa, Sparky Anderson, Whitey Herzog, Tom Kelly and others), Leyland wasn't much of a player—a .222 average and 4 home runs in six minor league seasons—so he had to use his head. And at Pittsburgh in the years of salary-shedding he learned how to wring maximum production from marginal players.

The Marlins' priciest free agent is a pitcher, Alex Fernandez, a Miami native. Before you come to his pages in the alphabetically arranged Marlins media guide, you encounter Luis Castillo from San Pedro de Macorís, Dominican Republic, a town that is to middle infielders what Saudi Arabia is to oil. The Marlins also have Felix Heredia, another Dominican; Livan Hernandez, a Cuban; Ralph Milliard, from Curaçao; Edgar Renteria, a Colombian; Devon White, born in Jamaica; Alex Delgado, a Venezuelan; and Hector Kuilan, from Puerto Rico.

Miami, of course, has a Latin accent, but so, increasingly, does Major League Baseball. Last season baseball's most common surname (11) was Martinez, the second most common (10) was Perez, the fifth most common (7) was Rodriguez. Baseball today owes much to the trail blazed by people named Aparicio, Clemente, Cepeda, Marichal and Carew.

Asia also is becoming an exporter to the major leagues, but no matter where players come from, the fundamental things apply, and the Marlins' fundamentals drill today is for base runners, practicing aggressive running when pitches are thrown in the dirt. Little things.

Jim Leyland celebrates the Marlins' victory in the 1997 World Series.

Like many modern managers, Leyland calls all his pitchers' throws to first base. Those "throw-overs" often are intended less to pick the runner off, or even to keep him close to the base, than to cause the runner to react in a way that might reveal his behavior when he is, or is not, planning to run. Leyland is paid to notice such small clues, and the other day he did.

An opposition base runner dug his left heel into the dirt when planning to steal on the next pitch. That means Leyland knows that man's habit and, perhaps by watching the other team's signals, he also knows its steal sign. "I want my guys to look like they're stealing on every pitch, because if you're playing someone like La Russa, and do one little thing different [when you are ready to steal], he's going to pitch out."

Who was the runner who dug in his heel? That is classified. I could tell you, but then I'd have to kill you.

ALOMAR IN CONTEXT

April 14, 1997

Roberto Alomar became a switch-hitter at the age of seven because his father, a major leaguer (he roomed with Henry Aaron), said that would help Roberto to be "an everyday player." Today Alomar, baseball's best second baseman, is giving new meaning to the phrase "everyday player." The Orioles' 1996 season was ended in mid-October by the Yankees (with an assist from an umpire's blown call on a catch by a kid in the right-field seats). By the first week of November Alomar, who earns $6 million a season from the Orioles, was playing winter ball back home in Puerto Rico for pocket change. He is baseball straight through. "Whenever I am done with this game, I am going to say, 'I played all those years and did not miss a chance to play.'"

When Alomar came to the Orioles, to play next to the then-shortstop Cal Ripken, Tony La Russa said that two of baseball's smartest players were now side by side. But to most fans Alomar is just the man who spit in the face of umpire John Hirschbeck. Alomar has repeatedly apologized for that inexcusable act, which happened this way:

In the first inning of a crucial late-September game—if the Orioles won they would go on to postseason play—Alomar took a pitch that was at least six inches outside and Hirschbeck called it strike three. Alomar protested and continued to complain as he went back to the dugout. The umpire followed, glaring at Alomar. Alomar, according to a player standing next to him, said two words that caused the umpire to eject him from the game. The words were: "Just play!" Alomar went ballistic and charged the umpire; he was pushed back by his manager, Davey Johnson, but not before Hirschbeck called Alomar a "motherfucker." In response to that epithet Alomar spit. That word, common in movies and on cable television, is an ingredient of the background buzz of vulgarity in an America that has defined decency down. But Alomar says, "I would advise everybody not to say that to Latin guys."

No baseball person condones what Alomar did. But many baseball people believe that baseball's biggest on-field problem is not the impulsive misbehavior of players in the heat of competition but the incompetence, confrontational surliness and premeditated misbehavior of some umpires. These factors threaten the integrity of the competition. Most players and managers are quick to affirm how good most umpires are. In today's ESPNized world their work is increasingly scrutinized from many television camera angles, and on replays, and they get things right, most of the time. (The Orioles' Brady Anderson recalls complaining about being called out on an attempted steal of second, then dashing up the tunnel behind the Camden Yards dugout to see the play on tape—players can check their at bats during a game—and seeing that he was six inches from the bag when tagged.) But there are some bush-league umpires, and there is no procedure for sending them where failing players are sent—back to the bushes. Furthermore, some umpires seem to be spoiling for fights.

This spring, when Mariners manager Lou Piniella asked an umpire not to chat with his rookie shortstop, the umpire ejected Piniella. And when a young shortstop asked an umpire to move a step or two left or right so the shortstop could see the batter better, the umpire glanced contemptuously over his shoulder at the shortstop and planted himself even more squarely in front of him. Some broadcasters believe that some umpires, displeased by coverage of their work, shorten between-inning breaks to disrupt broadcasts.

Fearing retaliation from the men in blue, nobody in baseball will say a critical syllable on the record. Many players and managers believe that American and National League umpires are different and that the Nationals are generally better. They call a bigger strike zone (although not as big as the rule book defines it), hustle more to be in position and keep a better grip on the game. However, one veteran of many seasons says: "If you question a ball-and-strike call of a National League umpire, the next pitch, if it's catchable, is a strike." Sometimes in both leagues a punitive call is communicated to a player in advance: "If you think that last call was bad, wait 'til you see the next one." And sometimes the punitive call is made with an emphasis clearly intended to provoke the player. Such behavior degrades a contest.

Part of the problem may be resentment arising from the widening disparities of players' and umpires' incomes. Another part is the declining professionalism of some players—arrogance, disrespect for the game and an inclination to blame their failures on umpires. Remember, it was a ballplayer to whom Ring Lardner gave the name Alibi Ike. Such a player, says one umpire, is a "chardon-

At their first meeting since the spitting incident, Roberto Alomar and John Hirschbeck shake hands.

nay." (Get it? A whiner.) And some teams (for example, the Orioles when managed by Earl Weaver) get a reputation for incessant complaining, a tactic intended to make umpires malleable in the late innings. Still, umpires are baseball's designated grown-ups and, like air-traffic controllers, are paid to handle pressure.

Some umpires, when wrong, admit it. Brady Anderson remembers an at bat late in a close game with the bases loaded, when the umpire called a low-and-outside pitch a strike. Even before Anderson could glance back at the umpire, the umpire said, "Yep, yep." Anderson, looking back, said: "Outside?" Umpire: "Yep."

What unites most players and umpires is affection for the game. Alomar talks with simple, unembarrassed love of "the smell of the ballpark—hot dogs, grass." He says, "This is what God chose me to do. He sent me here to play baseball." But Alomar is no stranger to the game's hard edges and ups and downs. He got his first major league hit in his first at bat, off Nolan Ryan, who was not amused. On Alomar's next at bat Ryan knocked him down. Alomar got back up and dug in, as he will do until he can't do it anymore.

THE ARGUMENT
AGAINST DEMOCRACY

July 3, 1997

QUESTION: *Should players select the All-Star rosters?*

Now here is a political question that should efficiently separate liberals from conservatives. It is a question first dealt with by Plato: What system for allocating offices and honors is most conducive to justice?

The liberal line states that pure democracy should prevail in All-Star balloting. Well, not exactly pure. Let's say Chicago-style democracy should prevail. The dead do not vote, Chicago-style, in All-Star balloting, but repeat voting is not just common, it is encouraged.

That is why in 1957, ballot stuffers of Cincinnati—how Mayor Daley must have admired them—voted seven Reds position players into the National League starting lineup. The only non-Red player elected was Stan Musial. So, Commissioner Ford C. Frick stepped in to purge two Reds.

The current system of mass voting gives an unfair leg up to players whose teams draw well, such as players for the Rockies. So a great player sentenced to play in the relatively empty caverns of, say, the Hubert H. Humphrey Metrodome, has a small home electorate through no fault of his own.

Now, real conservatives rather like the way popes are elected. It would be nice for a conclave of the cardinals of the Church of Baseball—perhaps elderly scouts and coaches and the like—to meet in private, pick a team and announce their decision with a puff of white smoke. Alas, that is impractical. So let the players do it.

They see and know things the rest of us do not about the game, and from them we would learn something more consequential than the whims of the multitude. Wouldn't the average fan like to know what American League players think about the relative merits of two young shortstops, Derek Jeter and Alex Rodriguez?

June 1957: Baseball Commissioner Ford Frick holds a press conference
to discuss the Cincinnati overload on the All-Star team.

I know my argument will be unavailing. So strong and undiscriminating
has been the democratic impulse since approximately July 14, 1789—the fall
of the Bastille—it is a bit late in the game to talk about contracting electorates.
But remember the iron law that obtains where electorates are concerned:
More means worse.

FANS TO OWNERS: "DOWN IN FRONT"

July 31, 1997

SAN DIEGO—Tony Gwynn, although having one of the better seasons in baseball history, recently endured a 5 for 28 minislump against sixteen pitchers during six games in six days in four time zones. (You think the achievements of earlier eras were somehow more impressive?) Then Gwynn used the fourth pitch he saw here at home to restore normality.

On a 2–1 count in the first inning, Pittsburgh's pitcher thought he would be safe if he kept the ball out of the strike zone. Silly him. Gwynn jerked a low-and-inside sinker into right field for a single. Gwynn swings at many pitches out of the strike zone "because I know I can handle them." He handled another pitch that night, producing his 47th multihit game in 96 games, the 826th of 2,042 games in his fifteen-year career.

At 6 P.M. the next night, ninety minutes before game time, he sits in the clubhouse, half-dressed in his game uniform and more than halfway through a workday that began with early-afternoon batting practice to correct the flaw that had driven his average down to a still-stratospheric .385. Reading the marks his feet made in the batter's box, he knew he had not been getting his front foot down properly. In fluent Gwynnspeak he explains that when his mechanics unravel, "my hands come forward too soon," "my upper body drifts forward," "my front foot floats. . . ."

Before he peels off his number 19 jersey this night he will have his 827th multihit game and hits 2,711 and 2,712. He started the season ranked 66th on the all-time career hit list. Any day now he will move past Lou Gehrig into 44th place, heading toward the 3,000-hit brotherhood.

In his clubhouse space this night is a pile of *Sports Illustrated*s, hot off the press with a cover photograph of him completing a swing, his eyes following the ball where he frequently flicks it, through the "5.5 hole," between third and short (the 5 and 6 positions, if you are keeping score). *SI*'s cover proclaims: "Baseball's Best Hitter Since Ted Williams." San Diegans, who know that if Gwynn played in New York he would be baseball's biggest star, think: "Nice of you to notice."

SI's Tom Verducci, a masterful sifter of statistics, notes that, measuring Gwynn's .339 career average against the .261 average of all major leaguers during his career, his differential of .0789 is the sixth best ever, behind Ty Cobb (.1029), Ted Williams, Rogers Hornsby, Nap Lajoie and Willie Keeler. Against the best pitcher of his era, Greg Maddux, Gwynn's career average is .459. Since 1995 he is hitting .425 with runners in scoring position. Can he become the first since Williams in 1941 to hit .400? The night the 1994 strike started Gwynn was an effortless 3 for 4, ending that truncated season at .394.

There is a paradox in the glittering performances of Gwynn and others. Maddux recently required just 78 pitches for a complete-game victory. The Mariners' Randy Johnson recently achieved history's second-best mark over a 50-decision span—44–6. The Yankees' brilliant twenty-three-year-old Derek Jeter may never be the American League's best shortstop, so gifted is the Mariners' twenty-two-year-old Alex Rodriguez. Baseball is unlike politics, education, popular culture and much else. Baseball is going against the grain of contemporary America by maintaining high quality. Yet some of baseball's owners are suffering a crisis of confidence in their product.

They are scrambling for gimmicks to entice customers who, these owners evidently think, cannot be attracted, as fans always have been, by what baseball alone among the professional sports has. Its unique advantage is more than a century of continuity that enables fans to savor Gwynn's greatness through meaningful comparisons with distant predecessors. These owners are threatening to rip the fabric of this most traditional sport by a stunning miscalculation.

Believing that this year's novelty of interleague play boosted attendance because of regional rivalries, they propose radical realignment of the teams, obliterating the identities of the National and American Leagues by creating geographic divisions. Here is one proposed division: Cubs, White Sox, Brewers, Twins, Cardinals, Royals, Rangers, Astros. With competition for the sports fans' dollar increasingly intense—the first NFL preseason game comes six weeks after the last NBA championship game—why does baseball contemplate jettisoning the traditionalism that makes it distinctive? Does it really want to become just another in the blur of constantly changing entertainment choices?

In baseball, unlike in, say, politics, it is not disheartening to compare the present and the past. Gwynn compares with Stan Musial more reassuringly than, say, President Clinton compares with President Truman, or Speaker Gingrich compares with Speaker Rayburn. So real fans, who understand how much the enjoyment of baseball derives from today's game being a linear extension of the game's past, should say to intrusive owners: "Down in front. Number 19 is on deck."

PURISTS VS. IMPURISTS

September 29, 1997

THE BALTIMORE ORIOLES played a night game at home two Sundays ago, and on the following Monday and Tuesday they played day-night doubleheaders (separate admissions for each game)—five games in fifty hours. Attendance for the five games was 220,183, not far behind what the Boston Braves drew in their entire 1952 season (281,278), the year before they decamped for Milwaukee, en route to Atlanta. Attendance on both Monday (88,712) and Tuesday (84,207) was more than the St. Louis Browns (who had been in Milwaukee until 1901 and who were to move to Baltimore in 1954) drew in the entire 1935 season (80,922). Put a good team in a pretty ballpark, people will come.

That is a concept the owners of the thirty teams (counting the Arizona Diamondbacks and Tampa Bay Devil Rays, coming next spring) might contemplate during breaks in their protracted deliberations about realignment. The idea of wholesale shuffling of the memberships of the two leagues suggests that the national pastime partakes of the national carelessness about the conservation of institutions, and of the national penchant for mismatching solutions to problems.

Baseball has serious organizational problems. Inadequate revenue sharing and huge disparities in local broadcast revenues produce today's situation, in which several players can have salaries larger than the payroll of the Pirates at the beginning of this season. Competitive balance is being jeopardized. Although attendance is still not back to the level of 1993 (the year before the most recent strike), it is beyond the dreams of baseball people just a generation ago. Yet most teams are losing money, and many owners seem to be mere conduits, passing money from fans and television contractors to players.

What would realignment do? Generate more money—maybe. But even if it did, baseball's structural imbalances would simply continue at a higher level of gross income. And realignment could cost money.

By forfeiting the century of tradition that is baseball's singular strength, realignment risks alienating the sport's base of support, the few million repeat customers who are buying a substantial portion of the approximately 63 million tickets that will be sold this season—10 million more than the NFL, NBA and NHL combined. When some owners suggested realigning fifteen teams, they claimed to have polls showing that "fans" favored that. But when the Cubs and Giants polled their season-ticket holders, they found, not surprisingly, strong opposition. (The Giants found 14 to 1 against.) Serious fans take tradition seriously.

The primary rationale for radical realignment is a highly dubious reading of the results of this season's interleague play. The assumption is: This year's interleague play was confined to regional rivalries (NL East against AL East, etc.) and stimulated attendance; therefore the higher attendance can be made permanent by concentrating most of each team's competition with regional rivals. Hence the original idea of putting the Cubs and White Sox in the same division, and likewise the Yankees and Mets.

But that would have meant that New Yorkers would have seen the realigned Expos, in town or on television, thirty-two times a season. Feel the excitement. Does baseball think it can simply decree new rivalries, as between, say, the Orioles and a new member of the American League, the Phillies? The Phillies are having a bad century—they are 1,439 games under .500 since 1900—and few fans want to see a lot more of them while seeing Ken Griffey Jr. and other West Coast stars a lot less. (Teams west of Detroit would come to Baltimore for one three-game series every four years.)

Interleague play has been enticing precisely because it involves carefully rationed contests between representatives of two leagues with distinctive heritages and current personalities. Radical realignment would turn a novelty into something ordinary. As regards regional rivalries, the Yankees and Red

Sox became storied rivals not because they are (sort of) near each other (not as near as the Yankees were to the Philadelphia Athletics), but because of a long tradition of competition. One of today's great rivalries is Yankees-Mariners. Over 100 years, Phillies-Pirates games have not been exceptional draws. Leonard Koppett, the Hall of Fame scribe, notes that when the Dodgers and Giants played each other in New York, the games were above-average draws only when at least one team was a contender. Today the Dodgers-Giants rivalry is hot, the Angels-A's rivalry is not. Regionalism alone does not guarantee great rivalries.

Perhaps one reason today's ownership group scants baseball's traditions is that the group is new. Once the sale of the Dodgers to Fox is consummated, Jerry McMorris of the expansion Rockies will be the senior owner in the NL West. In the last eleven years, nineteen of the twenty-eight teams playing this year have been sold. In those eleven years, the average career for a player now active who has played at least two years is 7.5 years. That is longer than the average tenure of the thirty owners whose teams will play next season.

Some owners stigmatize as "purists" all opponents of their most radical ideas. Surely those owners—do they wish to be known as impurists?—should credit fans for accepting considerable change. Until 1955 the westernmost team was in St. Louis. This year between June 4 and July 13 the Dodgers played thirty-six consecutive games in the Pacific time zone, thirty-four of them in California. Baseball is played on plastic grass, indoors and with "wild cards" that can make a mockery of a thrilling pennant race. (The Orioles and Yankees recently played eight September games to decide . . . who will play Cleveland and who will play Seattle in the playoffs.) Baseball's core constituency has been adaptable, but radical realignment, involving more than a few—say, five—teams, could break the ties that bind.

"THEM ARE THE BASES."

October 2, 1997

In 1962, at the New York Mets' first spring training, manager Casey Stengel took his ragged squad—it would lose 120 games that season—for a walk around the diamond. "Them are the bases," he explained.

Stengel sometimes muffed details, such as the name of his team. "It's a great honor for me to be joining the Knickerbockers," he said when announced as the Mets' manager. But he got basics right, as when he explained why the first player the Mets drafted was Hobie Landrith, an undistinguished catcher: "You have to have a catcher, because if you don't you're likely to have a lot of passed balls."

Baseball has recently been reacquiring a back-to-basics spirit, as with Camden Yards and the other intimate, baseball-only "retro" ballparks. About twenty-five years ago the general manager of the Cincinnati Reds wanted Riverfront Stadium—one of those ghastly concrete doughnuts built to accommodate both football and baseball—to smell like a bakery, so fans would be happy (and hungry). He was unable to find a satisfactory spray scent, which is just as well because ballparks like Riverfront do not need to be sprayed, they need to be dismantled.

Baseball's back-to-basics movement should be explained to Richie Phillips, the Philadelphia lawyer who speaks for the game's imperial judiciary, the umpires. As a crackerjack season reaches its postseason crescendo, baseball people are puzzling over a ukase issued by Phillips. He says umpires are oppressed and, having adopted at the beginning of the season a "low tolerance" policy toward what they consider on-field abuse, are now adopting "no tolerance."

He says players, managers, coaches and even trainers "physically assault umpires, spray tobacco in their faces, curse them and otherwise attempt to denigrate them and humiliate them." Certainly on-field relations have become increasingly confrontational, but this is partly because some umpires—including some whose language would occasion blushes below deck in a troop ship—have become intolerant of criticism, of their erratic and eccentric umpiring.

Phillips' grievances include "biased broadcasters" who are "second-guessing umpires, not only about judgment, but about things they know little or nothing about," including "mechanics, positioning and official rules." And Phillips says "networks continue to provide two-dimensional, contrived distortions to the viewers." People are second-guessing umpires? What a concept.

Granted, television can distort events. But umpires' work can be judged by using various camera angles. Most of their work is superb. Some of it is shoddy. And shoddy umpires, unlike failing players, are not sent back to the minor leagues.

Phillips should not raise the matter of rules because there is not an umpire in either league—not one—who administers baseball's most basic rule: who calls a strike zone as large as the one defined by the rule book. And it is not unusual for the dominant force in a game to be the home plate umpire. Stan Coveleski, who had a fine fourteen-season career, mostly in the 1920s with the Cleveland Indians, once pitched seven innings without a called ball. He was not pitching to anything like today's shrunken strike zone.

The disappearance of the high strike—of the upper third of the strike zone—has increased the number of pitches thrown, which is one reason games have become longer. On May 1, 1920, Brooklyn and Boston played to a 1–1 tie ended by darkness after twenty-six innings. The starting pitchers went the distance in the game, which lasted 3 hours and 50 minutes—about nine minutes an inning. This year the average game took 2 hours and 52 minutes, or about nineteen minutes

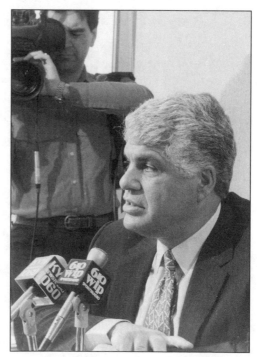

Richie Phillips, from "low tolerance" to "no tolerance."

an inning. In three World Series (1915, 1926, 1928) Grover Cleveland Alexander pitched four complete games averaging 1 hour and 58 minutes.

Change is a constant in baseball, so comparisons, although part of the fun, are problematic. Mark McGwire hit 58 home runs this year, as Jimmie Foxx did in 1932. Foxx was so strong he was said to have muscles in his hair—"He wasn't born, he was trapped," said Lefty Gomez, a pitcher. In 1932 Foxx hit nine shots that were kept in the Cleveland and St. Louis ballparks by fences that were not in place in 1927 when Babe Ruth hit his 60.

Baseball's hold on its fans' attention derives from the fact that what happens today invites comparison with a full century of competition. How strong can that hold be? In 1962 New York State abolished the death penalty, and the warden of Sing Sing said that when the news reached the twenty men on death row, "There was no reaction at all. They just kept listening to the ball game." They were listening to Stengel's Mets.

MILLER TIME

August 1997

IT IS FIVE-TWENTY on a Monday evening in July in San Diego and Jon Miller is dressed for radio. He is a sight that could curdle milk.

Miller is the play-by-play announcer of this Sunday's *Baseball Tonight* on ESPN telecasts, and at one time or another has been the radio voice of the Baltimore Orioles, Boston Red Sox and Texas Rangers. Furthermore, he has been a play-by-play announcer for the San Jose Earthquakes and Washington Diplomats soccer teams, and has honed his talent at swim meets, fast-pitch softball and something called broom ball, all in the city of Santa Rosa, California. But now, in his forty-sixth year, and in the midst of a broadcasting career nearly three decades long, he is above all else the radio voice of the San Francisco Giants. He performs that high office while dressed, from his shiny pate down to his unconfined feet, in a manner that might occasion adverse comments at even a broad-minded beach.

He is wearing sandals that are close kin to shower clogs, Bermuda shorts that have, or at least one hopes that have, seen better days, and a short-sleeved shirt, the print of which has, fortunately, faded, but unfortunately not enough. The shirttail is not tucked into the shorts, so Miller's barrel chest and ample girth takes on a draped look, like a statue before an unveiling. Or perhaps more like a sofa at a summer cottage that has been prepared for winter.

Gentlemen's Quarterly will not be doing a spread on Miller's radio

Jon Miller

wardrobe. Still, two words that describe him professionally are "tidy" and "elegant." He ranks right at the top of his profession, which means up there with Vin Scully. And Miller's story is a window on the world of baseball's supporting cast, which is not on the field but is part of the game.

Two hours before the Giants are to play the Padres, Miller is leaning on the doorjamb of the cramped, closet-sized room that serves as the visiting manager's office in the bowels of what once was called Jack Murphy Stadium. The stadium was named for a local sports columnist who was instrumental in getting San Diego awarded the Padres expansion franchise in 1969. In 1996 the Murph, as it was known, became Qualcomm Stadium, named for a corporation that ponied up $18 million for naming rights. Whirl is king in the world of today's sports. You can't identify the ball yards, let alone the ballplayers, without a scorecard.

The wonder is that Miller can tell what time zone, let alone what venue, he is in. On Saturday night the Giants played the Dodgers in Los Angeles. Miller got off the air at 10:45 P.M. and headed for the airport to catch a 12:15 A.M. flight to Atlanta for the Sunday evening ESPN game. At least he tried to head for LAX. He was in a rental car and the traffic leaving Chavez Ravine coagulated and he missed his flight. So he took a 1:35 A.M. flight, changing planes in Dallas, arriving in Atlanta at 10 A.M. In that night's game Atlanta blew a six-run lead, sending the game into extra innings. Miller got off the air at 11:30 P.M. Monday morning he caught an 8:55 A.M. nonstop arriving at 10 A.M. in San Diego, where his hotel room was, of course, not ready.

Never mind. Seasoned travelers are inured to such indignities, and often they have, as anodynes, on-the-road recreations. Miller enjoys rummaging around in small shops that specialize in artifacts from maritime history. While waiting for his room, Miller found a 1910 postcard from the old luxury liner *Mauritania.*

But enough play. Now to work, which at the moment means, for Miller, leaning there in the visiting manager's office, listening. In a few minutes he will tape the Giants' manager's show—a brief pregame conversation with Dusty Baker. As Miller leans and listens, Baker is in a recondite conversation with Dave Stewart, formerly a pitcher (he won 116 games in seven seasons, most of the wins coming with the Oakland A's). Stewart now is part of the Padres' front office. Baker and Stewart are talking in the sort of patois that specialists in any profession are apt to adopt, about some minor league pitchers. Listening to such shoptalk is for Miller a way of looking over baseball's horizon, and is part of his work. He is one of those fortunate few for whom there is a seamless continuity between work and play. His vocation is an extension of the form of play that filled his childhood from age eight on.

He was born at an Air Force base in Marin County, north of San Francisco. His father, whom he never knew, was an Air Force navigator who died in a noncombat accident during the Korean War. Miller was born October 11, 1951, a date he locates in the human drama as "eight days after Bobby Thomson's home run." One of the formative influences, and perhaps the decisive one, in young Jon's childhood was the man who was made famous nationally by his shouted repetition of five words when Thomson's fly ball settled into the left-field bleachers of New York's Polo Grounds: "The Giants win the pennant!"

Thomson's home run ended one of the most dramatic and famous games in baseball history, the third and final game of the playoff between the Giants and the Dodgers. In the billions of words spoken by baseball broadcasters, none are more famous than those five from Russ Hodges, the voice of the Giants in New York and for many years after their 1958 move to San Francisco.

Jon Miller became a fan at age eight, in 1960, the year the Giants moved into Candlestick Park. Back then, for almost all fans, almost all the time, baseball was still a radio experience, and a daytime experience. The Giants played night games only on Tuesdays and Fridays and they televised only the games they played in Los Angeles, so fans were connected to the team by Hodges and his partner, Lon Simmons (who in 1997 was seventy-three and substituted for Miller when he was discharging his ESPN duties).

In 1962 Miller's stepfather shelled out $2.50 for two reserved seats in the upper deck on the first-base side of Candlestick and Jon attended his first major league game. Does he remember who won? Are you kidding?

It was the Giants' first game of the season against the Dodgers. The Giants won 19–8 even though they only had 12 hits and the Dodgers had 15. The Dodgers made 3 errors. There were Giants home runs by Willie Mays (he would lead the league with 49 that year), Jim Davenport and Felipe Alou. Billy O'Dell pitched a complete game—a nifty 15-hitter—but he entered the ninth ahead 19–3 and the Giants had someone up in the bullpen before O'Dell got the twenty-seventh out. Stan Williams was the losing pitcher for the Dodgers, who walked 10. Attendance was 32,819. Miller remembers.

For a young fan, it was a vastly entertaining game, early in a crackerjack season that would end with the Giants of Mays, McCovey and Cepeda finishing in a dead heat with the Dodgers of Wills, Koufax and Drysdale and then winning the first and third games of a three-game playoff. "What if I had gone to a bad game?" Miller wonders, facetiously. Might his life have taken a different trajectory? Not likely. By 1962 his family lived in the hills of Hayward, across the bay from Candlestick, as the crow flies, and he could see the park from his house using a little telescope. At night he could see Candlestick's lights without a telescope. And there was the constant companionship of radio.

In the early 1960s Miller did not go to many games—usually only to doubleheaders, which meant when bad teams (such as the Cubs, Mets and Colt .45s, as the Astros then were called) were in town. But he passed many hours playing one of those tabletop baseball board games that used dice and statistics from the previous season to produce plausible big league games. As Miller played, usually against himself, he was both the public-address announcer and radio broadcaster.

In 1965 he bought a small reel-to-reel tape recorder to take to games to capture ballpark ambience—crowd noise, public-address announcer, vendors. He took it to the last game of the season, when Mays hit his fifty-second home run, which was saluted by Hodges with his trademark cry of "Tell it bye-bye baby—number fifty-two!" And what did Miller do during the long winter? He sat in front of the radio dubbing crowd noises from Candlestick onto tapes he made of his make-believe broadcasts of the then–San Francisco, now–Golden State Warriors basketball games.

After two years at the College of San Mateo he was offered a job in television, at channel 50 in Santa Rosa, about fifty miles north of the Golden Gate Bridge. Stan Atkinson, an anchor from KNBC in Los Angeles (where he worked with two rising stars, Tom Brokaw and Tom Snyder), had bought the station, which had an hour-long newscast every night. Miller was sports director. He was twenty years old.

The station found cheap programming in prime-time coverage of local sporting events—high-school football on Friday nights, junior-college football and basketball on Saturdays, auto racing, Arabian horse shows, swim meets, even broom ball. That last sport was played on ice supplied when a hockey fan from Minnesota—Charles Schulz, the creator of the "Peanuts" cartoon—moved to Santa Rosa and built an ice rink. Broom ball players wore tennis shoes and swatted a ball with brooms. (Think of it, if at all, as a sort of shuffleboard on ice, or hockey for pacifists, or degenerate curling. Miller thought of it as programming, period.)

Looking for programming a bit more glamorous than broom ball, Miller did a deal with Charlie Finley, who in addition to owning the Oakland A's owned the California Golden Seals of the National Hockey League. No one was televising the Seals, so Finley gave channel 50 the broadcasting rights. Miller would drive a truck down to the city, tape a game—he was doing major league hockey, such as it then was, as he turned twenty-one—and the station would air the tape the next night. It is a wonder the station managed to last even a year and a half before going broke in August 1973.

Unemployed at twenty-one, Miller took his tape recorder to Candlestick, sat in an empty section of the stands and made an audition tape of a Giants-Phillies game (which the Phillies won 5–4 when Bobby Bonds grounded out with the bases loaded in the ninth). He then sent copies to AAA minor league teams and to any major league teams that might be looking for broadcasters. But he got only one offer, from the Wichita Aeros, a Cubs farm team. Then fate, in the form of Charlie Finley's whim of iron, intervened.

After his A's won the 1973 World Series, Finley fired all his broadcasters, except for Monte Moore, to whom Miller sent his tape. Finley, recuperating at home from a heart attack, told Moore to play portions of four or five audition tapes for him over the phone. Moore told Finley he thought he would like the one from the young unknown, Miller. Finley, whose management style did not emphasize positive reinforcement of subordinates, listened, then said to Moore, "You were wrong about one thing. I didn't just like him. I liked him much better than I like you."

At age twenty-four Miller was hired for the 1974 season at $24,000 a year. It was a year-round job, and included selling advertising for the yearbook. He sold the back page to Jack in the Box. On such stepping-stones he has risen to his current glory.

He was looking forward to spring training at Mesa, Arizona, but there was one problem. As spring training began, the Athletics, who had just won two World Series, had neither a radio station nor a television station. Miller explains: "People didn't want to do business with Charlie." When Finley had moved the Athletics from Kansas City to Oakland, Senator Stuart Symington of Missouri had gone to the Senate floor to say, "The loss of the A's is more than recompensed by the pleasure of getting rid of Mr. Finley. Oakland is the luckiest city since Hiroshima." But Miller felt lucky to be Finley's employee.

On the day of the first exhibition game Finley phoned to tell Miller to fly to Arizona: A San Jose station agreed to carry the games on the simple understanding that any profits would be split with the club. This was how ramshackle some of baseball's neighborhoods were not long ago. It is hard to remember, but well to remember, that en route to their second consecutive World Series win in 1973, the A's drew just 840,000 at home. In the American League Championship Series that year the A's beat the Orioles, who had won their fifth division title in six years but had drawn only 910,000.

The A's opened their 1974 season, Miller's first as a big league broadcaster, against the Rangers in Arlington. Alvin Dark was the A's manager and Catfish Hunter was the starting pitcher. Reggie Jackson hit two home runs and when Miller tried to take him into the camera well for a postgame on-camera interview, Jackson sniffed the foul aroma of the several inches of standing water and balked: "Down *there*?" Then the little red light went on, the interview began and Jackson was the soul of geniality. Miller was on his way.

Except that two weeks before spring training the next year, he was unemployed.

At Chicago's winter Diamond Dinner, a baseball confabulation, Finley ran into Bob Waller, a White Sox broadcaster who had just been fired. Finley offered him Miller's job. Waller said: I'll think about it—let's have lunch. Finley, who wanted to make a splash at the dinner, said, No, it's now or never, so

I can make the announcement right now. Waller accepted. The *Chicago Tri-bune* reported the fact the next day and the *Oakland Tribune* called Miller for his reaction. That is how he found out that he was looking for work.

He looked in Cincinnati, where there was an opening. The team's sponsor, Hudepohl beer, wanted Ken Coleman. The television station wanted Miller. Beer was boss. So Miller became a soccer broadcaster at $150 a game for the San Jose Earthquakes. He also broadcast soccer for CBS. And basketball games of the University of the Pacific in Stockton and the University of San Francisco.

And Washington Diplomats soccer. He led something of a gypsy existence, and he rather liked it. The pay was not bad, and he did not even look for another job in baseball.

Then in the spring of 1978 the Rangers, whose lead broadcaster was ill, asked Miller to fly to Pompano Beach, Florida. There he broadcast the first two exhibition games as an audition for the Rangers' network. But before he did those broadcasts, the Rangers had decided to hire one of the Royals' broad-casters, who said he had no contract in Kansas City and would be interested in moving to Texas. So Miller went home. Then the Rangers called again, this time saying the Kansas City man had just used them to extort better terms from the Royals. The Rangers offered Miller the job and he was with Texas for the 1978 and 1979 seasons. Then he moved on to Boston to be the partner of the man who beat him out for the Cincinnati job, Ken Coleman. After three years in Boston, the station that had hired him lost the rights to the Red Sox games, and Miller was again looking for work.

He found it in Baltimore. "That was," he says, "the best thing I ever did."

The Orioles had been bought for $13 million in 1979 by Edward Bennett Williams, arguably the most admired lawyer in a town—Washington—where you cannot swing a fungo bat without hitting a lawyer, which is a good reason for swinging fungo bats. Until Williams' death from cancer in August 1988, he was an intense, involved, demanding owner, running the Orioles as he ran the Williams & Connolly law firm, impatiently insisting on excellence in all facets of the operation. Miller was one piece in the puzzle of producing a premier franchise and marketing it to the Chesapeake Bay region.

Before Williams owned the Orioles he owned Washington's football team, the Redskins, and he never quite got over the football mentality. Lose three early-season games in the NFL and life loses its savor. But the best team in baseball in any given year is apt to walk off the field beaten sixty-five times. Miller, repeating a saying once attached to Red Sox owner Tom Yawkey and applicable to lots of owners, recalls that Williams' idea of a good baseball game was one in which "the Orioles scored ten runs in the first inning and then slowly pulled away." Williams' idea of a good broadcaster, Miller recalls, was the Yankees' Phil Rizzuto, who was such a hometown rooter that when the news arrived, during a broadcast, that Pope Paul VI had died, he said, Holy cow, that would put a damper even on a Yankee win.

People who talk as much as sportscasters must are going to say some strange things, such as: "I don't think anywhere is there a symbiotic relationship between caddie and player like there is in golf." Or: "Anytime Detroit scores more than one hundred points and holds the other team below one hundred points, they almost always win." Because of baseball's intervals—between pitches, batters, innings—baseball announcers have ample time to trip up, as one did when broadcasting a Royals game in Kansas City, Missouri: "The sky is so clear today you can see all the way to Missouri." Verbal fender-benders happen all the time: "The Phillies scored two runs in the fourth, but the Braves countered with one run in the second." Or: "That was Benes' fifth strikeout on the day. He came in with ninety-four, so now he has one hundred and four strikeouts on the year." Or: "The Mets just had their first .500 or better April since July of 1992."

Because of Miller's professionalism, he has never added to baseball's considerable stock of such amusements. And Edward Bennett Williams would not have hired Miller if he were prone to verbal fender-benders. Williams was a sophisticate and he was marketing baseball to a sophisticated metropolitan area. Miller was what Williams was looking for: no trademark catchphrases, and a simple credo—"Speak good English and give good descriptions." Williams wanted a broadcaster whom fans would believe. He reasoned that when the team was going well, fans would not need to be coaxed to the ballpark, and when it was going badly and the broadcaster reported a silver lining, fans would trust him. Soon, Miller was part of a mix of ingredients that worked. Gone were the days when the Orioles did not even sell out playoff games.

In 1983, Miller's first season in the broadcast booth at Memorial Stadium, the Orioles beat the Phillies in a five-game World Series. Five years later the Orioles lost 12–0 on opening day and set a major league record by losing the first twenty-one games of the season. They lost 108 games that year, but radio ratings were better than in the season before. Getting good ratings for a good team is a piece of cake. Getting people to tune in to the struggles of a losing team requires a deft blend of journalism and evangelism, a triumph of hope over information. "We never sounded down, we didn't whine about it, didn't sound depressed," Miller recalls. "When there was excitement, we let people enjoy it."

Because even a good major league team loses about 40 percent of the time, a baseball fan's enjoyment on any given day cannot be contingent on winning. Hence the importance of the ambience—the experience—of the new-old parks like Camden Yards, and the importance of broadcasters who stress the integrity of the product more than the thrill of victory. Ask yourself: Why is there no generally recognized pantheon of great broadcasters who did, or do, football on radio? Surely the answer has to do with more than the fact that baseball broadcasters spend so much more time in the company, as it were, of their listeners. The answer must have something to do with the fact that baseball broadcasters' relationships with their listeners are colored by recurring disappointments and frustrations. It is a rare team that does not, over a span of even just three or four seasons, produce significant stretches in which the relationship between the broadcaster and the fan is predominantly one of shared melancholy.

In 1989 the Orioles came within a whisker—just a couple of pitches in Toronto in a season-ending three-game series—of winning the American League East. By then the Orioles had been bought, for $73 million, by Eli Jacobs, a businessman who oversaw the realization of Oriole Park at Camden Yards. By the time business reverses forced Jacobs to sell the team in 1993, the franchise was a hot commodity, attracting the interest of investors from out of town. Peter Angelos was not amused.

Angelos, like Williams, is a tough, gifted lawyer, an active Democrat and a fabulously successful self-made man. When Jacobs was forced to sell, Angelos, a son of East Baltimore, decided that the Orioles should be—*must* be—owned by a Baltimore resident. The sale went to an auction, the price went to $173 million and Angelos went to the owner's box.

He did not become successful by being bashful and he has not been deferential to professional baseball people. Regarding many things, from the signing of free agents to the making of trades to the mixing of the music played in the ballpark, he has had strong opinions and has acted on them. And has been right a lot. Over time, his feelings about Jon Miller's style—call it UnRizzuto—fell somewhat short of enthusiasm. His feelings crystallized during the Orioles' loss to the Yankees in 1996 in the five-game American League Championship Series. Angelos suffered like an ordinary fan and was dissatisfied that Miller did not seem to.

Now, as a friend of both Jon Miller and Peter Angelos (I am, and have been since the Williams era, an uncompensated member of the Orioles board of directors), I stress that there is a perennial, irresolvable tension in the craft of baseball broadcasting. On the one hand, the broadcaster is a journalist, reporting an ongoing story—that day's game and the unfolding season. But he does this on behalf of a team that is in the business of selling tickets and broadcast rights, hot dogs and hats. A broadcaster is important to a franchise because he makes fans. Miller knows this. Remembering Russ Hodges, he says, "A broadcaster turned me into a fan—taught me the game." And he asks rhetorically, "How many fans have Vin Scully and Harry Caray made over the years?" The answer is: a lot. Cardinal fans are still plentiful in Mississippi, Tennessee, Arkansas, Texas and Oklahoma because when St. Louis was Major League Baseball's westernmost outpost, KMOX's strong signal from St. Louis carried the voice of Caray, who had begun on "the Griesedieck Brothers [a beer, deceased] baseball network."

Angelos wanted a broadcaster who would bleed orange and black. After the 1996 ALCS, in which the Orioles lost to the Yankees, Miller's contract expired. Angelos felt that he was being unduly pressured by Miller's agent. Miller had in hand an offer from the Giants' owner, Peter Magowan, a passionate lifelong baseball fan. (He was at prep school at Groton with another baseball person, Peter Gammons.) Angelos decided to let Miller go west. And there he is, working for the only other big league team whose colors are orange and black.

But, back to that July night in San Diego—the Giants' starting pitcher is wild. "He just has no idea where the ball is going," says Miller, who is amusing, but not amused. He says that the catcher, diving to his left and right to prevent wild pitches, resembles a hockey goalie. And several pitches that are close enough to hit are hit to the Giants' third baseman,

"Tell it bye-bye, baby!" Broadcaster Russ Hodges.

who has several kinds of problems with them, problems that Miller blames, in part, on the stubbornness of the third baseman's resistance to coaches' recommendations that he use a bigger glove. The Giants have just lost three of four in Los Angeles, where, Miller reminds listeners, Giants batters were 1 for 18 with runners in scoring position. When a ball drops five feet in front of the Giants' right fielder, Miller reports, correctly, that it should have been caught.

A broadcaster goes to spring training with the team, and between the first of March and the end of September spends thousands of hours with the men whose performances he reports, and sometimes criticizes. He travels with them by plane and bus, stays in the same hotels. This involves an intimacy that, you might think, would be full of stress. Not so, says Miller, who can remember only one episode of awkwardness caused by remarks he made on the air. The episode, you will not be startled to learn, involved Charlie Finley and Reggie Jackson.

In a 1974 game he was broadcasting for the Athletics, the opposing team had a runner on second when the batter singled to right. Jackson fielded the ball and fired it to home—where there was no play at all. From the moment the ball was hit, it had been obvious that the runner would score from second. It had been so obvious that the Athletics did not even set up a cut off.

When a cut off is set up on a hit to right, the first baseman positions himself on the infield grass, in line between the right fielder and the catcher, and the second baseman loops around the runner and covers first base. There the second baseman is in position to receive a throw from the first baseman if the first baseman cuts off the right fielder's throw toward home. The batter rounding first must be wary of being picked off by the first baseman's redirecting the ball to the second baseman covering first.

On the 1974 play Miller remembers, because everyone on the Athletics—everyone except the right fielder—knew the runner would score from second, the first baseman was not in position to prevent the ball from going all the way to the catcher, so the batter did not pause rounding first and wound up at second. On the air Miller noted that Jackson had thrown to the wrong base, that he should have thrown to second, and had allowed the runner to advance.

Jackson's mistake did not matter because the next batter popped up for the third out. However, owner Finley was listening, and after the game he called Jackson with a lively rant: "My broadcaster says . . ." Finley's broadcaster had indeed said that Finley's twenty-two-year-old superstar had made a mistake. The next day Jackson spotted Miller in the lobby of the team's hotel and, adopting the manner of a revivalist preacher, began a parody of Finley's telephone call. Then Jackson explained to Miller why he had thrown to the wrong base.

You see, he said, Dick Green, the regular second baseman, was not playing, and Green usually keeps me in the game, giving me verbal cues to keep me thinking one play ahead. The second baseman that day had been Ted Kubiak, who was not so attentive to Jackson.

Oh, I see, Miller replied: "So if it happens again, I should say, 'Don't blame Reggie. Because if Dick Green is not in the game, Reggie has *no idea* where to throw the ball.'"

"That's not what I meant," Jackson replied. But he was mollified.

Miller is representative of the modern maturity of baseball broadcasting. His style is a far cry from the gush and syrup, the sentimentalism and romanticism of Grantland Rice and what has been called the "gargoyle school" of sports journalism. Reading today the most famous lead paragraphs in all of sportswriting, one can only cringe:

> "Outlined against a blue-gray October sky, the Four Horsemen rode again. In dramatic lore they are known as Famine, Pestilence, Destruction and Death. These are only aliases. Their real names are Stuhldreher, Miller, Crowley and Lay-

"One shudders to think."
Succinct, poetic Grantland Rice.

den. They formed the crest of the South Bend cyclone before which another fighting Army football team was swept over the precipice at the Polo Grounds yesterday afternoon as 55,000 spectators peered down on the bewildering panorama spread on the green plain below.

> "A cyclone can't be snared. It may be surrounded, but . . ."

Good grief.

Rice got into radio early. In 1922 he did the first live broadcast of a World Series game. Special transmitters had to be built to carry his voice the twenty miles from the Polo Grounds to WJZ in Newark. His biographer, Charles Fountain, writes that other New

York City radio stations went off the air during the game to minimize interference with Rice's voice being beamed from the Polo Grounds. It was hoped that WJZ's signal might reach to KDKA in Pittsburgh, which could pass it on west. The "reality fell somewhat short of that," but was impressive enough. Fountain writes that Rice's call of the game "was carried with stunning clarity over a three-hundred-mile radius, reaching an estimated one-and-a-half million people. In the history of the world to that point, no man had ever spoken to a larger audience." Broadcasting from a field box, gripping a handheld microphone and wearing earphones under his gray fedora, Rice, according to Fountain, "would wait until the play had concluded and then deliver a succinct, poetic report to his listeners." Poetic indeed. One shudders to think.

There are more reasons under the sun, and under the lights, to shudder than those that appeared in the gargoyle school of sports journalism. Miller, whose comic riffs can cause banquet audiences to laugh until their ribs squeak, says he once worked in Texas with a broadcaster who came to the park with a list of adjectives, verbs and nouns, and he would methodically work down the list, come what may, no matter what: "He swings and hits a nubber to left, it's off the wall on one bounce at the 390-foot mark. . . ." A 390-foot nubber?

In one game this broadcaster became bored by a pitcher's making a series of throws to first base to hold on the runner, Bump Wills. So the broadcaster began browsing though his sheet of statistics pertinent to the batter, Al Oliver. Suddenly the roar of the crowd brought the broadcaster back to the action, and he saw a runner breaking for second, rounding second and heading for third. On one of the throw-overs the pitcher had thrown the ball past the first baseman, down the right field line, and Wills was headed for third. But the broadcaster assumed Oliver had put the ball in play, and said: "Oliver rips the ball down the right field line, the ball caroms off the fence, Oliver rounds second and cruises into third with a stand-up triple. And now the next batter is"—here the broadcaster glanced down at the man standing next to the batter's box—"Al Oliver."

As Miller works, he keeps a detailed scorebook, using red ink pens for exceptional plays and defensive substitutions and pinch runners and pitchers who enter the game in the middle of an inning. He uses a blue ink pen for pinch hitters and relief pitchers who start an inning. He is constantly transmitting and storing the data generated by the game. Respect for listeners begins with respect for the data, and involves steering clear of mythic figures outlined against blue-gray skies.

The craft of broadcasting baseball began on August 5, 1921, in a ground-level box at Pittsburgh's Forbes Field, when Harold Arlin broadcast a Pirates-Phillies game. When station KDKA had gone on the air the previous November, its primary purpose had been to sell radio receivers. Sports helped broadcasting enormously in the sports-crazed 1920s, the decade of Babe Ruth and Red Grange, Jack Dempsey and Bobby Jones and Bill Tilden. Writer William Mead notes that by the 1930s more families had radios than had cars, or even indoor plumbing. Because of radio, and then television, the goal of professional sports was no longer just a business of getting fans to the game, it involved getting the game to the fans. Of course, the baseball owners, who are usually the last to learn, were slow to recognize that radio, which would be their greatest promotional instrument, was not a menace to be resisted. But promoting the team does not include applying a coat of varnish to a bad game like the one the Giants played that July night in San Diego.

It is an August Wednesday, it is Philadelphia, and Miller is dressed for television. He is resplendent in a dark suit, a blue shirt with a glistening white collar and cuffs and a broad necktie shimmering with various phosphorescent colors. On the preceding Saturday he had flown from San Francisco to Cleveland, where he broadcast ESPN's Sunday night game. Monday morning he flew to Baltimore to visit with his family, which had not yet moved to San Francisco. Tuesday morning he flew to San Francisco to broadcast that evening's Giants game, after which he flew with the team to Philadelphia, getting to his hotel at about 3 A.M. Wednesday. This will be a baseball rarity, a one-game series, a makeup game for one rained out early in the summer.

This night Miller will broadcast the middle innings on radio and the rest of the game on television. But an hour and a half before game time he is sit-

San Francisco Giants' manager
Dusty Baker.

ting in Dusty Baker's office, waiting to tape the manager's pregame radio show. Baker is covering his lineup card with small notations and is muttering about some pitcher being "slow to the plate." Might be a good night to run.

If base runners are not too scarce. The Phillies' starter, Curt Schilling, needs just ten strikeouts to reach three hundred for the season. It is drizzling. Schilling was supposed to pitch the rained-out game they are making up. Miller tells listeners he feels like Bill Murray in the movie *Groundhog Day*, in which one day keeps repeating itself. But this is a memorable day. The Giants win and go into first place. It is beginning to look like September might produce better memories than the Giants had any right to expect after finishing last in the previous two seasons.

Miller's aspiration is to be connected in baseball's memory with the broadcasters who have been, almost as much as the players, the makers of memories for millions of fans. And memories are made of this:

It is September 17, the Giants are two games behind the first-place Dodgers, there are eleven games to go, and Candlestick Park—sorry, 3-Com Stadium at Candlestick Point—is jumping. It took San Franciscans a long time to believe that this year's team was not like its last-place predecessors, but now they are in the park and in full throat for the first game of a two-game series. The Giants, hoping the past is prologue, have Orlando Cepeda, who is celebrating his sixtieth birthday, throw out the first pitch. And Miller makes the usual announcement in an unusual way, playing a tape of Russ Hodges saying:

"Today's broadcast is authorized under broadcasting rights granted by the San Francisco Giants solely for the entertainment of our listening audience and any publication, rebroadcast or other use of the description and accounts of this game without the express written consent of the San Francisco Giants is prohibited."

"Thanks, Russ," says Miller, and the nostalgia continues, thanks to the umpires, or to the airline that lost their equipment. They are wearing borrowed scraps of equipment, and the home plate umpire is wearing the old balloon "mattress-style" chest protector, which Miller notes has not been used since Jerry Neudecker became the last American League umpire to use it, about twenty years ago. When the American League abandoned that style, any umpire using it was allowed to continue until he retired.

Miller can draw upon a huge fund of such knowledge because, as part of what he calls his "ongoing preparation," he tries "to read everything I can get my hands on" in the way of baseball books. Everything, including, for example, a book of eyewitness reports of all of Babe Ruth's sixty home runs in 1927. And a book on the memorable 1908 season, when the Cubs won ninety-nine games and still needed, in order to win the pennant, the blunder that gave the Giants' Fred Merkle the lasting nickname "Bonehead."

His day-to-day preparation includes several hours devoted to devouring the daily baseball reports in the San Francisco, Oakland, San Jose and Sacramento papers, and then firing up his laptop to check the last three days of baseball reporting from the city whose team is next on the Giants' schedule. That was how Miller learned that, the day before the Rockies came to San Francisco for a series in 1997, the Rockies had blown a lead in an interesting way. Don Baylor, the Rockies' manager, had pinch-hit for his pitcher, planning to bring in Bruce Ruffin in relief. But Ruffin had told the bullpen coach—and Baylor had not been told—that he was not up to pitching that day. There was something to ask about—Is Baylor angry? Is Ruffin hurt?—when standing around the batting cage two hours before game time.

The Internet is all very well, but freewheeling conversation is and ever will be the primary means of research in the baseball community. The appearance of a home plate umpire in the old-fashioned mattress-style chest protector sets Miller off on a conversational ramble that takes him to memories of a friend, Satch Davidson, a retired umpire, who not only preferred calling pitches from directly behind the catcher, but would call a "catcher's balk" if the catcher complicated this by not crouching "directly back of the plate." (You never heard of a catcher's balk? You can look it up in the rule book, section 4.03.)

From this recondite subject, Miller moves—as is often the case with a great conversationalist, it is not clear how the words flow as they do, but the result is delightful—to memories of manager Bobby Bragan and a pitcher he had on the Pirates, Dick Hall. One year Bragan put into practice a theory devised by Hall. Miller says Hall was "great with numbers" and figured out that for every spot a player was moved up in the lineup, he would get, on average, seventeen more plate appearances in a season. So if a manager moved his three, four and five hitters up to the one, two and three spots, each would get thirty-four more appearances a year, and the three best hitters would get one hundred and two extra appearances a season.

That, Miller notes, was for a 154-game season. In a 162-game season, each move up means eighteen extra appearances. In 1984 Cal Ripken and Eddie Murray played every inning of every game for the Orioles, Ripken always batting third, Murray always fourth. And at the end of the season Ripken had eighteen more plate appearances than Murray.

Miller's conversation, turning and turning in a widening gyre, turns to spring training and the wisdom of watching drills. He remembers watching the Orioles practicing rundowns and learning that as the Orioles teach the technique, it is the responsibility of the player without the ball to call for the ball, and that "he can't call for the ball too early," because the later he calls for it, the more chance there is that the runner will get by him or that the ball will hit the runner.

And there is the problem of a single to right with a runner on second and a cutoff set up. The Orioles taught that in deciding whether to have the first baseman cut off the throw from right field or let it go through to the catcher, let the first baseman decide—if he is extraordinary, such as Eddie Murray or Don Mattingly. Otherwise, watch the other team's third base coach. If he sends the runner around third, it probably is wise to cut off the throw and hold the other runner at first because, Miller says, "when a third base coach *at this level* waves a runner home, he's not often wrong."

Miller, marinated in baseball since he first heard Russ Hodges' voice beamed from across the bay, usually gets things right. More remarkable is the fact that he never seems jaded, not in San Diego in July, not in Philadelphia in August, and certainly not now, September 17, Giants against the Dodgers, baseball's most resonant rivalry.

Well, certainly the National League's. And it is a rivalry right up there with the Yankees–Red Sox. In the first inning Barry Bonds homers into the right field upper deck and the Giants go on to win 2–1. The next day they tie the Dodgers for first place by winning on a home run in the eleventh. During both games Miller, like players in a pennant race, turns his game up a notch. The cadence of his delivery has an urgent crispness; the substance of his reporting has an edginess grounded in telling details.

In game one, when the Giants' second baseman Jeff Kent is late covering first on a bunt, Miller is acidic: "Jeff Kent fell asleep. And that is the kind of mental mistake that can kill you in a pennant race. . . . Jeff Kent is just not thinking out there." Miller's reporting covers not only the eighteen players on the field but the four umpires as well: "That strike zone is starting to shrink now. I mean, that pitch was called a strike the first three innings or so." When plate umpire Bruce Froemming makes an unusually emphatic gesture—a strike-three kind of call—on a called strike two on the Dodgers' Todd Zeile, Miller says, "I think Froemming forgot what the count was."

In the second game, on September 18, when Zeile takes a called third strike in a crucial situation, Miller explains that "he must have been thinking that [Rod] Beck was going to throw him a splitter. That was right at the knees and, of course, a splitter at the knees dips out of the strike zone."

On both of those September days Miller's listeners heard a broadcast laced with Russ Hodges:

"The two-and-oh delivery and Mays sends another one. Tell it 'bye-bye baby!' Aaron doesn't even move. It's going far up into the center-field bleachers. Willie Mays has tied a record, four home runs in a game. County Stadium is going mad."

And:

"Jack Fisher, up to his neck in trouble, to face Willie McCovey. Winds and throws to the plate. McCovey swings—and it's bye-bye baby! A grand slam for Willie McCovey up into the right-field bleachers, and it's his ninth grand slam. And Willie McCovey, now he is the all-time Giant in grand-slam home runs."

With such echoes of a voice that triggered remembered happiness, Miller brought to fans the braided eras of Bay Area baseball.

There is a paradoxical aspect of baseball. It is the most observable of team sports: It is a game of many discrete, observable episodes, rather than a game of flowing action, like, say, basketball. And the players are spread out thinly across a large green field. Yet this observable sport was, to a significant extent, popularized by disembodied voices heard through a veil of static emerging from wooden boxes whose only visual components were illuminated dials and the warm glow—this was when electricity still implied heat and fire, before the cool silicon world—of vacuum tubes. It remains especially suited to that nonvisual medium.

This writer was born in 1941 in central Illinois, in Champaign, and grew up there, about midway between Chicago and St. Louis. In the late 1940s and early 1950s, when I was catching the benevolent virus that produces baseball fever, baseball was in the air. The large radio in the living room pulled from the air the voices of Burt Wilson (Cubs), Bob Elson (White Sox), Harry Caray (Cardinals), Buddy Blattner (Browns). There was no television in the Will household until I was in graduate school, in 1964, and I was like most people who became fans between 1920 and 1950: Major League Baseball existed only in "the interior stadium" of the imagination, nourished by radio.

The phrase "the interior stadium" is from Roger Angell's essay of that title. His subject is the "inner game—baseball in the mind," in "the permanent interior pictures" of memory. Baseball, Angell says, "is intensely remembered because only baseball is so intensely watched." But it also is intensely listened to. And the listening is a form of watching, of watching the interior pictures of the imagination.

During the 1981 players' strike, Angell wrote an essay titled "The Silence," in which he described his intense sense of "the loss of that murmurous little ribbon of baseball-by-radio." Radio, which can be with fans while they work or garden or cook or drive, is essential, Angell wrote, to the "riverlike flow of baseball." Radio gives baseball its "sense of cool depth and fluvial steadiness" until the season reaches "the estuary of October." Jon Miller works on that river, on the radio, the medium most suited to the everydayness, and any-whereness, that gives baseball its special sweet penetration of the lives of its adherents.

CONCLUSION

I‍N 1954 BASEBALL had just rounded second, as it were, and was streaking into the second half of this century, when it instituted a small but portentous change. A new ruling required players to take their gloves with them when they left the field for their turn at bat. Until the end of the 1953 season, players could, and many did, just toss their gloves on the grass at the end of a half-inning.

The new rule was reasonable. Why leave the field littered with things the ball could hit or a player could trip over? Still, the new rule meant the end of an agreeable old informality, and was a portent of the game's growth into something more orderly and businesslike than it had been. Another portent was the addition, in 1952, of a fourth umpire. Baseball was becoming *serious.*

Today, at the end of a century that began just as baseball was acquiring its recognizable modern shape, the game is rounding third and heading for home, and perhaps for a collision at the plate. In the century's tenth decade more fans are passing through the turnstiles than ever before—more than could have been imagined in 1950 or anticipated in 1975—and the caliber of the play they are seeing is, I believe, generally better than that of any earlier era. However, there hangs over baseball a lowering cloud of anxiety about the game's current connection to American society, and about the trajectory of the sport that in this century came to be called the national pastime.

In 1900 home plate was changed from a 12-inch square to today's five-sided plate 17 inches wide. Seven years earlier the pitcher's mound, which had been 50 feet from the plate, had been moved back 10 feet 6 inches. (The origin—here we go again—of this change, which was a boon to bunters because it moved one fielder back, is said to have been fear that the fastest pitcher of the day, Amos Rusie, "the Hoosier Thunderbolt," was going to kill someone.) The 1900 season was the last in which batters could foul off pitches with no penalty: No foul was a strike. In 1901 the National League, and in 1903 the American League, decreed that any foul ball not caught on the fly would be a strike before the batter had two strikes.

There. Baseball, at least as it is defined by the rule book, was pretty much as we know it today. However, baseball is a case study of the fact that although rules frame a game, just as laws frame a society, they do not—not by a long shot—fully describe it. Important changes in the way the game is played have, cumulatively, made baseball remarkably different from the turn-of-the-century game.

The most abrupt and dramatic change, effected in the span of a few seasons at the end of the century's second decade, separated what are called baseball's two "eras," those of the dead ball and the lively ball. The change is dramatically defined by offensive statistics, but one small measurement of the change is in a lovely fact about defense. Four times in his career—twice in 1914—center fielder Tris Speaker made unassisted double plays, catching a fly and tagging second. Granted, he played a remarkably shallow center field even by the standards of the dead-ball era (he was sometimes used to take a pitcher's throw on pickoff plays at second), but in the lively-ball era not even a Speaker could play shallow enough to be, at times, a fifth infielder.

The transitions between baseball's eras seem, in distant retrospect, tidier than they really were. Like transitions between geological eras, they seem less messy and more inevitable than they were. For example, before the lively-ball era settled into stability there was one season of such gaudy hitting achievements that it threatened to make a mockery of baseball's new age of offense.

It was the notoriously aberrant season of 1930, when something was done to the ball—there is no other plausible explanation—that discombobulated baseball's equilibrium between hitting and pitching. The core of the ball was more resilient; the seams on the ball were flatter, making it harder for pitchers to make breaking balls break sharply. As a result, in 1930 the Phillies' Chuck Klein batted .386, hit 40 home runs and drove in 170 runs—and did not lead the league in any of those categories. He finished second to the Cubs' Hack Wilson—he of the 18-inch neck and size 6 shoes—in the home run and RBI races (Wilson had 56 and 190 respectively) and third in batting behind the Giants' Bill Terry's .401 and the Dodgers' Babe Herman's .393. The Giants team batted .316. Nine teams batted over .300—something only one team (the 1950 Boston Red Sox) has done since 1937. The American League batted .288 and the National League batted .303. (How good a pitcher was the Philadelphia Athletics' Lefty Grove? In 1930, the year of living dangerously for pitchers, he won 28 games, lost only 5 and had an ERA of 2.54.) After the 1930 cannonading, however, the owners decided that offense is a good thing but that Mae West's axiom that "too much of a good thing is wonderful" was not a good guide in all things.

Since 1930, the ball has not been tampered with, at least not in a way that produced an avalanche of indisputable statistical proof of the tampering. Since 1930, the most aberrant year was 1968, when baseball's balance seemed to tilt away from hitters, toward pitchers. That year the major league batting average was .237, the lowest ever, including the days of the dead ball. The Yankees' team average was .214, worse—much worse—than the .240 that the 1962 Mets hit while losing 120 games. Carl Yastrzemski won the American League batting title with an embarrassing .301. Twenty-one percent of all games were shutouts. Bob Gibson's ERA was 1.12 as he went 22–9, allowing a total of 27 runs in his 9 losses. Denny McLain became the first pitcher since Dizzy Dean in 1934 to win 30 games (his record was 31–6), Juan Marichal (26–9) pitched 30 complete games and Don Drysdale pitched 58⅔rds scoreless innings. Why did this happen? No one really knows. To make sure it didn't happen again, baseball's lords shaved the maximum height of the pitcher's mound from 15 to 10 inches and five teams moved their fences in. In 1968 only one batter (Frank Howard) had 40 home runs. In 1969 seven did.

Aberrations like the 1930 and 1968 seasons may briefly contradict a trend. However, it often happens in life that aberrations, and reactions to them, actually certify long-term trends. So it has been with baseball's history, which does fall remarkably neatly into two eras. Still, three other changes have been almost as transforming in their effect as the changed ball was on how players play and managers manage. These changes are the evolution of gloves, the rise of the relief pitcher and the rediscovery of speed as an offensive weapon and the melding of that weapon with the "big bang" baseball of the period from the 1920s through the 1950s.

To fans filing past the glass cases displaying baseball artifacts at the Hall of Fame in Cooperstown, nothing is more striking than the primitive nature of the gloves of early times. And regarding gloves, "early times" extend to more recent periods than the days when gloves had to be taken off the field at the end of each half-inning. The mitts—they *were* more like children's mittens than like today's gloves—that shortstops like the Yankees' Phil Rizzuto and the Cardinals' Marty Marion used are mute testimony to the range and dexterity of those men, who actually had to *get to* more balls than today's infielders do. Wearing those virtually flat little "pancake" gloves, without the precisely engineered pockets and capacious webs of today's gloves, infielders before the 1960s could not confidently reach to spear a sharply hit grounder. And today's outfielders who pull a potential home run back onto the playing field with a "snowcone" catch are doing something marvelous, but something made possible by marvelous new equipment.

Better groundskeeping and, beginning in 1966, the use of artificial turf have also made fielding easier. But it is the evolution of gloves that has moved baseball far from the days when a team could win a pennant and the World Series with a shortstop who made 65 errors. That shortstop, who is in the Hall of Fame, was Rabbit Maranville of the 1914 Braves. As early as 1908 *The Spalding Guide* said, "It may be that no more .400 hitters are likely to be born. It is certain that all batting will have its limitations, with the gloves now used by fielders and their speed." But fielders had barely begun the practice, considered unmanly by earlier generations, of wearing gloves. And baseball writer Jim Kaplan notes that it was not until the 1930s that the major league fielding average edged up over .970. (In 1997 it was .981.)

Kaplan believes that the fielding prowess born of better equipment changed baseball from a contest between the batter and the fielders to a contest between the batter and the pitcher. That is, before the advent of better gloves, putting the ball in play was, if not half the battle, at least a good start. As Kaplan notes, until 1887 the pitcher was supposed to pitch "to the bat." He was an enabler, helping the batter put the ball in play, so fielding was where the drama was. And in the 1880s, one of every two runs was unearned. One mark of today's modern era of defensive proficiency is that there are more throwing errors than fielding errors.

This is not to say that equipment wholly accounts for, and devalues, achievements such as Curt Flood's 1966 season, in which he handled 396 chances without an error as the Cardinals' center fielder. It is only reasonable to judge players by the standards of their day, and in doing so we salute the professionalism of Pete Rose, who played at least 500 games at each of three infield positions (first base, second base, third base) and 1,300 games in the outfield, where he won Gold Gloves in 1969 and 1970. The man could play.

Actually, fielding has acquired a new glamour as fielders have acquired new equipment that facilitates leaping, diving, sliding, lunging catches. The turning point, at which defense began to rise in the estimation of fans, may have been the 1970 World Series, the first played partially on artificial turf, at Cincinnati's Riverfront Stadium. The Reds had some strong right-handed pull hitters, including Johnny Bench, Tony Perez and Lee May. But the Orioles had

Brooks Robinson, who had, as the saying goes, a field day. A bunch of them. By the time he was done breaking the back of Reds rallies and the hearts of Reds fans, a national television audience had learned the truth of the axiom— repeated by football and basketball coaches as well as baseball managers—that offense wins games but defense wins championships. (It is almost a shame that Robinson somewhat diverted attention from his defensive contributions by getting 9 hits—4 of them for extra bases—in 21 at bats.)

Another contributor to the rising status of the fielders' skills was the Cardinals' Ozzie Smith, whose athleticism and showmanship brought fans to ballparks, and to their feet. In 2001 he will join Brooks Robinson and Luis Aparicio in the select ranks of those who are in the Hall of Fame primarily because of their defensive skills. When the appropriate people come to their senses, the Pirates' second baseman Bill Mazeroski will join them.

Aparicio inherited the White Sox shortstop position from a fellow Venezuelan, Chico Carrasquel, who was a harbinger of a development that was to mean a striking improvement in baseball generally, but especially in fielding. Perhaps it is partly because they hone their skills on unmanicured playing fields. Perhaps it is a penchant for showmanship rooted in the Latin baseball culture, which was influenced by barnstorming teams from America's Negro Leagues, long before baseball was integrated. For whatever reasons, baseball is being steadily enriched by the source of talent to the south, and not just from the storied city of San Pedro de Macorís. On one day in April 1986 nine Dominicans played shortstop in the major leagues, and four of them were from that city.

Among the indices of large and irreversible changes in baseball are the records that, it can be said with certainty, will never be broken. Here is one: Three times in one month in 1903 "Iron Man" Joe McGinnity of the Giants started, finished and won both ends of a doubleheader. Here is another: Cy Young completed all but 64 of his 815 starts. That was then. This is now: In 1974 Mike Marshall, the first relief pitcher to win the Cy Young Award, pitched in 106 of the Dodgers' 162 games, including 13 consecutive games. And he appeared in all five World Series games.

The prominence of relief pitchers is arguably the biggest change in pitching since 1872, when the rulesmakers decided that pitchers would be allowed to snap their wrists. Real pitching began then, and the profession of pitching did not change all that much until after the Second World War, when relief pitching became a recognized job description. Before that, although complete games were much more common than they are now, many pitchers—

often starting pitchers—appeared in relief. And a few were relief specialists. Today relief pitching includes two kinds of specialists: "set-up" men who are bridges between starting pitchers and closers, and closers who usually come into games in the ninth inning in "save" situations.

Tony La Russa, manager of the White Sox and then the Athletics and now the Cardinals, once said that if he were starting a franchise from scratch, the first player he would look for would be the one who could get the last three outs of a game. He was speaking from long and fond experience with Dennis Eckersley, whom La Russa brought with him from Oakland to St. Louis. As Whitey Herzog memorably put it, "If you don't have outstanding relief pitching, you might as well piss on the fire and call in the dogs."

He would get no disagreement from Sparky Anderson, the only manager to win a World Series in each league and the only one to win more than 100 games in a season in each league. In 1975 Anderson, a.k.a. "Captain Hook," managed Cincinnati's "Big Red Machine." En route to a World Championship the Reds went 45 consecutive games without anyone pitching a complete game—and won 32 of them. In 1984 Anderson managed the Tigers, who went wire to wire in first place, from game 1 through game 162, and won 104 games. They finished first by 15 games—and had only 19 complete games.

Relievers began to get their due when the Yankees' Joe Page finished third in the 1949 MVP voting. (The Cy Young Awards for the outstanding pitchers in each league were not established until 1956, and through 1966 there was only one award for both leagues.) By present standards, Page's record was not impressive. In 1950 Jim Konstanty of the pennant-winning Phillies' "Whiz Kids" was named the National League's MVP. His record was impressive. The still-unsettled nature of the reliever's role was reflected in the fact that Phillies manager Eddie Sawyer chose Konstanty to start the first game of the World Series (which Konstanty lost, 1–0, to the Yankees' Vic Raschi). In 1959, before the role of closer had become sharply defined, the Pirates' Elroy Face pitched 93 innings and had a won-lost record of 18–1. The stars of today's bullpens have records like Randy Myers' with the 1996 Orioles: just 2 wins, only 3 losses, but 45 saves.

(A pitcher gets a save when he enters the game with the tying run on deck. On August 22, 1997, Eddie Gaillard of the Tigers got a save in a 16–1 game against the Brewers. Go figure.)

Relief pitching changes the way starters pitch—with more intensity, all the way through the lineup—and it changes the experience of hitting. It was easier for batters early in the century to face a worn-down starting pitcher a fourth or even fifth time late in the game than it is for contemporary batters to face a second pitcher in the seventh inning and then a third pitcher—fresh and sometimes a bit crazed; closers have to like high levels of stress—in the ninth.

(Or perhaps, come to think about it, earlier conditions were not easier for batters. Is it not possible that a starting pitcher with a good arm and a great head—yes, I am talking about Greg Maddux—has such success *because* he faces the same batters three or four times a game? A pitcher like Maddux messes with batters' minds. Such a pitcher influences batters' expectations and guesses by offering particular pitches in particular circumstances, and not offering others. As the game progresses, the pitcher knows that the next time through the batting order the batters' experiences in the game up to that point will be on their minds. A Maddux can find advantages in what batters think they have learned about him in their first two or three at bats in a game.)

The trend to specialization in pitching is part of baseball's general discovery that the division of labor, which makes for efficiencies in most walks of life, makes special sense in a sport in which left-handers and right-handers have such different uses. In 1982 the Orioles' right fielder put up numbers that some MVPs would envy—51 home runs and 164 RBIs. But that right fielder, the product of manager Earl Weaver's deft platooning, was a composite of Gary Roenicke, John Lowenstein and Benny Ayala. The role of relief pitching in the elevation of the quality of play is clear: Fans see more innings of top-quality pitching, and the craft of batting has become more demanding.

Speaking of unbreakable records: Ty Cobb stole home 54 times. Rickey Henderson, whose career stolen base total (1,231 through 1997) will endure for a *very* long time, has stolen home only 4 times. Lou Brock, whose career record of 938 steals Henderson broke, never stole home. But Babe Ruth stole home 10 times. The most steals of home since the Second World War was Jackie Robinson's 19. But 17 of Rod Carew's 353 steals were of home, and some baseball people think that is why stealing home is an almost vanished art.

Now more than ever before, baseball success correlates with ever-finer refinements of techniques, and with increasing attention to individuals' tendencies, strengths and weaknesses. Carew's success as a stealer of home concentrated some good baseball minds on making that practice rare to the point of extinction. Nowadays pitchers are better than pitchers generally used to be at holding runners on and quicker delivery of the ball to the plate from the set position (for example, using the slide-step in pitching with a runner on base who is a base-stealing threat). So the fact that there are a lot fewer steals of home illustrates a paradox of baseball statistics and records: The reason some aspects of baseball achievements are less impressive than they used to be is that other aspects are better.

This is a constant baseball dialectic: Improvements in skill A beget improvements in skill B that diminish the statistical impressiveness of skill A—until practitioners of skill A make adjustments and make a comeback. In this regard, baseball replicates an evolutionary dynamic in biology: As species come under attack from diseases, the species generate defenses against the diseases—and the diseases acquire new modes of attack. The strong—species and diseases—survive. Consider the role of speed in baseball's evolution, with special reference to base stealing.

Begin with another exercise in originitis. We really do know the origin of shin guards, or at least the origin of the tradition of major league catchers wearing them. Roger Bresnahan, the Giants' catcher in the first decade of the century, decided to protect his suffering shins. When he put on guards, he dealt a blow to base stealers (and bunters) because protected catchers could play closer to the plate. Hence they received pitches quicker (and got to bunts quicker), and could get the ball winging its way to the appropriate base quicker.

But, of course, the running game was not inhibited all that much by anything as minor as improvements in catchers' equipment, or by improvements in catchers, for that matter. In 1922 the Pirates' Max Carey stole 51 bases and was caught stealing just twice, both times on hit-and-run plays when the batters swung and missed. What eventually produced a precipitous decline in base stealing was the Ruthian revolution—the home run. Why risk one of your 27 outs trying to steal an extra 90 feet when the baserunner might trot home in front of a slugger?

The debate about the supremacy of the home run was effectively ended by the 1929 season, the first season in which the number of home runs exceeded the number of triples. (In 1997 there were 4,640 home runs and 883 triples.) Writer Jim Kaplan notes that Honus Wagner, Ty Cobb, Home Run Baker, Shoeless Joe Jackson, Tris Speaker, George Sisler and Sam Crawford all retired with more triples than home runs. In 1901 Crawford, then with Cincinnati, led the league with 16 home runs, but his 16 triples ranked him only fifth in the league. (He retired after the 1917 season and eighty years later his career total of 312 triples remains unsurpassed.)

The eclipse of the art of base stealing is illustrated by the career of Joe DiMaggio, who had superb baseball instincts—he is said to have never made a baserunning error—and was fast enough to cover Yankee Stadium's then-cavernous center field. But he never stole more than six bases in a season (four times in this century—twice in the 1990s—players have stolen that many in a game), and his total for a thirteen-season career—30—is only slightly more than the 26 that Rickey Henderson stole in the month of May in 1982. In 1954 the Giants and Indians won pennants, and each team stole just 30 bases. In 1958 the muscular Milwaukee Braves of Henry Aaron, Eddie Mathews, Wes Covington, Del Crandall and Joe Adcock won the pennant while stealing just 26 bases. But the next year the White Sox won the American League pennant with a very different sort of team (see the essay in this volume on baseball in the 1950s) and in 1962 Maury Wills stole 104 bases (getting caught stealing just 13 times). Baseball was rediscovering the running game. More to the point, it was on the way to Lou Brock, who in 1967 became the first player in history to hit as many as 20 home runs while stealing as many as 50 bases.

Baseball has benefited mightily from the distinctively modern mix that Brock represented. There is nothing wrong with the splash of color that home runs apply to baseball. However, there is a lot wrong with a monochromatic game, even if the color is scarlet. And too many hitters were willing to pay too high a price for the long ball. They were, in short, too much like Hank Greenberg, who in 1946 hit 44 home runs while batting just .277, making him the first player in the American League ever to hit 40 or more home runs while batting under .290. As writer John Holway says, slugging and hitting were beginning to diverge. Not for everyone, of course. The greatest hitter of the postwar era, Ted Williams, never had a 200-hit season (his highest total was 194 in 1949; he had only 185 hits when he batted .406 in 1941) because he was willing to walk to first base. And as recently as 1961 eight players hit 40 or more home runs (Roger Maris, Mickey Mantle, Norm Cash, Rocky Colavito, Willie Mays, Orlando Cepeda, Jim Gentile and Harmon Killebrew) and all but three (Maris, Colavito, Killebrew) batted over .300.

One blemish on contemporary baseball is the amount of striking out that hitters do in pursuit of home runs. Babe Ruth never struck out more than 93 times in a season. The Giants' Bobby Bonds struck out more than twice that often—189 times—in 1970. In 1997 eighty-three hitters struck out more than 93 times. Ruth's career total of 1,330 no longer ranks in the top twenty. One of the prettiest parts of one of the game's most elegant careers is this fact: Joe DiMaggio struck out only eight more times than he homered (369 to 361). In 1947 Johnny Mize tied Ralph Kiner for the home run title with 51 while striking out only 42 times. Even Kiner struck out only 81 times. To be fair to today's game, neither Barry Bonds nor Ken Griffey, Jr.—both of whom are far better players than Mize and Kiner were—strikes out excessively. Not

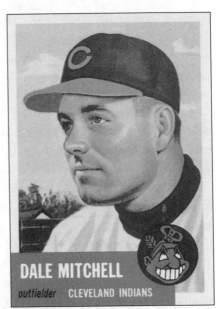

Dale Mitchell:
"Life is *really* unfair."

DALE MITCHELL
outfielder CLEVELAND INDIANS

Larry Walker hits his third home run of a game against the Montreal Expos.

since 1986, his first full season, has Bonds struck out more than 93 times (102), and Griffey has done so only once (104 in 1996).

(Life really is unfair. Dale Mitchell, whose career batting average over a distinguished eleven-year career was .312, struck out only 119 times in 3,984 at bats, but he is remembered for a strikeout—the last out of Don Larsen's perfect game in the 1956 World Series. Life is *really* unfair: The pitch was high and outside but the umpire, Babe Pinelli, evidently was eager to get the game over.)

Fortunately, contemporary baseball has room for the occasional player who reaches the highest levels of achievement without frequently reaching the bleachers. In 1972 Rod Carew became the first person to win a batting title with no home runs since Zack Wheat in 1918. Indeed, about 80 percent of his hits (all but 27 of the 170) were singles. And twenty-five years later Tony Gwynn won his fourth consecutive, and eighth overall, batting title with a .372 average, striking out just 28 times in a 220-hit season. So baseball still has aspects that Ty Cobb would have liked, had he had a knack for liking things.

It was difficult for events to make Cobb's disposition worse than Nature (and an unfortunate family life) had made it, but by 1925, when he was thirty-eight, he had a boiling disgust with the degradation, as he saw it, of baseball by Babe Ruth and the swing-from-the-heels batting that Ruth popularized. So on May 5 of that year, when the Tigers were in St. Louis, Cobb, who had never before hit more than 12 home runs in a season, said to some sportswriters, "Gentlemen, I would like for you to pay particular attention today because for the first time I will be deliberately going for home runs." He homered in the first, second and eighth innings. He also had a double and two singles, for 16 total bases, a record for a nine-inning game that survived until 1950, when Gil Hodges of the Dodgers hit four home runs and a single in a game. The next day Cobb hit two more home runs. Then, having convincingly made his point—that he could do pretty much what he wanted to do with a bat—he reverted to his kind of baseball.

In 1997 baseball showed both facets of its face at the end of the century. Between the white lines it sparkled with talents comparable to the best of earlier decades. But in the conduct of its affairs, and in the affections of the country, it was in a slump.

The performance of the Rockies' Larry Walker, who had one of the best seasons anyone has ever had, exemplified the balanced craftsmanship of the mature game. He hit .366 with 49 home runs and 130 RBIs. Before 1997, only thirteen players had achieved 400 total bases in a season. Walker's 409 were the most in the majors in fifty seasons, since Stan Musial's 429 in 1948.

Only nine players in history have topped that total. (Another reason why "Ruthian" is baseball's ultimate adjective: The record for total bases in a season is Ruth's 457 in 1921.) Four more hits and 11 more RBIs would have made Walker the National League's first Triple Crown winner in sixty years (since the Cardinals' Ducky Medwick in 1937). And Walker struck out only 90 times in 568 at bats. Only a season like Walker's could have kept the MVP award out of the hands of the Dodgers' Mike Piazza, who hit 40 home runs (the first Dodger to do so since Duke Snider in 1957) and whose average of .362 (actually .3615) missed by .0003 breaking the major league record for highest batting average by a catcher, Bill Dickey's .3617 in 1936.

Frank Thomas of the White Sox set a major league record by having his seventh season in which he hit .300 with at least 20 home runs, 100 RBIs, 100 runs and 100 walks. Marlins catcher Charles Johnson played 123 regular-season games without an error. The Blue Jays' Roger Clemens, who at age thirty-five was in what once was considered the sere and yellow leaf of a baseball life, was the first pitcher since 1945 (Hal Newhouser) to lead the American League in wins, ERA and strikeouts. It was Clemens' fifth ERA title and fourth strikeout title. (Sandy Koufax won that "pitcher's triple crown" in 1963, 1965 and 1966, and then retired at age thirty with an arthritic elbow. If he had been healthy he could have been a pretty good pitcher.) Tony Gwynn at age thirty-seven turned up his power enough to produce 17 home runs and 119 RBIs, both career highs. Baseball is beginning to be blasé about something notable, the pleasant fact of increasing productivity late in careers. Remember, Henry Aaron had his best year in 1971, hitting .327 with a career-high 47 home runs, when he was thirty-seven, the age Lou Gehrig was when he died.

In an earlier essay in this volume, written in the middle of the 1997 season, I wrote that the talent of the rising generation of players is so fine that Derek Jeter, the Yankees' superb young shortstop, might play twenty years and, because of the Mariners' Alex Rodriguez, never be the best shortstop in the American League. By the end of the 1997 season, it seemed possible that Jeter might never be considered the best shortstop in the American League's Eastern Division. This was because of the numbers put up by the Red Sox's Nomar Garciaparra, whose 209 hits helped him break the team's record for total bases by a rookie, a record set in 1939 by a kid named Williams.

So, one characteristic of baseball today is excellence. Another is turbulence.

The 1997 World Series was won by the Marlins, a franchise that began playing in 1993, and a team that was assembled—briefly rented, it turns out—for one season. Before the fans of south Florida could adequately savor

An embarassment of riches:
Shortstops Nomar Garciaparra
of the Boston Red Sox, Alex Rodriguez
of the Seattle Mariners and Derek Jeter
of the New York Yankees.

the Series victory—just a few days after the savory game seven—the disman-
tling of the team began. Before the 1997 season began, the Marlins spent $89
million in long-term contracts for free agents. It worked, and did not work.
They won the World Series but attendance rose only 600,000, to only 2.3
million, and they lost more money than any other team in an industry in
which most teams continued to lose money. Within a month of the Marlins'
Series victory it was clear that in 1998, for the first time ever, there would in
no meaningful sense be a defending champion: The 1997 Marlins would be
dispersed before the next opening day.

That was no great subtraction from baseball's supply of greatness. The
1997 Marlins were a team never far above mediocrity, but the team got hot at
the right time—late in the season, and in a season subsequent to baseball's
adoption of a multilayered playoff system that maximizes the chances for
mediocrity to suffice. The Marlins became the first wild-card team to win a
Series. In the regular season they did not just finish second in the National
League Eastern Division, they had only the *third*-best record in that division
against National League teams (that is, excluding interleague play). Well,
things could have been even more unsightly. As late as September 1997 it
seemed that the Houston Astros might win the National League Central
Division with a record under .500. (They won it with an 84–78 record.)
Someday something like that will happen and the people who administer
baseball (to the extent that there are such people) will wonder why the World
Series seems like something less than it used to be.

Less than two weeks after the 1997 World Series, voters said, in effect, an
emphatic "no" to spending public funds on new ballparks for the Minnesota
Twins and Pittsburgh Pirates. Baseball seemed to be approaching a new
period of franchise fluidity. In the 1880s franchises had been so evanescent
that the National League stopped listing its teams on its stationery. But after
that the Milwaukee Brewers moved to become the St. Louis Browns in 1902.
And why not? Missouri was the nation's fifth most populous state. It had sixteen congressional districts, seven more than it has today. Booming St. Louis,
the nation's fourth-largest city, was about to host the 1904 World's Fair. Then
as now, demography was destiny for baseball. However, after the Brewers'
rebirth as the Browns, Major League Baseball did not bend to charted demographic realities for fifty-one years.

That span of stability ended in 1953 when Milwaukee got back into the
big leagues by acquiring the Boston Braves. In 1954, not only were gloves
removed from the field during play, but the Browns became the Baltimore

Orioles. The most recent franchise shift occurred in 1972 when the second incarnation of the Washington Senators became the Texas Rangers. In 1961 the first incarnation had become the Twins, who by the end of 1997 seemed destined to decamp for North Carolina just as soon as baseball had a commitment from someone there to build a satisfactory ballpark. Ere long the sky may be darkened by flocks of migrating franchises. Even before their stadium was ruined to accommodate football's Raiders, it was clear that the Athletics could not long survive in Oakland. Are they headed for San Jose? Sacramento? Las Vegas? (The Athletics played some regular-season games in Las Vegas early in 1997, because work was in progress on the ruination of their Oakland facilities.) The Pirates and Expos seem likely to hemorrhage money and export talent as long as they stay where they are.

Furthermore, the demographics of baseball fandom are becoming increasingly ominous. Put bluntly, baseball's fan base is too old and too white. Anyone who regularly consorts with young people—say, those between twelve and twenty-five—knows that interest in sports has never been higher, and that interest in baseball runs a distant third to interest in the National Basketball Association and the National Football League. Time was, the "national pastime" thought it was unnecessary and, anyway, beneath its dignity to sell itself. But now there obviously is much marketing work for baseball to do. Fortunately, there is a favorable environment for it.

Various studies indicate astonishing levels of interest in sports among Americans generally. Huge majorities of Americans in every age cohort but the elderly express "strong" or "substantial" interest. We have come a long way from the America of President Calvin Coolidge, who thought that the Chicago Bears were an animal act, to the America of President George Bush, who worried about the intersection of the Gulf War and the Super Bowl. To Coolidge, the business of America was business. By the time Bush became president, the play of America was big business: It took 16 million avocados to make the guacamole consumed during the Super Bowl.

In terms of the number of people attending games, baseball is participating in the boom. Granted, it opens its gates more often than does any other professional sport. But people are pouring through those gates as never before. In the late nineteenth century teams raised ticket prices to 50 cents in order to keep some fans—the unruly elements of the lower orders—out of the park. Arguably the most dramatic game in baseball history—the third game of the Giants-Dodgers playoff in 1951, won by Bobby Thomson's home run—was played in the nation's largest city, the city that was home to both teams, and was played in front of more than 20,000 empty seats. In 1972 the transplanting of the Washington Senators brought Major League Baseball to Dallas–Fort Worth. Fewer than 700,000 fans showed up. In 1973 the Kansas City Royals opened a sparkling new ballpark, one that is still among the most pleasing, and more than doubled their 1972 attendance. But the doubling amounted to just 1,345,341. Nowadays most major league teams draw better than that every year (in 1997 the *worst* home attendance was the Oakland Athletics' 1,261,219), and the Rockies, Braves, Indians, Mariners and Orioles are apt to top that total well before the All-Star break.

Why, then, are so many teams in financial distress? Because (pick an explanation that suits your point of view) baseball has an indefensible compensation system, or because it has an inadequate system of revenue sharing, or because of both of those things.

Add to the list of problems the problem baseball has competing with entertainment giants—not just the NBA, NFL and NHL—for a portion of the ocean of dollars that the nation spends on entertainment. Remember, Major League Baseball is, in the scheme of things, a small—even tiny—business. In 1997, for the first time, major league salaries totaled more than a billion dollars—$1.2 billion. And in 1997 one team owner, Ted Turner, decided, on what seems to have been a kind of whim, to give a billion dollars to the United Nations. In 1997 Major League Baseball's revenues—gross, not net—exceeded $2 billion. Procter & Gamble's 1997 advertising budget was $3.3 billion.

It is difficult even to imagine, let alone implement, a structure of incentives for reforming baseball, given that the members of the ownership group have such radically different problems and such varied motives for being owners. As operators of businesses, what *do* Marge Schott and the Tribune Company have in common? Bud Selig and Rupert Murdoch? Kevin McClatchy in Pittsburgh and the Disney Corporation in Anaheim?

So far, free agency in the context of surging but vastly disparate team revenues has not had the consequence predicted: It has not resulted in diminished competitive balance. Quite the contrary. The era of free agency has been characterized by extraordinary fluidity in the standings. The era before that—before the mid-1970s—was different. In the supposed "good old days," such as during the twenty-four-year commissionership of Kenesaw Mountain Landis (1920–44), the Yankees and Giants made a total of twenty-one appearances in the World Series, which means that the other fourteen teams shared the other twenty-seven slots. In the thirteen seasons from 1927 through 1939, the

Yankees won four-game sweeps in the Series in 1927, 1928 and 1932, won in six games in 1936, in five games in 1937 and swept in 1938 and 1939, for a seven-series won-lost record of 28–3. In the forty-four-year span from 1921 to 1964 the Yankees won twenty-nine pennants and twenty World Series and the team carried the American League on its broad back: One in four fans who attended American League games saw the Yankees.

However, money matters. In the long run, large and chronic differences in teams' resources will destroy in many cities that which draws fans through the turnstiles—the hope that springs each spring. When the late Edward Bennett Williams owned the Orioles he said that life had taught him that money could not buy three things—love, happiness and the American League pennant. But money bought the 1997 World Championship for the Marlins, which event was not a happy harbinger for baseball.

Oh, well. In the long run, as John Maynard Keynes famously reminded us, we are all dead. But baseball somehow will abide. It will in spite of the mismanagement and shortsightedness all around. It will because although it is tiresome as a business, it is interesting and lovely as a game.

ACKNOWLEDGMENTS

WHEN KENESAW MOUNTAIN LANDIS was commissioner of baseball, a lawyer had the temerity to talk to him, or at least to try to, about the players' working conditions. In the course of their conversation, which must have been brief, Landis exclaimed, with unfeigned indignation, "I am shocked because you call playing baseball 'labor.'" The making of this book, which has been so much a labor of love that it can hardly be called labor, has been made easier in many ways and at every stage by my Cooperstown-caliber assistants, Dusa Gyllensvard and Mary Longnecker. Also pitching in were Chris Cillizza and Seth Meehan, students at Georgetown University, which I have found to be an unfailing source of cheerful, intelligent and industrious young people. Gail Thorin was the team's closer. Jim Gates, librarian, and Tim Wiles, director of research, at the Baseball Hall of Fame, in Cooperstown, and the fine people at the Elias Sports Bureau were generous with their time and resources in providing historical information. Eileen Miller, photo editor, is simply the best. This book bristles, as any baseball book must, with statistics. If any are wrong, that is my fault. My confidence that very few are wrong reflects the fact that the manuscript was scrutinized by the astonishing Frank Kelly, whose baseball knowledge is a sign of a misspent youth, but is very helpful. My editor at Scribner, Bill Rosen, also edited my earlier baseball book, *Men at Work*. He knows even more about baseball than he does about most things, which is a lot.

INDEX

Thomas, Frank, 324
Thompson, Hank, 229
Thomson, Bobby, 153, 192, 205, 225, 238, 296, 327
Three Rivers Stadium, 41, 232
throw-over, 14
Tiger Stadium, 179, 213, 244
Tilden, Bill, 115, 307
Titan, The (Dreiser), 175
Tocqueville, Alexis de, 264
Today, 39
Toledo Mud Hens, 182
Topeka Owls, 236
Toronto Blue Jays, 126, 138, 169, 192n, 205, 239, 242, 253–54, 324
Traynor, Pie, 263
Tribune Company, 328
Triple Crown winners, 324
Trollope, Frances, 195
True Grit, 187
Truman, Harry, 47, 289
Tucson Rockies, 235
Tudor, John, 123n
Tunney, Gene, 115
Turner, Ted, 328
Twain, Mark, 60, 104
twig, bent, 67, 133, 214
Tygiel, Jules, 88

Ueberroth, Peter, 65, 81
umpires, 58, 63, 80, 84–87, 198, 264
dignity of, 220
and Hurst at bat, 81–83
incompetence of, 283, 293
movements of, 220
in NL vs. AL, 283
pitchers and, 86
players in confrontations with, 282–84, 292–93
salaries of, 84–85, 283
second-guessing of, 293
standards of, 218–19
stress endured by, 86
strike zones and, 92–93, 116, 167, 246, 266, 274, 283, 293, 310
uniforms of, 308, 309

University of Pennsylvania Law Review, 265
Updike, John, 159–60, 188, 224

Vail, Mike, 69
Vancouver Capilanos, 236
Van Slyke, Andy, 232–34
Veeck, Bill, 50, 89, 175, 225
Verban, Emil, 31
Verducci, Tom, 288
Vernon, Mickey, 225
Vincent, Fay, 136, 138, 200, 223–24, 257
Vizquel, Omar, 15
Voiselle, Bill, 238
Volcker, Paul, 44–45

Waddell, Rube, 129
Wagner, Honus, 57, 231, 320
Walker, Larry, 323–24
Waller, Bob, 299–300
Wall Street Journal, 140
Walsh, Ed, 178
Washington Diplomats, 294, 300
Washington Post, 41, 48
Washington Redskins, 140, 300
Washington Senators, 44, 91, 111–12, 135, 225, 276, 327, 328
Watergate scandal, 113, 115, 202
Wayne, John, 187
Weaver, Earl, 50, 51–54, 284, 319
on managing, 53
Welch, Bob, 156
Wesley, John, 64
"wheel" ("rotation") play, 15, 16
White, Bill, 277
White, Devon, 280
White, G. Edward, 268
Whitman, Walt, 183
Whole Different Ball Game, A: The Sports and Business of Baseball (Miller), 204
Who's Who in Baseball, 35
Wichita Aeros, 298
"wild card" teams, 233, 248, 251, 291, 324
Wilde, Oscar, 38, 241

ART CREDITS AND TEXT PERMISSIONS